PROBABILISTIC GRAPHICAL MODELS

PRINCIPLES AND TECHNIQUES

PROBABILISTIC GRAPHICAL MODELS

PRINCIPLES AND TECHNIQUES

Ignacio Zurrian

Kruger Brentt
Publishers
2025

Kruger Brentt Publishers UK. LTD.
Company Number 9728962

Regd. Office: 68 St Margarets Road, Edgware, Middlesex HA8 9UU

ISBN: 978-1-78715-378-3

For information on all our publications visit our website at http://krugerbrentt.com/

PREFACE

Probabilistic graphical models (PGMs) represent a powerful framework for modeling uncertainty and complex dependencies in data, enabling effective reasoning, prediction, and decision-making in various domains, including artificial intelligence, machine learning, statistics, and engineering. PGMs provide a principled and intuitive way to represent probabilistic relationships among variables using graphical structures, such as Bayesian networks and Markov random fields, and offer a rich set of techniques for inference, learning, and reasoning under uncertainty. Understanding the principles and techniques of probabilistic graphical models is essential for researchers, practitioners, and students seeking to leverage the capabilities of graphical models for solving real-world problems and advancing the state of the art in data analysis and decision support.

This handbook, titled **"Probabilistic Graphical Models: Principles and Techniques"** is a comprehensive exploration of the foundational concepts, methodologies, and applications of probabilistic graphical models. Drawing upon the expertise of researchers, practitioners, and educators, this volume offers theoretical insights, practical guidance, and case studies for understanding and utilizing probabilistic graphical models in various domains.

From the basic principles of graphical model representation and inference to the advanced techniques of parameter estimation and model learning, "Probabilistic Graphical Models" covers a wide range of topics essential for mastering the field. Through clear explanations, algorithmic descriptions, and illustrative examples, readers will gain a deep understanding of the underlying principles and techniques used to build, analyze, and interpret graphical models.

Moreover, this handbook explores the applications of probabilistic graphical models across different domains and disciplines, including pattern recognition, computer vision, natural language processing, bioinformatics, and social network analysis. By examining case studies, research findings, and practical applications, we highlight the diverse ways in which graphical models are used to solve real-world problems, make predictions, and extract meaningful insights from data.

As we continue to generate and analyze increasingly large and complex datasets, the importance of probabilistic graphical models in enabling effective data-driven decision-making has never been greater. It is our hope that "Probabilistic Graphical Models: Principles and Techniques" will serve as a valuable resource for researchers, practitioners, and students in the field of machine learning and artificial intelligence. Whether you are developing new models, analyzing data, or applying machine learning techniques in your research or industry, this handbook invites you to explore the principles and techniques of probabilistic graphical models and contribute to the advancement of knowledge and innovation in this exciting field.

Ignacio Zurrian

CONTENTS

PREFACE V

1. INTRODUCTION 1

1.1 Theories 1

1.2 Overview of theory 3

1.3 Applications 17

1.4 Decisions- Emotions and Risky 18

1.5. Probabilistic Modeling: From Data to a Decisive Knowledge 20

References 22

2. GENERATIVE MODELS 25

2.1 Introduction 25

2.2. Types of generative models include: 26

2.3. Basic Generative Models 26

2.4 Building Generative Models 33

2.5 Representing working models with probabilistic programs 34

2.6 Prediction, Situation and Probabilities 38

References 43

3. CONDITIONING 47

3.1 Cognition and Conditioning 47

3.2 Hypothetical Reasoning with Infer 51

3.3 Rejection Sampling 58

3.4 Conditional Distributions 73

References 81

4. PATTERNS OF INFERENCE 89

4.1 Causal Dependence 89

4.2 Bayesian Networks and Causality 96

4.3 Statistical Dependence 115

4.4 Conditional Dependence 116

4.5 Graphical Notations for Dependence 120
4.6 Non-monotonic Reasoning 129
4.7 Modularity 135
References 137
5. MODELS FOR SEQUENCES OF OBSERVATIONS 141
5.1 Generative Models of Relations between Data Points 141
5.2 Independent and Exchangeable Sequences 145
5.3 Markov Models 155
5.4 Probabilistic Context-free Grammars 158
References 166
6. INFERENCE ABOUT INFERENCE 169
6.1 WebPPL function 169
6.2 Prelude: Assembly Lines 175
6.3 Social Cognition 177
6.4 Epistemic States of Model 182
6.5 Communication and Language 186
6.6 Algorithms for Inference 193
6.7 Cognitive Modeling 206
References 207
7. HIERARCHICAL MODELS 209
7.1 Hierarchical Generative Models 209
7.2 Dirichlet distribution 211
7.3 Learning Overhypotheses 215
7.4 X-Bar Theory 217
7.5 Lambda Abstraction 224
8. OCCAM'S RAZOR 227
8.1 Fitting Curves 227
8.2 Law of Conservation of Belief 229
8.3 The Size Principle 230
8.4 Bayesian Occam's Razor 232
References 234
9. MIXTURE MODELS 237
9.1 Introduction 237
9.2 Mixture model with Gaussian components 241

9.3 Latent Dirichlet Allocation 241

References 243

10. NON-PARAMETRIC MODELS **247**

10.1 Sampling from Discrete Distribution 247

10.2 The Dirichlet Processes 252

10.3 Markov Models 253

References 259

GLOSSARY **263**

INDEX **265**

1 Chapter INTRODUCTION

1.1 THEORIES

By default,Mathematical reasoning is understood to take place in *deterministic* mathematical universe. In such a universe, any given mathematical statement S (that is to say, a sentence with no free variables) is either true or false, with no intermediate truth value available. Similarly, any deterministic variable x can take on only one specific value at a time.

However, for a variety of reasons, both within pure mathematics and in the applications of mathematics to other disciplines, it is often desirable to have a rigorous mathematical framework in which one candiscuss *non-deterministic* statements and variables – that is to say, statements which are not always true or always false, but in some intermediate state, or variables that do not take one particular value or another with definite certainty, but are again in some intermediate state. In probability theory, which is by far the most widely adopted mathematical framework to formally capture the concept of non-determinism, non-deterministic statements are referred to as *events*, and non-deterministic variables are referred to *as random variables.* In the standard foundations of probability theory, as laid out by Kolmogorov, we can then *model* these *events* and *random* variables by introducing a sample space (which will be given the structure of a probability space)to capture all the ambient sources of randomness; *events* are then modeled as measurable subsets of this sample space, and *random* variables are modeled as measurable functions on this sample space.

Note carefully that sample spaces will be used to *model* probabilistic concepts, rather than to actually *be* the concepts themselves. This distinction (a mathematical analogue of the map-territorydistinction in philosophy) is implicit in much of modern mathematics, when we make a distinction between an abstract version of a mathematical object, and a concrete representation (or *model*) of that object. For instance:

In linear algebra, we distinguish between an abstract vector space V, and a concrete system of coordinates $\phi : V \to \mathbf{R}^n$ given by some basis of V.

In group theory, we distinguish between an abstract group G, and a concrete representation of that group $\phi : G \to \mathrm{Aut}(X)$ as Isomorphisms on some space X.

In differential geometry, we distinguish between an abstract manifold M, and a concrete atlas of coordinate systems that coordinateness that manifold.

Though it is rarely mentioned explicitly, the abstract number systems such as $\mathbf{N}, \mathbf{Z}, \mathbf{Q}, \mathbf{R}, \mathbf{C}$ are distinguished from the concrete numeral systems(e.g. the decimal or binary systems) that are used to represent them (this distinction is particularly useful to keep in mind when faced with the infamous identity $0.999\cdots = 1$, or when switching from one numeral representation system to another).

The distinction between abstract objects and concrete models can be fairly safely discarded if one is only going to use a single model for each abstract object, particularly if that model is "canonical" in some sense. However, one needs to keep the distinction in mind if one plans to switch between different models of a single object (e.g. to perform change of basis in linear algebra, change of coordinates in differential geometry, or base change in algebraic geometry). As it turns out, in probability theory it is often desirable to change the sample space model (for instance, one could *extend* the sample space by adding in new sources of randomness, or one could couple together two systems of random variables by *joining* their sample space models together). Because of this, we will take some care in this foundational set of notes to distinguish probabilistic concepts (such as events and random variables) from their sample space models.

From a foundational point of view, it is often logical to begin with some axiomatic description of the abstract version of a mathematical object, and discuss the concrete representations of that object later; for instance, one could start with the axioms of an abstract group, and then later consider concrete representations of such a group by permutations, invertible linear transformations, and so forth. This approach is often employed in the more algebraic areas of mathematics. However, there are at least two other ways to present these concepts which can be preferable from a pedagogical point of view. One way is to start with the concrete representations as motivating examples, and only later give the abstract object that these representations are modeling; this is how linear algebra, for instance, is often taught at the undergraduate level, by starting first with $\mathbf{R}^2$, $\mathbf{R}^3$, and $\mathbf{R}^n$, and only later introducing the abstract vector spaces.

Another way is to avoid the abstract objects altogether, and focus exclusively on concrete representations, but taking care to emphasise how these representations transform when one switches from one representation to another. For instance, in general relativity courses in undergraduate physics, it is not uncommon to see tensors presented purely through the concrete representation of coordinates indexed by multiple indices, with the transformation of such tensors under changes of variable carefully described; the abstract constructions of tensors and tensor spaces using operations such as tensor product and duality of vector spaces or vector bundles are often left to an advanced differential geometry class to set up properly.

The foundations of probability theory are usually presented (almost by default) using the last of the above three approaches; namely, one talks almost exclusively about sample space models for probabilistic concepts such as events and random variables, and only occasionally dwells on the need to extend or otherwise modify the sample space when one needs to introduce new sources of randomness (or to forget about some existing sources of randomness). However, much as in differential geometry one tends to work with manifolds without specifying any given atlas of coordinate charts, in probability one usually manipulates events and random variables without explicitly specifying any given sample space. For a student raised exclusively on concrete sample space foundations of probability, this can be a bit confusing, for instance it can give the misconception that any given random variable is somehow associated to its own unique sample space, with different random variables possibly living on different sample spaces, which often leads to nonsense when one then tries to combine those random variables together. Because of such confusions, we will try to take particular care in these notes to separate probabilistic concepts from their sample space models.

1.2 OVERVIEW OF THEORY

A probabilistic method or model is based on the theory of probability or the fact that randomness plays a role in predicting future events. The opposite is deterministic, which is the opposite of random which tells us something can be predicted exactly, without the added complication of randomness.

Probabailistic models incorporate random variables and probability distributions into the model of an event or phenomenon. While a deterministic model gives a single possible outcome for an event, a probabilistic model gives a probability distribution as a solution. These models take into account the fact that we can rarely know everything about a situation. There's nearly always an element of randomness to take into account. For example, life insurance is based on the fact we know with certainty that we will die, but we don't know when. These models can be part deterministic and part random or wholly random.

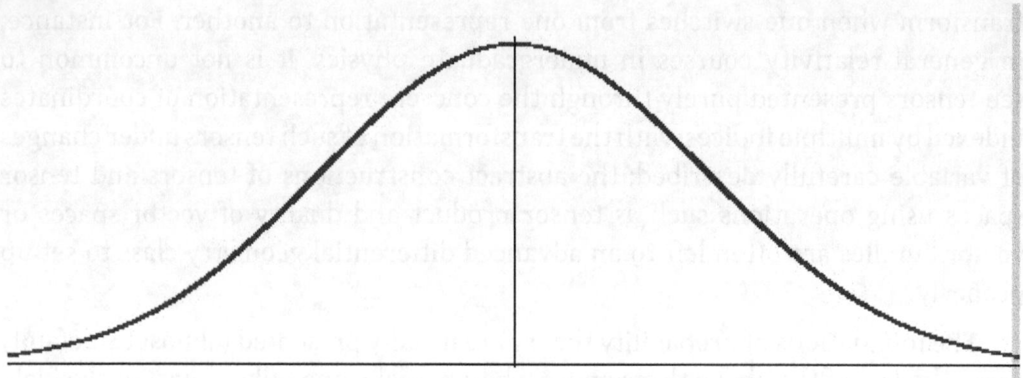

Fig A normal distribution curve

The probabilistic method, first introduced by Paul Erdős, is a way to prove the existence of a structure with certain properties in combinatorics. The idea is that you create a probability space, and choosing elements at random to prove than any random element from the space has both a positive probability and the properties sought after. The method is widely used in a variety of disciplines, including: statistical physics, quantum mechanics, and theoretical computer science.

The simplest models of probability theory are those generated by discrete probability spaces, which are adequate models for many applications, and which already capture much of the essence of probability theory while avoiding some of the finer measure-theoretic subtleties. We thus begin by considering discrete sample space models.

1.2.1 Discrete probability theory

D*iscrete probability space* $\Omega = (\Omega, (p_\omega)_{\omega \in \Omega})$ is an at most countable set Ω (whose elements $\omega \in \Omega$ will be referred to as *outcomes*), together with a non-negative real number p_ω assigned to each outcome ω such that $\sum_{\omega \in \Omega} p_\omega = 1$; we refer to p_ω as the *probability* of the outcome ω. The set Ω itself, without the structure $(p_\omega)_{\omega \in \Omega}$, is often referred to as the *sample space*, though we will often abuse notation by using the sample space Ω to refer to the entire discrete probability space $(\Omega, (p_\omega)_{\omega \in \Omega})$.

In discrete probability theory, we choose an ambient discrete probability space Ω as the randomness model. We then model *events* E by subsets E_Ω of the sample space Ω. The *probability* $\mathbf{P}(E)$ of an event E is defined to be the quantity

$$\mathbf{P}(E) := \sum_{\omega \in E_\Omega} p_\omega;$$

note that this is a real number in the interval $[0, 1]$. An event E is *surely true* or is the *sure event* if $E_\Omega = \Omega$, and is *surely false* or is the *empty event* if $E_\Omega = \emptyset$.

We model random variables X taking values in the range R by functions $X_\Omega : \Omega \to R$ from the sample space Ω to the range R. Random variables taking values in $\mathbf{R}$ will be called *real random variables* or *random real numbers*. Similarly for random variables taking values in $\mathbf{C}$. We refer to real and complex random variables collectively as *scalar random variables*.

We consider two events E, F to be equal if they are modeled by the same set: $E = F \iff E_\Omega = F_\Omega$. Similarly, two random variables X, Y taking values in a common range R are considered to be equal if they are modeled by the same function: $X = Y \iff X_\Omega = Y_\Omega$. In particular, if the discrete sample space Ω is understood from context, we will usually abuse notation by identifying an event E with its model E_Ω, and similarly identify a random variable X with its model X_Ω.

As discussed in the preceding section,, the distinction between a collection of events and random variable and its models becomes important if one ever wishes to modify the sample space, and in particular to extend the sample space to a larger space that can accommodate new sources of randomness (an operation which we will define formally later, but which for now can be thought of as an analogue to change of basis in linear algebra, coordinate change in differential geometry, or base change in algebraic geometry). This is best illustrated with a simple example.

Example

Suppose one wishes to model the outcome X of rolling a single, unbiased six-sided die using discrete probability theory. One can do this by choosing the discrete proability space Ω to be the six-element set $\{1, 2, 3, 4, 5, 6\}$, with each outcome $i \in \{1, 2, 3, 4, 5, 6\}$ given an equal probability of $p_i := 1/6$of occurring; this outcome i may be interpreted as the state in which the die roll X ended up being equal to i. The outcome X of rolling a die may then be identified with the identity function $X_\Omega : \Omega \to \{1, \dots, 6\}$, defined by $X_\Omega(i) := i$ for $i \in \Omega$. If we let E be the event that the outcome X of rolling the die is an even number, then with this model Ω we have $E_\Omega = \{2, 4, 6\}$, and

$$\mathbf{P}(E) = \sum_{\omega \in E_\Omega} p_\omega = 3 \times \frac{1}{6} = \frac{1}{2}.$$

Now suppose that we wish to roll the die again to obtain a second random variable Y. The sample space $\Omega = \{1, 2, 3, 4, 5, 6\}$ is inadequate for modeling both the original die roll X and the second die roll Y. To accommodate this new source of randomness, we can then move to the larger discrete probability space $\Omega' := \{1, \dots, 6\} \times \{1, \dots, 6\}$, where each outcome $(i, j) \in \Omega'$ now having probability $p'_{(i,j)} := \frac{1}{36}$; this outcome (i, j) can be interpreted as the state in which the die roll X ended up being i, and the die roll Y ended up being j. The random variable X is now modeled by a new function $X_{\Omega'} : \Omega' \to \{1, \dots, 6\}$ defined by $X_{\Omega'}(i, j) := i$ for $(i, j) \in \Omega'$; the random variable Y is similarly modeled by the function $Y_{\Omega'} : \Omega' \to \{1, \dots, 6\}$ defined by $Y_{\Omega'}(i, j) := j$ for $(i, j) \in \Omega'$. The event E that X is even is now modeled by the set

$$E_{\Omega'} = \{2, 4, 6\} \times \{1, 2, 3, 4, 5, 6\}.$$

This set is distinct from the previous model E_Ω of E (for instance, $E_{\Omega'}$ has eighteen elements, whereas E_Ω has just three), but the probability of E is unchanged:

$$\mathbf{P}(E) = \sum_{\omega' \in E_{\Omega'}} p'_{\omega'} = 18 \times \frac{1}{36} = \frac{1}{2}.$$

One can of course also combine together the random variables X, Y in various ways. For instance, the sum $X + Y$ of the two die rolls is a random variable taking values in $\{2, \ldots, 12\}$; it cannot be modeled by the sample space Ω, but in Ω' it is modeled by the function

$$(X + Y)_{\Omega'} : (i, j) \mapsto i + j.$$

Similarly, the event $X = Y$ that the two die rolls are equal cannot be modeled by Ω, but is modeled in Ω' by the set

$$(X = Y)_{\Omega'} = \{(i, i) : i = 1, \ldots, 6\}$$

and the probability $\mathbf{P}(X = Y)$ of this event is

$$\mathbf{P}(X = Y) = \sum_{\omega' \in (X=Y)_{\Omega'}} p'_{\omega'} = 6 \times \frac{1}{36} = \frac{1}{6}.$$

We thus see that extending the probability space has also enlarged the space of events one can consider, as well as the random variables one can define, but that existing events and random variables continue to be interpretable in the extended model, and that probabilistic concepts such as the probability of an event remain unchanged by the extension of the model.

The set-theoretic operations on the sample space Ω induce similar boolean operations on events:

- The conjunction $E \wedge F$ of two events E, F is defined through the intersection of their models: $(E \wedge F)_\Omega := E_\Omega \cap F_\Omega$.
- The disjunction $E \vee F$ of two events E, F is defined through the the union of their models: $(E \vee F)_\Omega := E_\Omega \cup F_\Omega$.
- The symmetric difference $E \Delta F$ of two events E, F is defined through the symmetric difference of their models: $(E \Delta F)_\Omega := E_\Omega \Delta F_\Omega$.
- The complement $\overline{E}$ of an event E is defined through the complement of their models: $\overline{E}_\Omega := \Omega \backslash E_\Omega$.
- We say that one event E is contained in or implies another event F, and write $E \subset F$, if we have containment of their models: $E \subset F \iff E_\Omega \subset F_\Omega$. We also write "$F$ is true on E" synonymously with $E \subset F$.

- Two events E, F are disjoint if their conjunction is the empty event, or equivalently if their models E_Ω, F_Ω are disjoint.

Thus, for instance, the conjunction of the event that a die roll X is even, and that it is less than 3, is the event that the die roll is exactly 2. As before, we will usually be in a situation in which the sample space Ω is clear from context, and in that case one can safely identify events with their models, and view the symbols $\vee$ and $\wedge$ as being synonymous with their set-theoretic counterparts $\cup$ and $\cap$.

With these operations, the space of all events thus has the structure of a boolean algebra. We observe that the probability $\mathbf{P}$ is finitely additive in the sense that

$$\mathbf{P}(E \vee F) = \mathbf{P}(E) + \mathbf{P}(F)$$

whenever E, F are disjoint events; by induction this implies that

$$\mathbf{P}(E_1 \vee \cdots \vee E_n) = \mathbf{P}(E_1) + \cdots + \mathbf{P}(E_n)$$

whenever $E_1, \ldots, E_n$ are pairwise disjoint events. We have $\mathbf{P}(\emptyset) = 0$ and $\mathbf{P}(\overline{\emptyset}) = 1$, and more generally

$$\mathbf{P}(\overline{E}) = 1 - \mathbf{P}(E)$$

for any event E. We also have monotonicity: if $E \subset F$, then $\mathbf{P}(E) \leq \mathbf{P}(F)$.

Now we define operations on random variables. Whenever one has a function $f : R \to S$ from one range R to another S, and a random variable X taking values in R, one can define a random variable $f(X)$ taking values in S by composing the relevant models:

$$f(X)_\Omega := f \circ X_\Omega,$$

thus $f(X)_\Omega$ maps ω to $f(X_\Omega(\omega))$ for any outcome $\omega \in \Omega$. Given a finite number $X_1, \ldots, X_n$ of random variables taking values in ranges $R_1, \ldots, R_n$, we can form the joint random variable $(X_1, \ldots, X_n)$ taking values in the Cartesian product $R_1 \times \cdots \times R_n$ by concatenation of the models, thus

$$(X_1, \ldots, X_n)_\Omega : \omega \mapsto ((X_1)_\Omega(\omega), \ldots, (X_n)_\Omega(\omega)).$$

Combining these two operations, given any function $f : R_1 \times \cdots \times R_n \to S$ of n variables in ranges $R_1, \ldots, R_n$, and random variables $X_1, \ldots, X_n$ taking values in $R_1, \ldots, R_n$ respectively, we can form a random variable $f(X_1, \ldots, X_n)$ taking values in S by the formula

$$f(X_1, \ldots, X_n)_\Omega : \omega \mapsto f((X_1)_\Omega(\omega), \ldots, (X_n)_\Omega(\omega)).$$

Thus for instance we can add, subtract, or multiply two scalar random variables to obtain another scalar random variable.

A deterministic element x of a range R will (by abuse of notation) be identified with a random variable x taking values in R, whose model in Ω is constant: $x_\Omega(\omega) = x$ for all $\omega \in \Omega$. Thus for instance 37 is a scalar random variable.

Given a relation $F : R_1 \times \cdots \times R_n \to \{\text{ true, false}\}$ on n ranges $R_1, \ldots, R_n$, and random variables $X_1, \ldots, X_n$, we can define the event $F(X_1, \ldots, X_n)$ by setting

$$F(X_1, \ldots, X_n) := \{\omega \in \Omega : F((X_1)_\Omega(\omega), \ldots, (X_n)_\Omega(\omega)) \text{ true}\}.$$

Thus for instance, for two real random variables X, Y, the event $X > Y$ is modeled as

$$(X > Y)_\Omega := \{\omega \in \Omega : X_\Omega(\omega) > Y_\Omega(\omega)\}$$

and the event $X = Y$ is modeled as

$$(X = Y)_\Omega := \{\omega \in \Omega : X_\Omega(\omega) = Y_\Omega(\omega)\}.$$

At this point we encounter a slight notational conflict between the dual role of the equality symbol $=$ as a logical symbol and as a binary relation: we are interpreting $X = Y$ both as an external equality relation between the two random variables (which is true if the functions X_Ω, Y_Ω are identical), and as an internal event (modeled by $(X = Y)_\Omega$). However, it is clear that $X = Y$ is true in the external sense if and only if the internal event $X = Y$ is surely true. As such, we shall abuse notation and continue to use the equality symbol for both the internal and external concepts of equality (and use the modifier "surely" for emphasis when referring to the external usage).

It is clear that any equational identity concerning functions or operations on deterministic variables implies the same identity (in the external, or surely true, sense) for random variables. For instance, the commutativity of addition $x + y = y + x$ for deterministic real numbers x, y immediately implies the commutativity of addition: $X + Y = Y + X$ is surely true for real random variables X, Y; similarly $X + 0 = X$ is surely true for all scalar random variables X, etc.. We will freely apply the usual laws of algebra for scalar random variables without further comment.

Given an event E, we can associate the indicator random variable 1_E (also written as $\mathbf{I}(E)$ in some texts) to be the unique real random variable such that $1_E = 1$ when E is true and $1_E = 0$ when E is false, thus $(1_E)_\Omega(\omega)$ is equal to1 when $\omega \in E_\Omega$ and 0 otherwise. We record the trivial but useful fact that Boolean operations on events correspond to arithmetic manipulations on their indicators. For instance, if E, F are events, we have

$$1_{E \wedge F} = 1_E 1_F$$
$$1_{\overline{E}} = 1 - 1_E$$

and the inclusion-exclusion principle

$$1_{E \vee F} = 1_E + 1_F - 1_{E \wedge F}. \qquad (1)$$

In particular, if the events E, F are disjoint, then

$$1_{E \vee F} = 1_E + 1_F.$$

Also note that $E \subset F$ if and only if the assertion $1_E \leq 1_F$ is surely true. We will use these identities and equivalences throughout the course without further comment.

Given a scalar random variable X, we can attempt to define the expectation $\mathbf{E}(X)$ through the model X_Ω by the formula

$$\mathbf{E}(X) := \sum_{\omega \in \Omega} X_\Omega(\omega) p_\omega.$$

If the discrete sample space Ω is finite, then this sum is always well-defined and so every scalar random variable has an expectation. If however the discrete sample space Ω is infinite, the expectation may not be well defined. There are however two key cases in which one has a meaningful expectation. The first is if the random variable X is unsigned, that is to say it takes values in the non-negative reals $[0, +\infty)$, or more generally in the extended non-negative real line $[0, +\infty]$. In that case, one can interpret the expectation $\mathbf{E}(X)$ as an element of $[0, +\infty]$. The other case is when the random variable X is absolutely integrable, which means that the absolute value $|X|$ (which is an unsigned random variable) has finite expectation: $\mathbf{E}|X| < \infty$. In that case, the series defining $\mathbf{E}(X)$ is absolutely convergent to a real or complex number (depending on whether X was a real or complex random variable.).

We have the basic link

$$\mathbf{P}(E) = \mathbf{E}(1_E)$$

between probability and expectation, valid for any event E. We also have the obvious, but fundamentally important, property of linearity of expectation: we have

$$\mathbf{E}(cX) = c\mathbf{E}(X)$$

and

$$\mathbf{E}(X+Y) = \mathbf{E}(X) + \mathbf{E}(Y)$$

whenever c is a scalar and X, Y are scalar random variables, either under the assumption that c, X, Y are all unsigned, or that X, Y are absolutely integrable. Thus for instance by applying expectations, we obtain the identity

$$\mathbf{P}(E \vee F) = \mathbf{P}(E) + \mathbf{P}(F) - \mathbf{P}(E \wedge F).$$

We close this section by noting that discrete probabilistic models stumble when trying to model continuous random variables, which take on an uncountable number of values. Suppose for instance one wants to model a random real number X drawn uniformly at random from the unit interval $[0, 1]$, which is an uncountable set. One would then expect, for any subinterval $[a, b]$ of $[0, 1]$, that X will fall into this interval with probability $b - a$. Setting $a = b$ (or, if one wishes instead, taking a limit such as $b \to a^+$), we conclude in particular that for any real number a

in $[0, 1]$, that X will equal a with probability 0. If one attempted to model this situation by a discrete probability model, we would find that each outcome ω of the discrete sample space Ω has to occur with probability $p_\omega = 0$ (since for each ω, the random variable X has only a single value $X_\Omega(\omega)$). But we are also requiring that the sum $\sum_{\omega \in \Omega} p_\omega$is equal to 1, a contradiction. In order to address this defect we must generalise from discrete models to more general probabilistic models, to which we now turn.

We now present the more general measure-theoretic foundation of Kolmogorov which subsumes the discrete theory, while also allowing one to model continuous random variables. It turns out that in order to perform sums, limits and integrals properly, the finite additivity property of probability needs to be amplified to *countable* additivity

We begin with the notion of a measurable space.

(Measurable space) Let Ω be a set. A Boolean algebra in Ω is a collection $\mathcal{F}$ of subsets of Ω which

- contains $\emptyset$ and Ω;
- is closed under pairwise unions and intersections (thus if $E, F \in \mathcal{F}$, then $E \cup F$ and $E \cap F$ also lie in $\mathcal{F}$); and
- is closed under complements (thus if $E \in \mathcal{F}$, then $\Omega \backslash E$ also lies in $\mathcal{F}$.

(Note that some of these assumptions are redundant and can be dropped, thanks to de Morgan's laws.) A σ-algebra in Ω (also known as a σ-field) is a Boolean algebra $\mathcal{F}$ in Ω which is also

- closed under countable unions and countable intersections (thus if $E_1, E_2, E_3, \cdots \in \mathcal{F}$, then $\bigcup_{n=1}^{\infty} E_n \in \mathcal{F}$ and $\bigcap_{n=1}^{\infty} E_n \in \mathcal{F}$).

Again, thanks to de Morgan's laws, one only needs to verify closure under just countable union (or just countable intersection) in order to verify that a Boolean algebra is a σ-algebra. A *measurable space* is a pair $(\Omega, \mathcal{F})$, where Ω is a set and $\mathcal{F}$ is a σ-algebra in Ω. Elements of $\mathcal{F}$ are referred to as *measurable sets* in this measurable space.

If $\mathcal{F}, \mathcal{F}'$ are two σ-algebras in Ω, we say that $\mathcal{F}$ is *coarser than* $\mathcal{F}'$ (or $\mathcal{F}'$ is *finer than* $\mathcal{F}$) if $\mathcal{F} \subset \mathcal{F}'$, thus every set that is measurable in $(\Omega, \mathcal{F})$ is also measurable in $(\Omega, \mathcal{F}')$.

In probabilistic terms, one can interpret the space Ω in the above construction as a sample space, and the function ϕ as some collection of "random variables" or "measurements" on that space, with R being all the possible outcomes of these measurements. The pullback then represents all the "information" one can extract from that given set of measurements.

In probability theory, we choose an ambient probability space $\Omega = (\Omega, \mathcal{F}_\Omega, \mu)$ as the randomness model, and refer to the set Ω (without the additional structures $\mathcal{F}_\Omega, \mu$) as the *sample space* for that model. We then model an *event* E by an element E_Ω of σ-algebra $\mathcal{F}_\Omega$, with each such element describing an event. The *probability* $\mathbf{P}(E)$ of an event E is defined to be the quantity

$$\mathbf{P}(E) := \mu(E_\Omega).$$

An event E is *surely true* or is the *sure event* if $E_\Omega = \Omega$, and is *surely false* or is the *empty event* if $E_\Omega = \emptyset$. It is *almost surely true* or an *almost sure event* if $\mathbf{P}(E) = 1$, and *almost surely false* or a *null event* if $\mathbf{P}(E) = 0$.

We model random variables X taking values in the range R by measurable functions $X_\Omega : \Omega \to R$ from the sample space Ω to the range R. We define real, complex, and scalar random variables as in the discrete case.

As in the discrete case, we consider two events E, F to be equal if they are modeled by the same set: $E = F \iff E_\Omega = F_\Omega$. Similarly, two random variables X, Y taking values in a common range R are considered to be equal if they are modeled by the same function: $X = Y \iff X_\Omega = Y_\Omega$. Again, if the sample space Ω is understood from context, we will usually abuse notation by identifying an event E with its model E_Ω, and similarly identify a random variable X with its model X_Ω.

As in the discrete case, set-theoretic operations on the sample space induce similar boolean operations on events. Furthermore, since the σ-algebra $\mathcal{F}_\Omega$ is closed under countable unions and countable intersections, we may similarly define the countable conjunction $\bigwedge_{n=1}^{\infty} E_n$ or countable disjunction $\bigvee_{n=1}^{\infty} E_n$ of a sequence $E_1, E_2, \ldots$ of events; however, we do *not* define uncountable conjunctions or disjunctions as these may not be well-defined as *events*.

The axioms of a probability space then yield the Kolmogorov axioms for probability:

- $\mathbf{P}(\emptyset) = 0$.
- $\mathbf{P}(\overline{\emptyset}) = 1$.
- If $E_1, E_2, \ldots$ are disjoint events, then $\mathbf{P}(\bigvee_{n=1}^{\infty} E_n) = \sum_{n=1}^{\infty} \mathbf{P}(E_n)$.

We can manipulate random variables just as in the discrete case, with the only caveat being that we have to restrict attention to *measurable* operations. For instance, if X is a random variable taking values in a measurable space R, and $f : R \to S$ is a measurable map, then $f(X)$ is well defined as a random variable taking values in S. Similarly, if $f : R_1 \times \cdots \times R_n \to S$ is a measurable map and $X_1, \ldots, X_n$ are random variables taking values in $R_1, \ldots, R_n$ respectively, then $f(X_1, \ldots, X_n)$ is a random variable taking values in S. Similarly we can create events $F(X_1, \ldots, X_n)$ out of *measurable* relations $F : R_1 \times \cdots \times R_n \to \{\text{true}, \text{false}\}$ (giving the boolean range $\{\mathrm{true}, \mathrm{false}\}$ the discrete σ-algebra, of course). Finally, we continue to view deterministic elements of a space X as a special case of a random element of X, and associate the indicator random variable 1_E to any event E as before.

We say that two random variables X, Y *agree almost surely* if the event $X = Y$ is almost surely true; this is an equivalence relation. In many cases we are willing to consider random variables up to almost sure equivalence. In particular, we can generalise the notion of a random variable slightly by considering random variables X whose models $X_\Omega : \Omega \to R$ are only defined almost surely, i.e. their domain is not all of Ω, but instead Ω with a set of measure zero removed. This is, technically, not a random variable as we have defined it, but it can be associated canonically with an equivalence class of random variables up to almost sure equivalence, and so we view such objects as random variables "up to almost sure equivalence". Similarly, we declare two events E and F *almost surely equivalent* if their symmetric difference $E \Delta F$ is a null event, and will often consider events up to almost sure equivalence only.

We record some simple consequences of the measure-theoretic axioms:

Let $(\Omega, \mathcal{F}_\Omega, \mu)$ be a measure space.

(Monotonicity) If $E \subset F$ are measurable, then $\mu(E) \leq \mu(F)$.

(Subadditivity) If $E_1, E_2, \ldots$ are measurable (not necessarily disjoint), then $\mu(\bigcup_{n=1}^\infty E_n) \leq \sum_{n=1}^\infty \mu(E_n)$.

(Continuity from below) If $E_1 \subset E_2 \subset \ldots$ are measurable, then $\mu(\bigcup_{n=1}^\infty E_n) = \lim_{n\to\infty} \mu(E_n)$.

(Continuity from above) If $E_1 \supset E_2 \supset \ldots$ are measurable and $\mu(E_1)$ is finite, then $\mu(\bigcap_{n=1}^\infty E_n) = \lim_{n\to\infty} \mu(E_n)$. Give a counterexample to show that the claim can fail when $\mu(E_1)$ is infinite.

Variants of the standard foundations (optional) –

We have focused on the orthodox foundations of probability theory in which we model events and random variables through probability spaces. In this section, we briefly discuss some alternate ways to set up the foundations, as well as alternatives to probability theory itself. (Actually, many of the basic objects and concepts in mathematics have multiple such foundations; see for instance this blog post exploring the many different ways to define the notion of a group.) We mention them here in order exclude them from discussion in subsequent notes, which will be focused almost exclusively on orthodox probability.

One approach to the foundations of probability is to view the event space as an *abstract* σ-algebra $\mathcal{E}$ – a collection of abstract objects with operations such as $\wedge$ and $\vee$ (and $\bigwedge_{n=1}^\infty$ and $\bigvee_{n=1}^\infty$) that obey a number of axioms. The probability map

$E \mapsto \mathbf{P}(E)$ can then be viewed as an abstract probability measure on $\mathcal{E}$, that is to say a map from $\mathcal{E}$ to $[0, 1]$ that obeys the Kolmogorov axioms. Random variables X taking values in a measurable space $(R, \mathcal{B})$ can be identified with their pullback map $X^* : \mathcal{B} \to \mathcal{E}$, which is the morphism of (abstract) σ-algebras that sends a measurable set $S \in \mathcal{B}$ to the event $X \in S$ in $\mathcal{E}$; with some care one can then redefine all the operations in previous sections (e.g. applying a measurable map $f : R \to S$ to a random variable X taking values in R to obtain a random variable $f(X)$ taking values in S) in terms of this pullback map, allowing one to define random variables satisfactorily in this abstract setting. The probability space models discussed above can then be viewed as *representations* of abstract probability spaces by concrete ones. It turns out that (up to null events) any abstract probability space can be represented by a concrete one, a result known as the *Loomis-Sikorski theorem*

Another, related, approach is to start not with the event space, but with the space of scalar random variables, and more specifically with the space L^∞ of *almost surely bounded* scalar random variables X (thus, there is a deterministic scalar C such that $|X| \leq C$ almost surely). It turns out that this space has the structure of a commutative tracial (abstract) von Neumann algebra. Conversely, starting from a commutative tracial von Neumann algebra one can form an abstract probability space (using the idempotent elements of the algebra as the events), and thus represent this algebra (up to null events) by a concrete probability space. This particular choice of probabilistic foundations is particularly convenient when one wishes to generalise classical probability to*noncommutative* probability, as this is simply a matter of dropping the axiom that the von Neumann algebra is commutative. This leads in particular to the subjects of quantum probability and free probability, which are generalisations of classical probability that are beyond the scope of this course

It is also possible to model continuous probability via a nonstandard version of discrete probability (or even finite probability), which removes some of the technicalities of measure theory at the cost of replacing them with the formalism of nonstandard analysis instead.

One can generalise the traditional, countably additive, form of probability by replacing countable additivity with finite additivity, but then one loses much of the ability to take limits or infinite sums, which reduces the amount of analysis one can perform in this setting. Still, finite additivity is good enough for many applications, particularly in discrete mathematics. An even broader generalisation is that of *qualitative* probability, in which events that are neither almost surely true nor almost surely false are not assigned any specific numerical probability between 0 or 1, but are simply assigned a symbol such as I to indicate their indeterminate status.

There have been multiple attempts to move more radically beyond the paradigm of probability theory and its relatives as discussed above, in order to more accurately capture mathematically the concept of non-determinism. One family of approaches is based on replacing deterministic *logic* by some sort of probabilistic logic; another is based on allowing several parameters in one's model to be unknown (as opposed to being probabilistic random variables), leading to the area of uncertainty quantification. These topics are well beyond the scope of this study material

1.2.2 Discrete Probability Distribution

In statistics and probability theory, a discrete probability distribution is a distribution characterized by a probability mass function. This distribution is commonly used in computer programs which help to make equal probability random selections between a number of choices. The most common applications of discrete probability distribution are binomial distribution, Poisson distribution, Geometric distribution and Bernoulli distribution. If a random variable is a discrete variable, its probability distribution is called a discrete probability.

Distribution. Any random variable is called discrete random variable which is the part of discrete distribution. A random variable can take two types of values, either fix numbers that is discrete values or a range that is continuous type of values. In continuous type data, the values can lie anywhere within the specified range. For example: the number of apples in the basket is discrete while the time needed to drive from school to home is continuous.So the probability distribution over a random variable 'X' where 'X' takes discrete values, is commonly said to be discrete probability distribution.

Formula

When we say that the probability distribution of an experiment is discrete then the sum of probabilities of all possible values of the random variable must be equal to 1. That is if X is a discrete random variable, then,

$\Sigma eP(X=e)=1\Sigma eP(X=e)=1$

Here, 'e' is the set of all values that the variable X can take.

Example1 : Suppose you flip a coin two times. This simple statistical experiment can have four possible outcomes: HH, HT, TH, and TT. Now, let the random variable X represent the number of Heads that result from this experiment. The random variable X can only take on the values 0, 1, or 2, so it is a discrete random variable. The probability distribution for this statistical experiment appears below.

Number of heads	Probability
0	0.25
1	0.50
2	0.25

The above table represents a discrete probability distribution because it relates each value of a discrete random variable with its probability of occurrence. With a discrete probability distribution, each possible value of the discrete random variable can be associated with a non-zero probability. Thus, a discrete probability distribution can always be presented in tabular form.

Example 2: We flip a coin 10 times. Find the probability that 6 heads are obtained. **Solution:**We solve this using binomial distribution.A binomial distribution is expressed by B (n, p) where n is the number of trials made, k is the number of successes out of n trials and p is the probability of a success in each trial. So (1 – p) will be the probability of failure in each trial. Then, the binomial distribution is calculated as below.

p(X=k)=(nk)pk.(1-p)n-kp(X=k)=(nk)pk.(1-p)n-k

The term (nk)(nk) is known as the binomial coefficient and is calculated as:n!((k!)(n-k)!)n!((k!)(n-k)!)Here, n = 10, k = 6, p = 1212 = 0.5. So, 1 – p = 0.5Using this we get, P(X = 6) = 0.2051

Changing Data into Probability

Imagine if you were given a set of numbers representing the number of cell phones in different households. In order to understand data, it is often necessary to tabulate the data. As data is collected, it also has to be decided whether the data is discrete or continuous since this will affect the way the data is tabulated. Let's take an example of a set of discrete data.

Suppose a research team gathers some data on the number of cell phones in households in the fictitious town of Phonyville. The first step would be to decide what the random variable represents. Since we are looking at the number of cell phones, it is natural to let X, the random variable, be the number of cell phones per household.

Also note that X is discrete because it represents distinct numbers, since one cannot really have a fraction of a cell phone! Thus, X could range from 0 to a very large number. However, let's assume the percentage of homes having 5 or more cell phones was negligible. If we tabulated the results, it could look like the following:

X = Number of Cell Phones	Number of Households
0	457
1	18,763
2	22,345
3	12,534
4	9,830
5 or more	11
	Total number surveyed: 63,940

If we look at the table, we see that there were 457 households with no cell phones, 18,763 households with 1 cell phone, 22,345 households with 2 cell phones and so on. Also, 5 or more is grouped as one category, since relative to the sample size, the amount of households with 5 or more cell phones was very small. Also notice that a grand total of 63,940 households were surveyed to collect this data.

So, we have a count of the number of households with the different amount of cell phones, but we need to convert these numbers to a percentage or probability. Well, we do this by dividing each count of the number of households by the total number of households to create a decimal or proportion for each category. The decimal is also an empirical probability.

X = Number of Cell Phones	Number of Households	P(X)
0	457	0.007147
1	18,763	0.293447
2	22,345	0.349468
3	12,534	0.196028
4	9,830	0.153738
5 or more	11	0.000172
	Total surveyed: 63,940	**Total of P(X): 1**

Looking at the table, we see that the probability of a household with no cell phones (or probability that X = 0) is 457 divided by 63,940, which is 0.007147. The probability of selecting a household with only one cell phone (or probability that X = 1) is 18,763 divided by 63,940, which is 0.293447, or about 29%, and so on. If you want, you can pause the video to take a minute here and calculate the rest of the probabilities in the table to make sure your results match those in the table.

You should have calculated the same probabilities as the table and note the probability for 5 or more cell phones is very small at 0.00017, which is the reason 5 or more cell phones were grouped into one category. Also note that all the probabilities sum to a total of 1, or 100%, which is the property of a probability distribution.

1.3 APPLICATIONS

The fundamental ingredient of probability theory is an experiment that can be repeated, at least hypothetically, under essentially identical conditions and that may lead to different outcomes on different trials. The set of all possible outcomes of an experiment is called a "sample space." The experiment of tossing a coin once results in a sample space with two possible outcomes, "heads" and "tails." Tossing two dice has a sample space with 36 possible outcomes, each of which can be identified with an ordered pair (i, j), where i and j assume one of the values 1, 2, 3, 4, 5, 6 and denote the faces showing on the individual dice. It is important to think of the dice as identifiable, so that the outcome (1, 2) is different from (2, 1). An "event" is a well-defined subset of the sample space. For example, the event "the sum of the faces showing on the two dice equals six" consists of the five outcomes (1, 5), (2, 4), (3, 3), (4, 2), and (5, 1).

A third example is to draw n balls from an urn containing balls of various colours. A generic outcome to this experiment is an n-tuple, where the ith entry specifies the colour of the ball obtained on the ith draw (i = 1, 2,..., n). In spite of the simplicity of this experiment, a thorough understanding gives the theoretical basis for opinion polls and sample surveys. For example, individuals in a population favouring a particular candidate in an election may be identified with balls of a particular colour, those favouring a different candidate may be identified with a different colour, and so on. Probability theory provides the basis for learning about the contents of the urn from the sample of balls drawn from the urn; an application is to learn about the electoral preferences of a population on the basis of a sample drawn from that population.

Another application of simple urn models is to use clinical trials designed to determine whether a new treatment for a disease, a new drug, or a new surgical procedure is better than a standard treatment. In the simple case in which treatment can be regarded as either success or failure, the goal of the clinical trial is to discover whether the new treatment more frequently leads to success than does the standard treatment. Patients with the disease can be identified with balls in an urn. The red balls are those patients who are cured by the new treatment, and the black balls are those not cured. Usually there is a control group, who receive the standard treatment. They are represented by a second urn with a possibly different fraction of red balls. The goal of the experiment of drawing some number of balls from each urn is to discover on the basis of the sample which urn has the larger fraction of red balls. A variation of this idea can be used to test the efficacy of a new vaccine. Perhaps the largest and most famous example was the test of the Salk vaccine for poliomyelitis conducted in 1954. It was organized by the U.S. Public Health Service and involved almost two million children. Its success has led to the almost complete elimination of polio as a health problem in the industrialized parts of the world. Strictly speaking, these applications are problems of statistics, for which the foundations are provided by probability theory.

Because of their comparative simplicity, experiments with finite sample spaces are discussed first. In the early development of probability theory, mathematicians considered only those experiments for which it seemed reasonable, based on considerations of symmetry, to suppose that all outcomes of the experiment were "equally likely." Then in a large number of trials all outcomes should occur with approximately the same frequency. The probability of an event is defined to be the ratio of the number of cases favourable to the event—i.e., the number of outcomes in the subset of the sample space defining the event—to the total number of cases. Thus, the 36 possible outcomes in the throw of two dice are assumed equally likely, and the probability of obtaining "six" is the number of favourable cases, 5, divided by 36, or 5/36.

Now suppose that a coin is tossed n times, and consider the probability of the event "heads does not occur" in the n tosses. An outcome of the experiment is an n-tuple, the kth entry of which identifies the result of the kth toss. Since there are two possible outcomes for each toss, the number of elements in the sample space is 2n. Of these, only one outcome corresponds to having no heads, so the required probability is 1/2n.

1.4 DECISIONS- EMOTIONS AND RISKY

Many decision makers depends on emotions in making judgments concerning risky decisions. Many people are afraid of the possible unwanted consequences. However, do we need emotions in order to be able to judge whether a decision and its concomitant risks are morally acceptable. This question has direct practical implications: should engineers, scientists and policy makers involved in developing risk regulation take the emotions of the public seriously or not? Even though emotions are subjective and irrational, they should be a part of the decision making process since they show us our preferences. Since emotions and rationality are not mutually exclusive, because in order to be practically rational, we need to have emotions. This can lead to an alternative view about the role of emotions in risk assessment: emotions can be a normative guide in making judgments about morally acceptable risks.

Most people often make choices out of habit or tradition, without going through the decision-making process steps systematically. Decisions may be made under social pressure or time constraints that interfere with a careful consideration of the options and consequences. Decisions may be influenced by one's emotional state at the time a decision is made. When people lack adequate information or skills, they may make less than optimal decisions. Even when or if people have time and information, they often do a poor job of understanding the probabilities of consequences. Even when they know the statistics; they are more likely to rely on personal experience than information about probabilities. The fundamental concerns of decision making are combining information about probability with information about desires and interests.

Business decision making is almost always accompanied by conditions of uncertainty. Clearly, the more information the decision maker has, the better the decision will be. Treating decisions as if they were gambles is the basis of decision theory. This means that we have to trade off the value of a certain outcome against its probability.

To operate according to the canons of decision theory, we must compute the value of a certain outcome and its probabilities; hence, determining the consequences of our choices. The origin of decision theory is derived from economics by using the utility function of payoffs. It suggests that decisions be made by computing the utility and probability, the ranges of options, and also lays down strategies for good decisions:

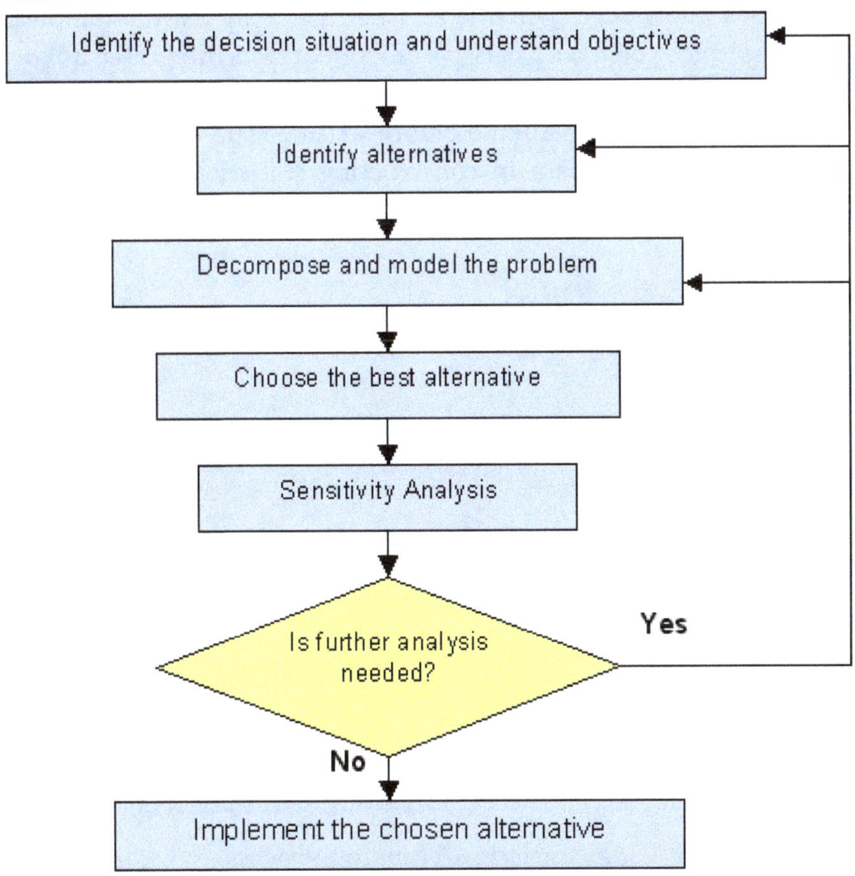

1.5. PROBABILISTIC MODELING: FROM DATA TO A DECISIVE KNOWLEDGE

1.5.1 Introduction

Knowledge is what we know while information is communication of knowledge. In case of all exchange of knowledge, there appears a sender and receiver. The sender make common what is private, does the informing and communicating. Information can be classified as explicit and tacit forms. The explicit information is explained in structured form, while tacit information is inconsistent and fuzzy to explain. Know that data are only crude information and not knowledge by themselves.

Data is known to be crude information and not knowledge by itself. The sequence from data to knowledge is: from Data to Information, from Information to Facts, and finally, from Facts to Knowledge. Data becomes information, when it becomes relevant to your decision problem. Information becomes fact, when the data can support it. Facts are what the data reveals. However the decisive instrumental knowledge is expressed together with some statistical degree of confidence.

Fact becomes knowledge, when it is used in the successful completion of a decision process. Once you have a massive amount of facts integrated as knowledge, then your mind will be superhuman in the same sense that mankind with writing is superhuman compared to mankind before writing. The figure shows statistical thinking process based on data in constructing statistical models for decision making under uncertainties.

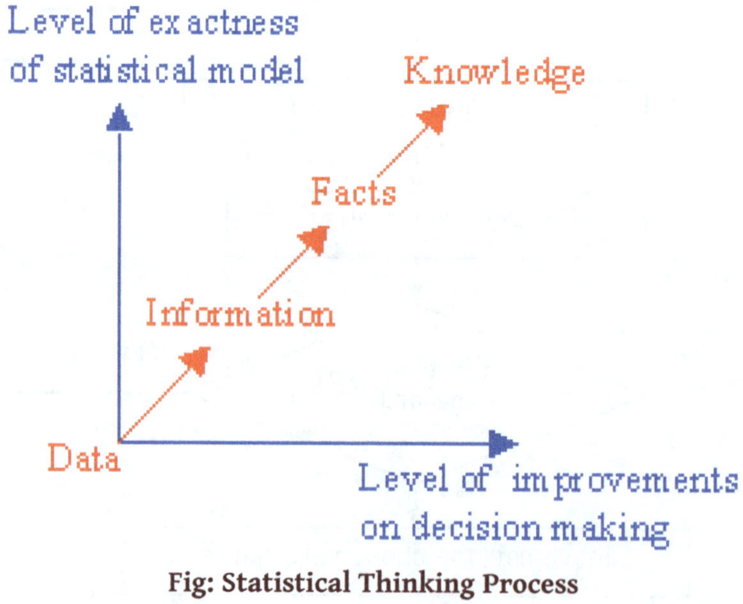

Fig: Statistical Thinking Process

The figure describes that when exactness of statistical model increases, level of improvements in decision-making also increases. With this, a probabilistic model is required. Probabilistic modeling arose from the need to place knowledge on a systematic evidence base. This required a study of the laws of probability, the development of measures of data properties and relationships, and so on.

Statistical inference aims at determining whether any statistical significance can be attached that results after due allowance is made for any random variation as a source of error. Intelligent and critical inferences cannot be made by those who do not understand the purpose, the conditions, and applicability of the various techniques for judging significance.

Knowledge is more than knowing something technical. Knowledge needs wisdom. Wisdom is the power to put our time and our knowledge to the proper use. Wisdom comes with age and experience. Wisdom is the accurate application of accurate knowledge and its key component is to knowing the limits of your knowledge. Wisdom is about knowing how something technical can be best used to meet the needs of the decision-maker. Wisdom, for example, creates statistical software that is useful, rather than technically brilliant. For example, ever since the Web entered the popular consciousness, observers have noted that it puts information at your fingertips but tends to keep wisdom out of reach.

Considering the uncertain environment, the chance that good decisions are made increases with the availability of good information. The chance that good information is available which increases with level of structuring the process of Knowledge Management. Knowledge Management and Decision Analysis are indeed interrelated as one influences other in time and space. The notion of wisdom in sense of practical wisdom entered Western civilization by biblical texts. Making decisions is certainly the most important task of a manager and it is often a very difficult one. This site offers a decision making procedure for solving complex problems step by step.

1.5.2 Decision-Making Process

Unlike the deterministic decision-making process, in the decision making process under uncertainty the variables are often more numerous and more difficult to measure and control. However, the steps are the same. They are:

Simplification:

Building a decision model

Testing the model

Using the model to find the solution

- It is a simplified representation of the actual situation

- It need not be complete or exact in all respects
- It concentrates on the most essential relationships and ignores the less essential ones.
- It is more easily understood than the empirical situation and, hence, permits the problem to be more readily solved with minimum time and effort.
- It can be used again and again for like problems or can be modified.

Fortunately the probabilistic and statistical methods for analysis and decision making under uncertainty are more numerous and powerful today than even before. The computer makes possible many practical applications.

REFERENCES

Bertsekas, D. P., J. N. Tsitsiklis, Introduction to Probability, Athena Scientific, Belmont, Massachusetts, 2002.

Gordon, H., Discrete Probability, Springer Verlag, 2010.

Lipschutz, S., Theory and Problems of Probability, Schaum's Outline Series, McGraw Hill, 1965.

Ross, S. M., A First Course in Probability, Prentice Hall, 5th edition, 1998.

Stone, C. J., A Course in Probability and Statistics, Duxbury Press, 1996.

Freedman, D., R. Pisani, R. Purves, Statistics, W. W. Norton & Company, 4th edition, 2007.

Johnson, R., P. Kuby, Elementary Statistics, Brooks/Cole, Cengage Learning, 11th edition, 2012.

Shao, J., Mathematical Statistics, Springer Verlag, 1998.

Spiegel, M. R., L. J. Stephens, Theory and Problems of Statistics, McGraw Hill, 3rd edition, 1999.

Berger J., Statistical Decision Theory and Bayesian Analysis, Springer, 1978.

Corfield D., and J. Williamson, Foundations of Bayesianism, Kluwer Academic Publishers, 2001. Contains Logic, Mathematics, Decision Theory, and Criticisms of Bayesianism.

GrÃ¼nig R., KÃ¼hn, R., and M. Matt, (Eds.), Successful Decision-Making: A Systematic Approach to Complex Problems, Springer, 2005.

Lapin L., Statistics for Modern Business Decisions, Harcourt Brace Jovanovich, 1987.

Lindley D., Making Decisions, Wiley, 1991.

Pratt J., H. Raiffa, and R. Schlaifer, Introduction to Statistical Decision Theory, The MIT Press, 1994.

Press S., and J. Tanur, The Subjectivity of Scientists and the Bayesian Approach, Wiley, 2001. Comparing and contrasting the reality of subjectivity in the work of history's great scientists and the modern Bayesian approach to statistical analysis.

Tanaka H., and P. Guo, Possibilistic Data Analysis for Operations Research, Physica-Verlag, 1999.

Chapter 2 GENERATIVE MODELS

2.1 INTRODUCTION

Generative model is a model for generating all values for a phenomenon, both those that can be observed in the world and "target" variables that can only be computed from those observed. By contrast, discriminative models provide a model only for the target variable(s), generating them by analyzing the observed variables. In simple terms, discriminative models infer outputs based on inputs, while generative models generate both inputs and outputs, typically given some hidden parameters.

Generative models are used in machine learning for either modeling data directly (i.e., modeling observations drawn from a probability density function), or as an intermediate step to forming a conditional probability density function. Generative models are typically probabilistic, specifying a joint probability distribution over observation and target (label) values. A conditional distribution can be formed from a generative model through Bayes' rule.

Shannon gives an example in which a table of frequencies of English word pairs is used to generate a sentence beginning with "representing and speedily is an good"; which is not proper English but which will increasingly approximate it as the table is moved from word pairs to word triplets etc.

Despite the fact that discriminative models do not need to model the distribution of the observed variables, they cannot generally express complex relationships between the observed and target variables. They don't necessarily perform better than generative models at classification and regression tasks. The two classes are seen as complementary or as different views of the same procedure.

2.2. TYPES OF GENERATIVE MODELS INCLUDE:

- Gaussian mixture model and other types of mixture model
- Hidden Markov model
- Probabilistic context-free grammar
- Naive Bayes
- Averaged one-dependence estimators
- Latent Dirichlet allocation
- Restricted Boltzmann machine
- Generative adversarial networks

If the observed data are truly sampled from the generative model, then fitting the parameters of the generative model to maximize the data likelihood is a common method. However, since most statistical models are only approximations to the true distribution, if the model's application is to infer about a subset of variables conditional on known values of others, then it can be argued that the approximation makes more assumptions than are necessary to solve the problem at hand.

2.3 BASIC GENERATIVE MODELS

Here are three popular generative model approaches which gives sense of variation:

2.3.1 Generative Adversarial Networks (GANs):

Initially before looking at GANs, first review the generative and discriminative models:

- Discriminative model learns a function that maps the input data (x) to some desired output class label (y). In probabilistic terms, they directly learn the conditional distribution P(y|x).
- Generative model tries to learn the joint probability of the input data and labels simultaneously, i.e. P(x,y). This can be converted to P(y|x) for classification via Bayes rule, but the generative ability could be used for something else as well, such as creating likely new (x, y) samples.

Both models are useful, but generative models have one interesting advantage over discriminative models as they have the potential to understand and explain the underlying structure of the input data even when there are no labels. This is very desirable when working on data modelling problems in the real world, as unlabelled data is of course abundant, but getting labelled data is often expensive at best and impractical at worst.

The main idea behind a GAN is to have two competing neural network models. One takes noise as input and generates samples (and so is called the generator). The other model (called the discriminator) receives samples from both the generator and the training data, and has to be able to distinguish between the two sources. These two networks play a continuous game, where the generator is learning to produce more and more realistic samples, and the discriminator is learning to get better and better at distinguishing generated data from real data.

In a training process, a generator network and discriminative network tries to classify samples as either coming from true distribution p(x) or model distribution p(x). Every time the discriminator notices a difference between the two distributions the generator adjusts its parameters slightly to make it go away, until at the end (in theory) the generator exactly reproduces the true data distribution and the discriminator is guessing at random, unable to find a difference. The figure of 2-layer network from scalar to scalar for modeling both generator and discriminator network are shown:

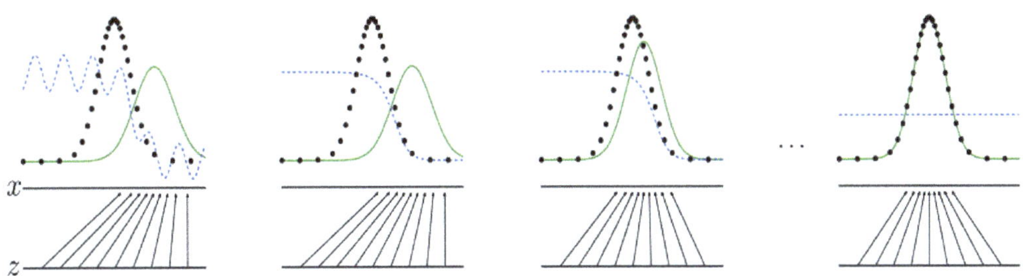

Fig Two layer network

In order to fully understand GANs, one has to understand the difference between Supervised and Unsupervised learning machines. Supervised machines are trained and tested based on large quantities of "labeled" samples. In other words, they require large datasets containing the "features" or "predictors" as well as its corresponding labels. As an example, a supervised image classifier engine would require a set of images with correct labels. Unsupervised learners don't have this luxury and they learn on the job as they go. They learn from mistakes and try not to make similar errors in the future.

The disadvantage of supervised machines is their need for large sums of labeled data. Labeling large number of samples is costly and time consuming. Unsupervised learners don't have this disadvantage but they tend to be less accurate. Naturally there is a strong motivation to improve the unsupervised machines and to lessen the reliance on the supervised ones. You can view GANs and RLs means of improving unsupervised machines.

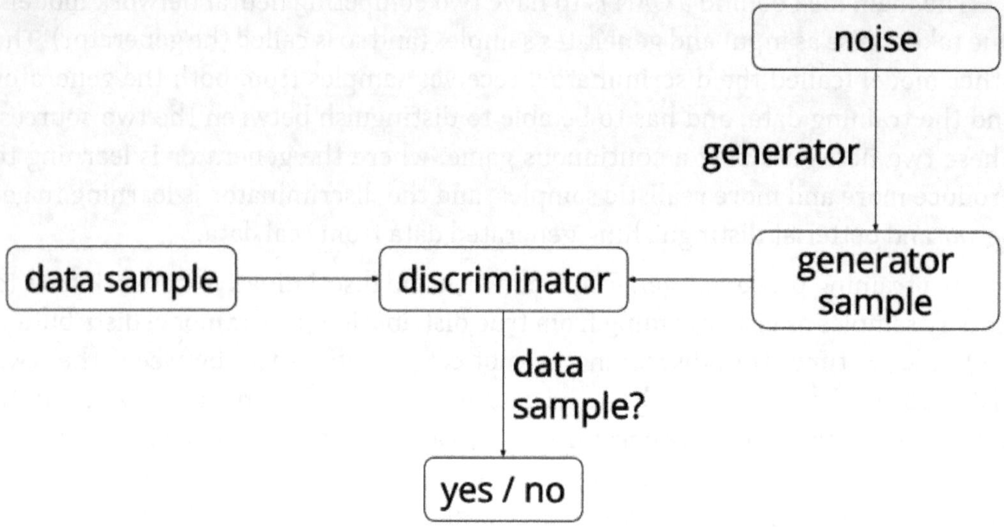

Fig: GAN overview

The analogy that is often used here is that the generator is like a forger trying to produce some counterfeit material, and the discriminator is like the police trying to detect the forged items. This setup may also seem somewhat reminiscent of reinforcement learning, where the generator is receiving a reward signal from the discriminator letting it know whether the generated data is accurate or not. The key difference with GANs however is that it propagates gradient information from discriminator back to generator network, so generator knows how to adapt its parameters in order to produce output data that can fool the discriminator.

Keeping these two concepts in mind, we now can tackle GANs. You can view a GAN as a new architecture for an unsupervised neural network able to achieve far better performance compared to traditional nets. To be more precise GANs are a new way of training a neural net. GANs contain not one but two independent nets that work separately and act as adversaries. The first neural net is called the Discriminator (D) and is the net that has to undergo training. D is the classifier that will do the heavy lifting during the normal operation once the training is complete. The second network is called the Generator (G) and is tasked to generate random samples that resemble real samples with a twist rendering them as fake samples.

Consider image classifier D designed to identify a series of images depicting various animals. Now consider an adversary (G) with the mission to fool D using carefully crafted images that look almost right but not quite. This is done by picking a legitimate sample randomly from training set (latent space) and synthesizing a new image by randomly altering its features (by adding random noise). As an example, G can fetch the image of a cat and can add an extra eye to the image converting it to a false sample. The result is an image very similar to a normal cat with the exception of the number of eye.

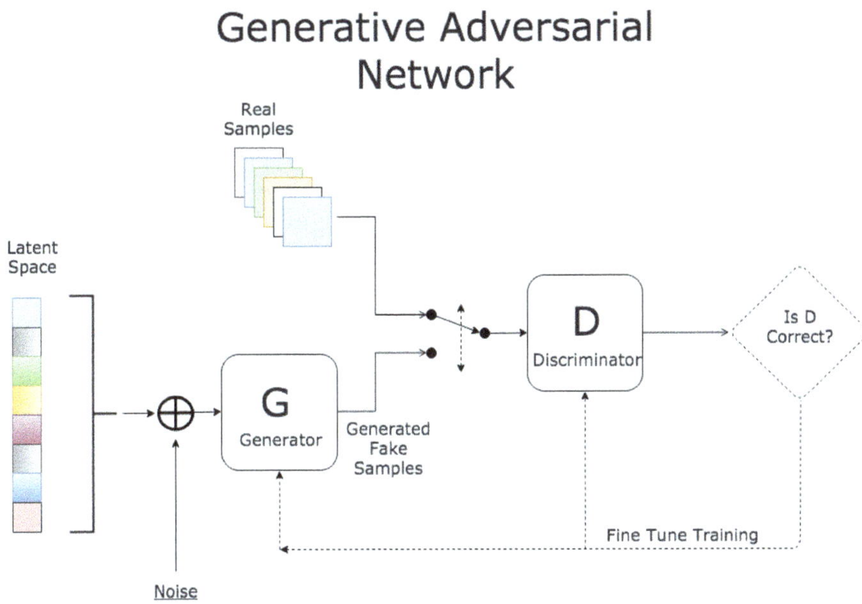

Fig: Network

During training, D is presented with a random mix of legitimate images from training data as well as fake images generated by G. Its task is to identify correct and fake inputs. Based on the outcome, both machines try to fine-tune their parameters and become better in what they do. If D makes the right prediction, G updates its parameters in order to generate better fake samples to fool D. If D's prediction is incorrect, it tries to learn from its mistake to avoid similar mistakes in the future. The reward for net D is the number of right predictions and the reward for G is the number D's errors. This process continues until an equilibrium is established and D's training is optimized.

One of the weaknesses of early GANs was stability but we have seen very promising work that can alleviate this problem. In a way of an analogy, GANs act like the political environment of a country with two rival political parties. Each party continuously attempts to improve on its weaknesses while trying to find and leverage vulnerabilities in their adversary to push their agenda. Over time both parties become better operators.

GANs rely on the idea that a data generator is good if we cannot tell fake data apart from real data. In statistics, this is called a two-sample test - a test to answer the question whether datasets $X=\{x1,...xn\}$X={x1,...xn} and X′={x′1,...x′n}X′={x1′,... xn′} were drawn from the same distribution. The main difference between most statistics papers and GANs is that the latter use this idea in a constructive way. In other words, rather than just training a model to say 'hey, these two datasets don't look like they came from the same distribution, they use the two-sample test to provide training signal to a generative model. This allows us to improve the data generator until it generates something that resembles the real data. At the very least, it needs to fool the classifier.

As you can see, there are two pieces to GANs - first off, we need a device that might potentially be able to generate data that looks just like the real thing. If we are dealing with images, this needs to generate images. If we're dealing with speech, it needs to generate audio sequences, and so on. It is a generator network which is the second component that attempts to distinguish fake and real data from each other. Both networks are in competition with each other. The generator network attempts to fool the discriminator network. At that point, the discriminator network adapts to the new fake data. This information, in turn is used to improve the generator network, and so on.

Generator

Drawing some parameter z from a source of randomness, e.g. a normal distribution z~N(0,1). Apply a function f such that it get x′=G(u,w) and compute the gradient with respect to w to minimize log p(y=fake|x′)

Discriminator

Improve the accuracy of a binary classifier *ff*, i.e. maximize log p(y=fake|x′) and log p(y=true|x) for fake and real data respectively.

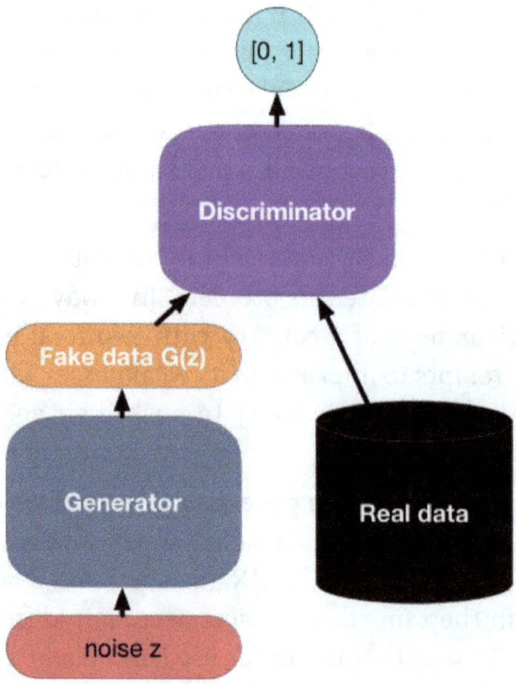

In short, there are two optimization problems running simultaneously, and the optimization terminates if a stalemate has been reached. There are lots of further tricks and details on how to modify this basic setting. For instance, we could try solving this problem in the presence of side information. This leads to cGAN, i.e. conditional Generative Adversarial Networks. We can change the way how we detect whether real and fake data look the same. This leads to wGAN, kernel-inspired GANs and lots of other settings, or we could change how closely we look at the objects. E.g. fake images might look real at the texture level but not so at the larger level, or vice versa.

2.3.2 Variational Autoencoders (VAEs)

VAEs tries to reconstruct output from input and consist of an encoder and decoder, which are encoding and decoding the data. However, instead of direct link among these two, there is a sampling layer in between them which samples from distribution and then feeds the generated samples to the decoder. With this, VAEs can be used as generative model that is able to generate specific features like specific digits or letters. It allows to formalize this problem in the framework of probabilistic graphical models where we are maximizing a lower bound on the log likelihood of the data.

A common way of describing a neural network is an approximation of some function we wish to model. However, they can also be thought of as a data structure that holds information.

Let's say we had a network comprised of a few deconvolution layers. We set the input to always be a vector of ones. Then, we can train the network to reduce the mean squared error between itself and one target image. The data for that image is contained in the network's parameters.

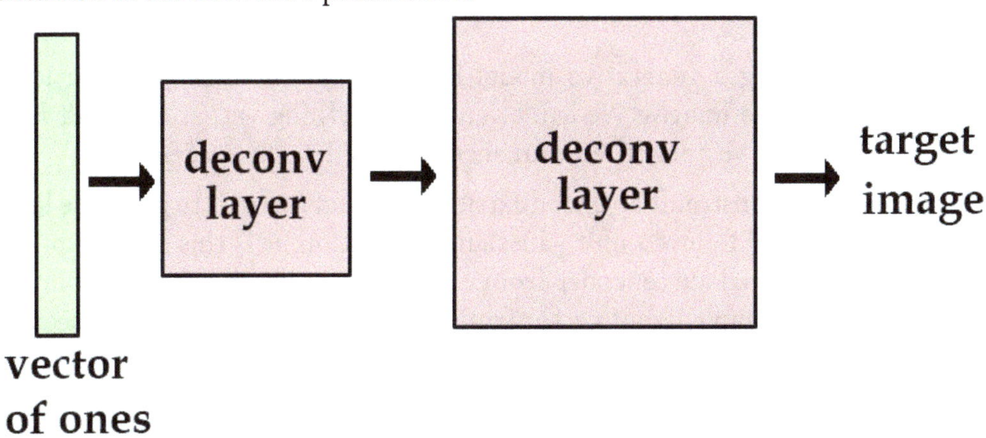

Fig: Neural Network

Now, let's try it on multiple images. Instead of a vector of ones, we'll use a one-hot vector for the input. [1, 0, 0, 0] could mean a cat image, while [0, 1, 0, 0] could mean a dog. This works, but we can only store up to 4 images. Using a longer vector means adding in more and more parameters so the network can memorize the different images.

For fixing this, use a vector of real numbers instead of a one-hot vector in shape of a code for an image, where the terms encode/decode come from. For example, [3.3, 4.5, 2.1, 9.8] could represent the target image, while [3.4, 2.1, 6.7, 4.2] could represent other image. This initial vector is known as our latent variables.

Selecting latent variables randomly, like as shown, is obviously a bad idea. In auto-encoder, add another component which takes in original images and encodes them into vectors. The de-convolutional layers then decode the vectors back to the original images.

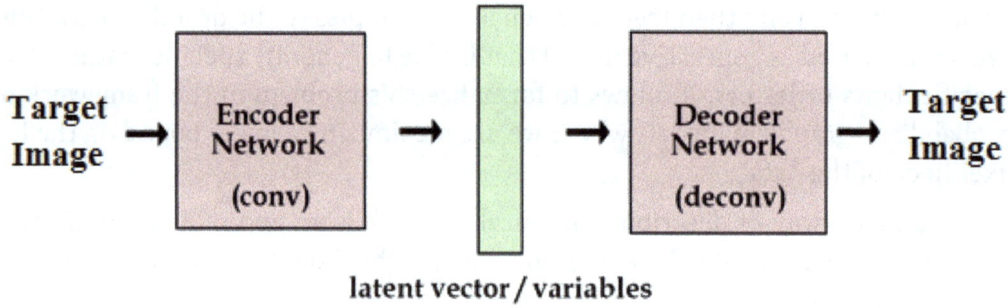

Fig: Model

Now finally, a stage appears where the model has some hint of practical use. Here we can train our network on as many images as required. If we save the encoded vector of an image, we can reconstruct it later by passing it into the decoder portion.

Further, building a generative model here, is not just fuzzy data structure which can memorize images. We can't generate anything yet, as we don't know how to create latent vectors other than encoding them from images.

For this, add a constraint on encoding network, that forces it to generate latent vectors that roughly follow a unit gaussian distribution. It is this constraint that separates a variational autoencoder from a standard one. Generating new images is easy as it needs sample latent vector from unit gaussian and pass it to decoder.

2.3.3 Autoregressive models

Autoregressive models are remarkably flexible at handling a wide range of different time series patterns. Autoregressive models are a fundamental class of time series models which take advantage of fact that time series data is sequential and is required to preserve the order or sequence of data for making accurate forecasts.

It includes Pixel RNN instead train a network that models the conditional distribution of every individual pixel given previous pixels. This is similar to plugging the pixels of the image into a char-rnn, but the RNNs run both horizontally and vertically over the image instead of just a 1D sequence of characters.

The forecasts of autoregressive models are regressed on previous observations in the time series. It shows past values of time series that has effect on current and future values of that series. Autoregressive models use weighted sums of past values to forecast future values. The equation that governs the forecasts takes the form of a linear model:

$$Y_t = A_0 + A_1 X_{t-1} + A_2 X_{t-2} + A_3 X_{t-3} + \dots + A_N X_{t-N} + e$$

For autoregressive models, coefficients of the model (A_1, A_2, A_3, ... , A_N) define the importance of lagged values. The largest coefficients are multiplied by observations in time series that holds the most weight. On rewriting this equation with contrived numbers for clarity, lets say we had 10 observations where every observation are used to build the model as shown:

$$Y_t = 0.9X_{t-1} + 0.7X_{t-2} + 0.5X_{t-3} + \dots + 0.2X_{t-10} + e$$

Here, the equation is showing the prediction where Y_t is dependent on most recent values X_{t-1} and least dependent on most lagged values in time series, X_{t-10}. This is indicative of how many time series work. However, the coefficients don't necessarily have to follow this decreasing pattern as shown in the equation above. The main takeaway is that the coefficients help define how correlated a time series is with past values of itself.

All of these approaches have their pros and cons. For example, Variational Autoencoders allow us to perform both learning and efficient Bayesian inference in sophisticated probabilistic graphical models with latent variables. However, their generated samples tend to be slightly blurry. GANs currently generate the sharpest images but they are more difficult to optimize due to unstable training dynamics. Pixel RNNs have a very simple and stable training process and currently give the best log likelihoods. However, they are relatively inefficient during sampling and don't easily provide simple low-dimensional codes for images.

2.4 BUILDING GENERATIVE MODELS

Generative modeling is an approach to computer-assisted geometric modeling. The goal of the approach is to allow convenient and high-level specification of shapes, and provide tools for rendering and analysis of the specified shapes. Shapes include curves, surfaces, and solids in 3D space, as well as higher-dimensional entities such as surfaces deforming in time, and solids with a spatially varying mass density.

Shape specification in the approach involves combining low-dimensional entities, especially 2D curves, into higher-dimensional shapes. This combination is specified through a powerful shape description language which builds multidimensional parametric functions. The language is based on a set of primitive operators on parametric functions which include arithmetic operators, vector and matrix operators, integration and differentiation, constraint solution and global optimization. Although each-primitive operator is fairly simple, high-level shapes and shape building operators can be defined using recursive combination of the primitive operators.

The approach encourages the modeler to build parameterized families of shapes rather than single instances. Shapes can be parameterized by scalar parameters (e.g., time or joint angle) or higher-dimensional parameters (e.g., a curve controlling how the scale of a cross section varies as it is translated). Such parameterized shapes allow easy modification of the design, since the modeler can interact with parameters that relate to high-level properties of the shape. In contrast, many geometric modeling systems use a much lower-level specification, such as through sets of many 3D control points.

Tools for rendering and analysis of generative models are developed using the concept of interval analysis. Each primitive operator on parametric functions has an inclusion function method, which produces an interval bound on the range of the function, given an interval bound on its domain. With these inclusion functions, robust algorithms exist for computing solutions to nonlinear systems of constraints and global minimization problems, when these problems are expressed in the modeling language. These algorithms, in turn, are developed into robust approximation techniques to compute intersections, CSG operations, and offset operations.

2.5 REPRESENTING WORKING MODELS WITH PROBABILISTIC PROGRAMS

A generative model describes a process, usually one by which observable data is generated. Generative models represent knowledge about the causal structure of the world which simplified as working models of domain. These models may then be used to answer many different questions, by conditional inference. This contrasts to a more procedural or mechanistic approach in which knowledge represents the input-output mapping for a particular question directly. While such generative models often describe how we think the "actual world" works, there are many cases where it is useful to have a generative model even if there is no "fact of the matter".

A prime example of the latter is in linguistics, where generative models of grammar can usefully describe the possible sentences in a language by describing a process for constructing sentences.

It is possible to use deterministic generative models to describe possible ways a process could unfold, but due to sparsity of observations or actual randomness there will often be many ways that our observations could have been generated. How can we choose amongst them? Probability theory provides a system for reasoning under exactly this kind of uncertainty. Probabilistic generative models describe processes which unfold with some amount of randomness, and probabilistic inference describes ways to ask questions of such processes.

Probabilistic programming language aim to close this representational gap, unifying general purpose programming with probabilistic modeling; literally, users specify a probabilistic model in its entirety (e.g., by writing code that generates a sample from the joint distribution) and inference follows automatically given the specification. These languages provide the full power of modern programming languages for describing complex distributions, and can enable reuse of libraries of models, support interactive modeling and formal verification, and provide a much-needed abstraction barrier to foster generic, efficient inference in universal model classes.

We believe that the probabilistic programming language approach within AI has the potential to fundamentally change the way we understand, design, build, test and deploy probabilistic systems. This approach has seen growing interest within AI over the last 10 years, yet the endeavor builds on over 40 years of work in range of diverse fields including mathematical logic, theoretical computer science, formal methods, programming languages, as well as machine learning, computational statistics, systems biology, probabilistic AI.

2.5.1 Probabilistic Programming Systems

Below we have compiled a list of probabilistic programming systems including languages, implementations/compilers, as well as software libraries for constructing probabilistic models and toolkits for building probabilistic inference algorithms.

- Alchemy is a software package providing a series of algorithms for statistical relational learning and probabilistic logic inference, based on the Markov logic representation.
- Anglican is a portable Turing-complete research probabilistic programming language that includes particle MCMC inference.

- BLOG, or Bayesian logic, is a probabilistic programming language with elements of first-order logic, as well as an MCMC-based inference algorithm. BLOG makes it relatively easy to represent uncertainty about the number of underlying objects explaining observed data.
- BUGS is a language for specifying finite graphical models and accompanying software for performing B(ayesian) I(nference) U(sing) G(ibbs) S(ampling), although modern implementations (such as WinBUGS, JAGS, and OpenBUGS) are based on Metropolis-Hastings. BiiPS is an implementation based on interacting particle systems methods like Sequential Monte Carlo.
- Church is a universal probabilistic programming language, extending Scheme with probabilistic semantics, and is well suited for describing infinite-dimensional stochastic processes and other recursively-defined generative processes (Goodman, Mansinghka, Roy, Bonawitz and Tenenbaum, 2008). The active implementation of Church is webchurch. Older implementations include MIT-Church, Cosh, Bher, and JSChurch. See also Venture below.
- Dimple is a software tool that performs inference and learning on probabilistic graphical models via belief propagation algorithms or sampling based algorithms.
- Edward is a python library for probabilistic modeling that builds on top of TensorFlow to support distributed training and hardware such as GPUs.
- FACTORIE is a Scala library for creating relational factor graphs, estimating parameters and performing inference.
- Figaro is a Scala library for constructing probabilistic models that also provides a number of built-in reasoning algorithms that can be applied automatically to any constructed models.
- HANSEI is a domain-specific language embedded in OCaml, which allows one to express discrete-distribution models with potentially infinite support, perform exact inference as well as importance sampling-based inference, and model inference over inference.
- Hakaru is a simply-typed probabilistic programming language which offers composable and pluggable inference engines as well as computer-algebra guided program optimization.
- Hierarchical Bayesian Compiler (HBC) is a language for expressing and compiler for implementing hierarchical Bayesian models, with a focus on large-dimension discrete models and support for a number of non-parametric process priors.

- LibBi is a library for Bayesian inference, based largely on the sequential Monte Carlo framework.
- Markov the Beast is a software package for statistical relational learning and structured prediction based on Markov logic.
- NIMBLE is a system for building and sharing analysis methods for statistical models, especially for hierarchical models and computationally-intensive methods. NIMBLE is built in R but compiles your models and algorithms using C++ for speed. NIMBLE borrows the syntax of BUGS.
- PRISM is a general programming language for logic-based probabilistic modeling that offers various learning methods for generative modeling (Bayesian and non-Bayesian), discriminative modeing and rank learning.
- Infer.NET is a software library developed by Microsoft for expressing graphical models and implementing Bayesian inference using a variety of algorithms.
- PRAiSE is a system performing probabilistic inference without grounding random variables or sampling, but instead performing it exactly and directly over an expressive higher-level language involving difference arithmetic over integers, linear real arithmetic, equality over categorical types, with relational random variables and algebraic data types coming next.
- Probabilistic-C is a C-language probabilistic programming system that, using standard compilation tools, automatically produces a compiled parallel inference executable from C-language generative model code.
- ProbLog is a probabilistic extension of Prolog based on Sato's distribution semantics. While ProbLog1 focuses on calculating the success probability of a query, ProbLog2 can calculate both conditional probabilities and MPE states.
- Probabilistic Soft Logic is a machine learning framework for developing probabilistic models. Models are defined using a straightforward logical syntax and solved via convex optimization.
- PyMC is a python module that implements a suite of MCMC algorithms as python classes, and is extremely flexible and applicable to a large suite of problems. PyMC includes methods for summarizing output, plotting, goodness-of-fit and convergence diagnostics.
- PyMLNs is a toolbox and software library for learning and inference in Markov logic networks.
- R2 is a probabilistic programming system that employs powerful techniques from programming language design, program analysis and verification for scalable and efficient inference.

- Stan exposes a language for defining probability density functions for probabilistic models. Stan includes a compiler, which produces C++ code that performs Bayesian inference via a method similar to Hamiltonian Monte Carlo sampling.
- Tuffy is a highly scalable inference engine for Markov logic networks using a database backend.
- Venture is an interactive, Turing-complete, higher-order probabilistic programming platform that aims to be sufficiently expressive, extensible and efficient for general-purpose use. Its virtual machine supports multiple scalable, reprogrammable inference strategies, plus two front-end languages: VenChurch and VentureScript.
- WebPPL A PPL based on and implemented in Javascript. Include MH, SMC, variational, and other experimental inference engines.

2.6 PREDICTION, SITUATION AND PROBABILITIES

The basic idea is to build two models and to pit them against each other. The generative model takes random inputs and tries to generate output data that "look like" real data. The discriminative model takes as input data from both the generative model and real data and tries to correctly distinguish between them. By updating each model in turn iteratively, an equilibrium is achieved where neither discriminator nor generator improves. At this point, generator is doing it's best to fool discriminator, and discriminator is doing it's best not to be fooled. The result is a generative model which, given some random inputs, will output data which appears to be a plausible sample from your dataset

Suppose that we flip two fair coins, and return the list of their values:

(list (flip) (flip))

For predicting the return value of the program, a probability is a number between 0 and 1 that expresses the answer to such a question which served as a degree of belief that we will see a given outcome, such as (#t #f). The probability if an event A as shown returns (#t #f)) which is written as: $P(A)$.

As did above, we can sample many times and examine the histogram of return values:

(define (random-pair) (list (flip) (flip)))

It is observed that parentheses around random-pair makes an object that can be sampled many times in a single execution of the program as described below.

We see by examining this histogram as (#t #f) which with 0.25 of time. So probability of a return value is defined to be the fraction of times as this value is returned from evaluating the program, then probability of (#t #f) from above results as 0.25.

Even for very complicated programs we can predict the probability of different outcomes by simulating (sampling from) the program. It is also often useful to compute these probabilties directly by reasoning about the sampling process.

2.6.1 Product Rule

In an example, considering three steps to find the output value that can be sample from first (flip), then from second and finally making list from the values. For this, re-write the program as:

- (define A (flip))
- (define B (flip))

It is observed that the probability of #t for A is 0.5 while probability of #f from B is 0.5. Can we use these two probabilities to arrive at the probability of 0.25 for the overall outcome C=(#t #f)? Yes, using the product rule of probabilities:

The probability of two random choices is the product of their individual probabilities.

The probability of many random options together is often known as joint probability and is written as $P(A,B)$. Since the first and second random choices must each have their specified values in order to get (#t #f) in the example, the joint probability is their product: 0.25.

You need to be careful while using this rule, as probability of a choice can depend on probabilities of earlier choices. For instance, compute the probability of (#t #f) resulting from this program:

- (define a (flip))
- (define b (flip (if a 0.3 0.7)))

In general, the joint probability of two random choices A and B made sequentially, in that order, can be written as $P(A,B) = P(A) P(B|A)$. This is read as the product of the probability of <math>A</ math> and the probability of "B given A", or "B conditioned on A" -- that is, the probability of making choice B given that choice A has been made in a certain way.

It is noted that when the second choice is independent of first choice, will the expression reduces to the product of simple probabilities of each choice individually:

$P(A,B) = P(A) P(B)$.

What is the relation between $P(A,B)$ and $P(B,A)$, the joint probability of the same choices written in the opposite order? The only logically consistent definitions of probability require that these two probabilities be equal, so $P(A) P(B|A) = P(B) P(A|B)$.

2.6.2 Sum Rule or Marginalization

Now let's consider an example where we can't determine from the overall return value the sequence of random choices that were made:

(or (flip) (flip))

We can sample from this program and determine that the probability of returning #t is about 0.75. We cannot simply use the product rule to determine this probability because we don't know the sequence of random choices that led to this return value. However we can notice that the program will return true if the two component choices are #t,#t, or #t,#f, or #f,#t. To combine these possibilities we use another rule for probabilities:

'If there are two alternative sequences of choices that lead to the same return value, the probability of this return value is the sum of the probabilities of the sequences.'

If there are two alternative sequences of choices that lead to the same return value, the probability of this return value is the sum of the probabilities of the sequences. We can write this using probability notation as:

$P(A) = \sum_{B} P(A,B)$

where we see A as final value and B as sequence of random choices on way to that value.

Using product rule we can determine that the probability in example as 0.25 for each sequence that leads to return value #t, then, by sum rule, where probability of #t is 0.25+0.25+0.25=0.75.

Using sum rule to find the probability of a final value is known as marginalization. From the point of view of sampling processes, marginalization is ignoring intermediate random values that are created on the way to final return value. From the point of view of directly computing probabilities, marginalization is summing over all the possible "histories" that could lead to a return value.

2.6.3 Building Functions and Distributions

The power of lambda calculus as a model of computation comes from the ability to make new functions. To do so, we use the lambda primitive. For example, we can construct a function that doubles any number it is applied to:

(define double (lambda (x) (+ x x)))

The general form of a lambda expression is: lambda arguments body

The first sub-expression of lambda, the arguments, is a list of symbols that tells us what the inputs to the function will be called; the second sub-expression, the body, tells us what to do with these inputs. The value which results from a lambda expression is called a compound procedure. When a compound procedure is applied to input values we imagine identifying (also called binding) the argument variables with these inputs, then evaluating the body. As another simple example, consider this function:

```
   (lambda              (x)               (+     x     4))
      ↑                  ↑                 ↑     ↑     ↑
the procedure   of an argument x   that adds   x and 4
```

We also use lambda to construct more complex stochastic functions from primitive ones. Here is a stochastic function which only sometimes double its input:

(define noisy-double (lambda (x) (if (flip) x (+ x x))))

In lambda calculus we can build procedures that manipulate any kind of value -- even other procedures. Here we define a function twice which takes a procedure and returns a new procedure that applies the original twice:

(define double (lambda (x) (+ x x)))

This ability to make higher-order functions is what makes the lambda calculus a universal model of computation. Since we often want to assign names to functions, (define (foo x) ...) is short ("syntactic sugar") for (define foo (lambda (x) ...)). For example we could have written the previous example:

(define (double x) (+ x x))

A lambda expression with an empty argument list, (lambda () ...), is called a thunk which acts as a function that takes no input arguments. If we apply a thunk, we get a return value back, for example (flip), and on doing it many times, we can locate the marginal probability of each return value. Thus thunk is an object that shows whole probability distribution. By using higher-order functions we can construct and manipulate probability distributions.

Example: Flipping Coins

The following program defines a fair coin, and flips it 20 times:

(define fair-coin (lambda () (if (flip 0.5) 'h 't))) ;the thunk is a fair coin

(hist (repeat 20 fair-coin) "fair coin")

This program defines a "trick" coin that comes up heads most of the time (95%), and flips it 20 times:

(define trick-coin (lambda () (if (flip 0.95) 'h 't)))

(hist (repeat 20 trick-coin) "trick coin")

A common mistake when defining names for new functions and using them with higher-order functions like repeat is to confuse the name of a thunk with the name of a variable that stands for the output of a single function evaluation. For instance, why doesn't this work?

(define trick-coin-1 (if (flip 0.95) 'h 't))

(hist (repeat 20 trick-coin-1) "trick coin")

The higher-order function repeat requires as input a thunk, a procedure (or function) with no arguments, as returned by lambda in the examples above. Consider the difference in what is returned by these two code fragments:

(define trick-coin-1 (if (flip 0.95) 'h 't))

trick-coin-1

trick-coin-1 names a variable that is defined to be the result of evaluating the (if ...) expression a single time (either h or t), while below trick-coin-2 names a thunk that can serve as the input to the higher-order function repeat.

(define trick-coin-2 (lambda () (if (flip 0.95) 'h 't)))

trick-coin-2

The difference between these two programs becomes particularly subtle when using the (define (name) ...) syntax. Simply putting the name to be defined in parentheses turns a variable definition into a thunk definition:

(define (trick-coin-2) (if (flip 0.95) 'h 't))

trick-coin-2

To Church the last two definitions of trick-coin-2 are the same both output a thunk -- although superficially the last one looks more similar to the variable definition that assigns trick-coin-1 to a single value of h or t.

The higher-order function make-coin takes in a weight and outputs a function (a thunk) describing a coin with that weight. Then we can use make-coin to make the coins above, or others.

```
(define (make-coin weight) (lambda () (if (flip weight) 'h 't)))
(define fair-coin (make-coin 0.5))
```

We can also define a higher-order function that takes a "coin" and "bends it":

```
(define (make-coin weight) (lambda () (if (flip weight) 'h 't)))
(define (bend coin)
```

REFERENCES

Shah, S.A., Mohamadpour, M., Askin, G., Nakase-Richardson, R., Stokic, D.S., Sherer, M., Yablon, S.A., Schiff, N.D. (2017) Focal electroencephalographic changes index post-traumatic confusion and outcome. J. Neurotrauma, doi: 10.1089/neu.2016.4911.

Forgacs, P.B., Frey, H.-P., Velazquez, A., Thompson, S., Brodie, D., Moitra, V., Rabani, L, Park, S., Agarwal, S., Falo, M.C., Schiff, N.D., and Claassen, J. (2017) Dynamic regimes of neocortical activity linked to corticothalamic integrity correlate with outcomes in acute anoxic brain injury after cardiac arrest. Ann Clin. Transl. Neurol. 4, 119-129.

Shah, S.A., Goldin, Y., Conte, M.M., Goldfine, A.M., Mohamadpour, M., Fidali, B.C., Cicerone, K., and Schiff, N.D. (2017) Executive attention deficits after traumatic brain injury reflect impaired recruitment of resources. Neuroimage: Clinical 14, 233-241.

Adams, Z.M., Forgacs, P.B., Conte, M.M., Nauvel, T.J., Drover, J.D., Schiff, N.D. (2016) Late and progressive alterations of sleep dynamics following central thalamic deep brain stimulation (CT-DBS) in chronic minimally conscious state. Clinical Neurophysiology. doi: 10.1016/j.clinph.2016.06.028.

Melman, T., and Victor, J.D. (2016) Robust power spectral estimation for EEG data. J. Neurosci. Meth. 268, 14-22.

Reichenbach, C.S., Braiman, C., Schiff, N.D., Hudspeth, A.J., and Reichenbach, T. (2016) The auditory brainstem response to continuous, non-repetitive speech is modulated by the speech envelope and reflects speech processing. Front. Comput. Neurosci. doi: 10.3389/fncom.2016.00047.

Meltzer, B., Reichenbach, C.S., Braiman, C., Schiff, N.D., Hudspeth, A.J., and Reichenbach, T. (2016) The steady-state response of the cerebral cortex to the beat of music reflects both the comprehension of music and attention. Front. Hum. Neurosci. doi: 10.3389/fnhum.2015.00436.

Forgacs, P.B., Conte, M.M., Fridman, E.A., Voss, H.U., Victor, J.D., and Schiff, N.D. (2015) A proposed role for routine EEGs in patients with consciousness disorders. Annals of Neurology 77, 185-186.

Forgacs, P.B., Conte, M.M., Fridman, E.A., Voss, H.U., Victor, J.D., and Schiff, N.D. (2014) Preservation of EEG organization in patients with impaired consciousness and imaging-based evidence of command-following. Annals of Neurology 76, 869-79.

Schiff, N.D., Nauvel, T., and Victor, J.D. (2014) Large-scale brain dynamics in disorders of consciousness. Current Opinion in Neurobiology 25, 7-14.

Williams, S.T., Conte, M.M., Goldfine, A.M., Noirhomme, Q., Gosseries, O., Thonnard, M., Beattie, B., Hersh, J., Katz, D.I., Victor, J.D., Laureys, S., and Schiff, N.D. (2013) Common resting brain dynamics indicate a possible mechanism underlying zolpidem response in severely brain-injured subjects. eLife 2013;2:e01157.

Schiff, N.D., Nauvel, T., and Victor, J.D. (2013) Large-scale brain dynamics in disorders of consciousness. Current Opinion in Neurobiology, accepted.

Goldfine, A.M., Bardin, J.C., Noirhomme, Q., Fins, J.J., Schiff, N.D., and Victor, J.D. (2013) Reanalysis of "Bedside detection of awareness in the vegetative state: a cohort study." Lancet 381, 289-291.

Goldfine, A.M., Victor, J.D., Conte, M.M., Bardin, J.C., and Schiff, N.D. (2012) Bedside detection of awareness in the vegetative state (Letter re Cruse et al. (2011)) The Lancet, 379, 1701-1702.

Goldfine, A.M., Victor, J.D., Conte, M.M., Bardin, J.C., and Schiff, N.D. (2011) Determination of awareness in patients with severe brain injury using EEG power spectral analysis. Clinical Neurophysiology 122, 2157-2168.

Victor, J.D., Drover, J.D., Conte, M.M., and Schiff, N.D. (2011) Mean-field modeling of thalamocortical dynamics, and a model-driven approach to EEG analysis. Proc. Natl. Acad. Sci. USA 108, 15631-15638.

Drover, J.D., Schiff, N.D., and Victor, J.D. (2010) Dynamics of coupled thalamocortical modules. Journal of Computational Neuroscience 28, 605-616.

Kobylarz, E.J., and Schiff, N.D. (2005)Neurophysiological correlates of persistent vegetative and minimally conscious states. Neuropsychol. Rehabil. 15, 323-332.

Repucci, M.A., Schiff, N.D., and Victor, J.D. (2001) General strategy for hierarchical decomposition of multivariate time series: implications for temporal lobe seizures. Annals of Biomedical Engineering 29, 1135-1149.

Schiff, N.D., Labar, D.R., and Victor, J.D. (1999) Common dynamics in temporal lobe seizures and absence seizures. Neuroscience 91, 417-428.

Schiff, N.D., Victor, J.D., Canel, A., and Labar, D.R. (1995) Characteristic nonlinearities of the 3/second ictal EEG identified by nonlinear autoregressive analysis. Biological Cybernetics 72, 519-526.

Schiff, N.D., Victor, J.D., and Canel, A. (1995) Nonlinear autoregressive analysis of the 3/second ictal EEG: implications for underlying dynamics. Biological Cybernetics 72, 527-532.

Victor, J.D., and Canel, A. (1992) A relation between the Akaike criterion and reliability of parameter estimates, with application to nonlinear autoregressive modelling of ictal EEG. Annals of Biomedical Engineering 20, 167-180.

Victor, J.D., and Mast, J. (1991) A new statistic for steady-state evoked potentials. Electroenceph. Clin. Neurophysiol. 78, 378-388.

Mast, J., and Victor, J.D. (1991) Fluctuations of steady-state VEP's: Interaction of driven evoked potentials and the EEG. Electroenceph. Clin. Neurophysiol. 78, 389-401.

Gutowitz, H., Zemon, V., Victor, J.D., and Knight, B.W. (1986) Source geometry and dynamics of the visual evoked potential. Electroenceph. Clin. Neurophysiol. 64, 308-327.

3 Chapter
CONDITIONING

3.1 COGNITION AND CONDITIONING

3.1.1 Introduction

The computational theory of mind will involve in answering about thought and in describing the intelligent inferences that made in everyday human reasoning and learning. Using computational theory of mind, starting from the hypothesis that the mind is a computer, mental representations are computer programs, and thinking is a computational process till running a computer program are covered.

A natural assumption is that such program take the inputs, percepts from the senses, facts from memory, etc and find the outputs with intelligent behaviors. Thus the mental representations that lead to thinking are functions from inputs to outputs. However, this input-output view suffers from a combinatorial explosion: we must posit an input-output program for each task in which humans draw intelligent inferences. A different approach is to assume that mental representations are more like theories: pieces of knowledge that can support many inferences in many different situations.

For instance, Newton's theory of motion makes predictions about infinitely many different configurations of objects and can be used to reason both forward in time and from the consequences of an interaction to the initial state. The generative approach posits that mental representations are more like theories in this way: they capture more general descriptions of how the world works hence, the programs of the mind are models of the world that can be used to make many inferences.

Generative model describes a process, one by which observable data is generated. Generative models shows knowledge about the causal structure of the world, working models of a domain. These models may then be used to answer many different questions, by conditional inference. This contrasts to a more procedural or mechanistic approach in which knowledge represents the input-output mapping for a particular question directly. While such generative models often describe how we think the "actual world" works, there are many cases where it is useful to have a generative model even if there is no "fact of the matter". A prime example of the latter is in linguistics, where generative models of grammar can usefully describe the possible sentences in a language by describing a process for constructing sentences.

It is possible to use deterministic generative models to describe possible ways a process could unfold, but due to sparsity of observations or actual randomness there will often be many ways that our observations could have been generated. How can we choose amongst them? Probability theory provides a system for reasoning under exactly this kind of uncertainty. Probabilistic generative models describe processes which unfold with some amount of randomness, and probabilistic inference describes ways to ask questions of such processes. This tutorial is concerned with the knowledge that can be represented by probabilistic generative models and the inferences that can be drawn from them.

In order to make the idea of generative models precise we want a formal language that is designed to express the kinds of knowledge individuals have about the world. This language should be universal in the sense that it should be able to express any (computable) process. We build on the λ-calculus (as realized in functional programming languages) because the λ-calculus describes computational processes and captures the idea that what is important is causal dependence—in particular the λ-calculus does not focus on the sequence of time, but rather on which events influence which other events. We introduce randomness into this language to construct a stochastic λ-calculus, and describe conditional inferences in this language.

3.1.2 Conditioning

We have built up a tool set for constructing probabilistic generative models. These can represent knowledge about causal processes in the world: running one of these programs samples a particular outcome by sampling a "causal history" for that outcome. However, the power of a causal model lies in the flexible ways it can be used to reason about the world. For instance, if we have a generative model in which X depends on Y, we may ask: "assuming I have observed X, how must Y have been?" In this section we describe how a wide variety of inferences can be made from a single generative model by conditioning the model on an assumed or observed fact.

Much of cognition can be understood in terms of conditional inference. In its most basic form, causal reasoning is conditional inference: given some observed effects, what were the likely causes? Predictions are conditional inferences in the opposite direction: given that I have observed some known cause, what are its likely effects? These inferences come from conditioning a probabilistic program expressing a "causal model", or an understanding of how effects depend on causes. The acquisition of that causal model, or learning, is also conditional inference at a higher level of abstraction: given our general knowledge of how causal relations operate in the world, and some observed events in which candidate causes and effects co-occur in various ways, what specific causal relations are likely to hold between these observed variables?

To see how these concepts apply in a domain that is not usually thought of as causal, consider language. The core questions of interest in the study of natural language are all at heart conditional inference problems. Given beliefs about the syntactic structure of my language, and an observed sentence, what should it is seen about the syntactic structure of that sentence? This is just the parsing problem. The complementary problem of speech production is as follows: given some beliefs about the syntactic structure of a language and a particular thought that is expressed on how to encode the thought syntactically. Finally, the discovery or acquisition problem: given general knowledge about universal grammar and some data from a particular language, what should we believe about that language's structure? This problem is simultaneously the problem facing the linguist and the child trying to learn a language.

Parallel problems of conditional inference arise in visual perception, theory of mind (or intuitive psychology), and virtually every other domain of cognition. In visual perception, we observe an image or image sequence that is the result of rendering a three-dimensional physical scene onto our two-dimensional retinas. A probabilistic program can model both the physical processes at work in the world that produce natural scenes, and the imaging processes (the "graphics") that render images from scenes. Perception is then conditioning this program on some observed output image and inferring the scenes most likely to have given rise to it. In interacting with other people, we observe the actions of intentional agents that are the outputs of planning processes: programs that take as input an agent's mental states (beliefs and desires) and produce action sequences -- typically, for a rational agent, actions that are likely to produce the agent's desired states as reliably or efficiently as possible, given the agent's beliefs. A rational agent can plan their actions by conditional inference to infer what steps would be most likely to achieve their desired state. Action understanding, or interpreting an agent's observed behavior, can be expressed as conditioning a planning program (a "theory of mind") on the observed actions to infer the mental states that most likely gave rise to those actions, and to predict how the agent is likely to act in the future.

Hypothetical Reasoning with Query

Suppose that we know some fixed fact, and we wish to consider hypotheses about how a generative model could have given rise to that fact. On using special function called as query with following interface:

(query

generative-model

what-we-want-to-know

what-we-know)

query takes three arguments.

The first is some generative model expressed as a series of define statements. The second is an expression, called the query expression, which represents the aspects of the computation that we are interested in. The last argument is the condition that must be met; this may encode observations, data, or more general assumptions. It is called the conditioner.

Consider the following simple generative process.

(define A (if (flip) 1 0))

(define B (if (flip) 1 0))

This process samples three digits 0/1 and adds the result. The value of the final expression here is either 0, 1, 2 or 3. A priori, each of the variables A, B, C has .5 probability of being 1 or 0. However, suppose that we have observed that the sum D is equal to 3. How does this change the space of possible values that variable A can take on? It is obvious that A must be equal to 1 for this result to happen. We can see this in the following Church:

(define (take-sample)

(rejection-query

The output of rejection-query is a "guess" about the likely value of A, conditioned on D being equal to 3. We use repeat to take 100 guesses, which are then turned into a bar graph representing relative probabilities using the hist function. Because A must necessarily equal 1, the histogram shows 100% of the samples on that value.

Now suppose that we condition on D being greater than or equal to 2. Then A need not be 1, but it is more likely than not to be. The corresponding histogram shows the appropriate distribution of "guesses" for A conditioned on this new fact:

(define (take-sample)

(rejection-query

Predicting the outcome of a generative process is simply a special case of querying, where we condition on no restrictions (simply true) and ask about the outcome:

(define (take-sample)

(rejection-query

Conditional Distributions

The definition of conditional distribution in terms of rejection sampling is equivalent to the formal definition of conditional probability in probability theory. Conditional probabilities are often written $P(A=a|B=b)$ for the probability that "event" A has value a given that B has value b. (The meaning of events A and B must be given elsewhere, unlike a Church program, which contains the full model specification.) In the case of a Church query, $A=a$ is the "event" of the query expression returning value a, while $B=b$ will be the conditioner returning true (so b will be true). The conditional probability can be defined the ratio:

$P(A=a|B=b)=\frac{P(A=a,B=b)}{P(B=b)}.$

That is, the conditional probability is the ratio of the joint probability to the probability of the condition.

We can use the process of rejection sampling to understand this alternative definition of the conditional probability $P(A=a|B=b)$. We imagine sampling many times, but only keeping those samples in which the condition is true, i.e. $B=true$. The frequency of the query expression returning a particular value a (i.e. $A=a$) given that the condition is true, will be the number of times that $A=a$ and $B=true$ divided by the number of times that $B=true$. Since the frequency of the conditioner returning true will be $P(B=true)$ in the long run, and the frequency that the condition returns true and the query expression returns a given value a will be $P(A=a,B=true)$, we get the above formula for the conditional probability.

3.2 HYPOTHETICAL REASONING WITH INFER

3.2.1 Marginal distribution

If X and Y are discrete random variables and f (x,y) is the value of their joint probability distribution at (x,y), the functions given by:

g(x) = Σy f (x,y) and h(y) = Σx f (x,y) are the marginal distributions of X and Y , respectively.

If you're great with equations, that's probably all you need to know. It tells you how to find a marginal distribution. But if that formula gives you pain, you can use a frequency distribution table to find a marginal distribution.

A marginal distribution gets it's name because it appears in the margins of a probability distribution table.

Table: Probability Distribution Table

i/j	1	2	3	4	5	6	px(i)
1	1/36	1/36	1/36	1/36	1/36	1/36	1/6
2	1/36	1/36	1/36	1/36	1/36	1/36	1/6
3	1/36	1/36	1/36	1/36	1/36	1/36	1/6
4	1/36	1/36	1/36	1/36	1/36	1/36	1/6
5	1/36	1/36	1/36	1/36	1/36	1/36	1/6
6	1/36	1/36	1/36	1/36	1/36	1/36	1/6
py(j)	1/6	1/6	1/6	1/6	1/6	1/6	

Of course, it's not quite as simple as that. You can't just look at any old frequency distribution table and say that the last column (or row) is a "marginal distribution." Marginal distributions follow a couple of rules:

The distribution must be from bivariate data. Bivariate is just another way of saying "two variables," like X and Y. In the table above, the random variables i and j are coming from the roll of two dice.

A marginal distribution is where you are only interested in one of the random variables . In other words, either X or Y. If you look at the probability table above, the sum probabilities of one variable are listed in the bottom row and the other sum probabilities are listed in the right column. So this table has two marginal distributions.

A marginal distribution of a variable is a frequency or relative frequency distribution of either the row or column variable in the contingency table.

Consider a survey given to 82 students in a Basic Algebra course at ECC, with the following responses to the statement "I enjoy math."

	Strongly Agree	Agree	Neutral	Disagree	Strongly Disagree
Men	9	13	5	2	1
Women	12	18	11	6	5

To study this relationship and finding a way to tell if gender and whether the student enjoys math, it needs background work.

If we consider the example:

	Strongly Agree	Agree	Neutral	Disagree	Strongly Disagree
Men	9	13	5	2	1
Women	12	18	11	6	5

The entire table is referred to as the contingency table. The marginal distribution for gender removes the effect of whether or not the student enjoys math:

	Strongly Agree	Agree	Neutral	Disagree	Strongly Disagree	Total
Men	9	13	5	2	1	**30**
Women	12	18	11	6	5	**52**

Whereas, the marginal distribution for whether or not the student enjoys math removes the effect of gender:

	Strongly Agree	Agree	Neutral	Disagree	Strongly Disagree
Men	9	13	5	2	1
Women	12	18	11	6	5
Total	**21**	**31**	**16**	**8**	**6**

We can also create a relative frequency marginal distribution, which, as expected, is simply relative frequencies rather than frequencies.

Example:

The combined relative frequency marginal distributions would look like this:

	SA	A	N	D	SD	Total
Men	9	13	5	2	1	30
Women	12	18	11	6	5	52
Total	21	31	16	8	6	82

We might now be interested in comparing the two variables. For example:

What proportion of women strongly agreed with the statement "I enjoy math"?

What proportion of women disagreed?

What proportion of men were neutral?

What proportion of men strongly agreed?

Solution:

There were 12 women who strongly agreed, and 52 women in all, so $12/52 \approx 0.23$

Similarly, there were 6 women who disagreed, and 52 overall, so $6/52 \approx 0.12$

$5/30 \approx 0.17$

$9/30 \approx 0.30$

If we completed the table in this fashion, we get something called a conditional distribution. A conditional distribution lists the relative frequency of each category of variable, given a specific value of the other variable in the contingency table.

One thing we can use conditional distributions for is to identify an association between qualitative variables. The best way to do this is a side-by-side bar graph.

Example:

In Example, we found the conditional distribution of gender by how the student feels regarding math:

	SA	A	N	D	SD
Men	9/21≈ 0.43	13/31≈ 0.42	5/16≈ 0.31	2/8= 0.25	1/6≈ 0.17
Women	12/21≈ 0.57	18/31≈ 0.58	11/16≈ 0.69	6/8= 0.75	5/6≈ 0.83
Total	21/21= 1	31/31= 1	16/16= 1	8/8= 1	6/6= 1

Since it's difficult to gain much from this table alone, a good way to analyze this would be to make a side-by-side bar graph.

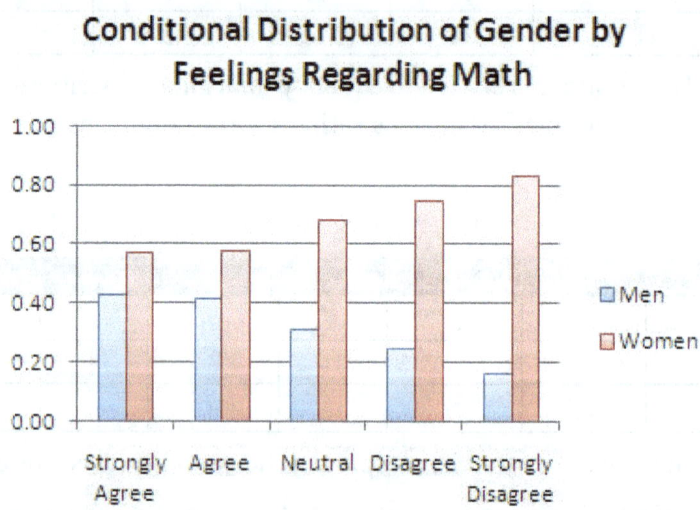

From the graph, we can see that there definitely appear to be some differences between the different responses. The proportions of responses were similar for both "Strongly Agree" and "Agree", but very different for "Neutral" and "Disagree". As we go down the scale, the proportion of the responses that are by women increases.

3.2.2 Inference on marginal distribution

Clustered data problems are encountered everywhere in biomedical research and, not surprisingly, the statistical methods involving the analysis of cluster correlated data have been subject to intensive research even until today. A typical situation is that instead of sampling N independent and identically distributed (i.i.d.) random variables, the researcher samples observations in (say) M clusters with known cluster memberships. Observations within a cluster tend to be similar in some way but can be assumed independent across clusters.

To be more specific, write $Y_{i1},\ldots, Y_{iN_i}$ for the N_i observations in the i th cluster, $i = 1,\ldots, M$. Let X_{ij} be a possible vector of (random or fixed) explanatory variables for the response valueY_{ij}, $i = 1,\ldots, M; j = 1,\ldots, N_i$.

The cluster sizes $N_1,\ldots, N_M$ are often simply thought to be fixed design constants. In the linear regression model it is then assumed that, for a correct value β,

- The marginal distributions of $\varepsilon_{ij} = Y_{ij} - \beta' X_{ij}$ are all the same,
- All the bivariate distributions of $(\varepsilon_{ij}, \varepsilon_{ij}'), j \neq j'$ are the same,
- ε_{ij} and $\varepsilon_{i'j'}, i \neq i'$ are independent.

If multivariate normality of the random errors ε_{ij} can be assumed, for example, the most popular technique for valid statistical inference for the parameter β is to employ mixed models with cluster effects as random effects. Alternatively, one can work out the variance terms for different test statistics, and modify the tests accordingly. Introduction of weights (indirectly present in likelihood inference for mixed models) can potentially improve the efficiency of the analysis, but variance adjusted test and estimating procedures based on different weighting schemes all provide valid statistical inference in this model. If $N_1,\ldots, N_M$ are random and the joint distribution of the random errors ε_{ij} does not depend on $N_1,\ldots, N_M$, it is still reasonable to assume that (i–iii) hold.

A much more complex setting arises when the cluster size may have an influence on the measured values, or vice versa, or possibly they are both influenced by a third, unobservable latent variable. The setting is termed informative cluster size, because the cluster size which is now also a random variable will carry information about the quantities or parameters of interest.

Models for Informative Cluster Size

A reasonable basis for statistical modeling is to assume that the measurements in the ith cluster are: the cluster size N_i and a realization of a stochastic process $(Yij)\infty j=1$, that is, $(N_i; Y_{i1}, Y_{i2}, \ldots)$. The stochastic process may be finite or infinite, and possibly multivariate. In practice we only observe N_i and $Y_i = (Y_{i1},\ldots, Y_{iN_i})'$, and the observed data consists of

$$V_i = (N_i; Y_{i1}, \ldots, Y_{iN_i}), i = 1, \ldots, M.$$

The cluster variables $V_1,\ldots, V_M$ are assumed to be independent and identically distributed with some probability measure $\mathbb{P}(V)$. The goal is to make valid and efficient statistical inference on the marginal distribution of Y_{ij}'s, which can be a result of an unconventional data generating mechanism. Any violation of the first condition in Definition 1 means that the cluster size cannot be ignored while making inference on the marginal distribution of Y_{ij}'s, but needs to be accounted for.

Remark 1

A formal way of definition of probability distributions of $V = (N, Y_1, \ldots, V_N)$, where N is the cluster size, can be written as follows. Let $(\Omega, \mathcal{F}, P)$ be the common probability space on which $N, Y_1, Y_2, \ldots$ are defined. Then V is a random element on $(\Omega, \mathcal{F}, P)$ taking values in

$\chi = \cup_{k \geq 1} \{k\} \times R^k$.

The appropriate σ-algebra on $\mathcal{X}$ is the σ-algebra generated by the π-class $\Pi = \emptyset \cup \{\{k\} \times B_1 \times \cdots \times B_k : B_i = [c_i, d_i)$ is a semi-open interval in $\Re$; $1 \leq i \leq k, k \geq 1\}$.

We define $\mathbb{P}_V$ on such sets by $\mathbb{P}_V(\emptyset) = 0$, and

$\mathbb{P}_V(\{k\} \times B_1 \times \cdots \times B_k) = P(N = k)P(Y_1 \in B_1, \cdots, Y_k \in B_k | N = k)$.

Note that $\mathbb{P}_V$ is σ-additive on Π. Let $A_i = \{k_i\} \times B_{i1} \times \cdots \times B_{iki} \in \Pi$, $i \geq 1$, such that $A_i \cap A_j = \emptyset$, for $i \neq j$, and $\cup_{i=1}^{\infty} A_i = A = \{k\} \times B_1 \times \cdots \times B_k \in \Pi$ Then we must have $k_i = k$, $\forall_i$ and $C = \cup_{i=1}^{\infty} C_i$ where $C = B_1 \times \cdots \times B_k$, $C_i = B_{i1} \times \cdots \times B_{ik}$; furthermore, $C_i \cap C_j = \emptyset$, for $i \neq j$.

Since the distribution of $(Y_1, \ldots, Y_k)$ given $N = k$, denoted $\mathbb{P}^k$, say, is a proper probability distribution,

$P^k(\cup_{i=1}^{\infty} C_i) = \Sigma_{i=1}^{\infty} P^k(C_i)$,

and hence

$P_V(\cup_{i=1}^{\infty} A_i) = P(N=k) P^k(\cup_{i=1}^{\infty} C_i) = P(N=k) \Sigma_{i=1}^{\infty} P^k(C_i) = \Sigma_{i=1}^{\infty} P(N=k) P^k(C_i) = \Sigma_{i=1}^{\infty} P_V(A_i)$.

Therefore, by the π-λ theorem, $\mathbb{P}_V$ has a unique extension on σ(Π). For designed experiments, we also may have a fixed sequence of design variables $(X_{ij})_{j=1}^{\infty}$ so that the cluster variables are

$(N_i; Y_{i1}, Y_{i2}, \ldots; X_{i1}, X_{i2}, \ldots)$

but only N_i, $Y_i = (Y_{i1}, \ldots, Y_{iN_i})'$ and $X_i = (X_{i1}, \ldots, X_{iN_i})'$ are observed. Inference on the conditional distribution of $Y_{ij} | X_{ij}$ may again be confounded by the cluster size.

Parametric Models

Informative cluster size settings frequently appear in the biomedical literature. There are three natural ways to generate these type of data. If the parametric model for the data generating mechanism can be correctly identified, maximum likelihood estimates and likelihood ratio tests can be employed for statistical inference.

Models where the cluster size is assumed to have an influence on the outcomes

The data can then be thought to be generated in the following way: First, N_i is generated from its marginal distribution. Second, (Yij)∞j=1 are generated from a conditional distribution conditioned on N_i. If the unobserved are integrated out, the likelihood for what we observe is

∏i=1MP(Ni)f(Yi1,...,YiNi|Ni).

These types of models are frequently found in the literature. The joint density $f(Y_{i1},..., Y_{i\,Ni}|N_i)$ can be for instance a multivariate normal with a intracluster correlation coefficient $\rho(N_i)$.

Models where cluster size is dependent on outcomes

We suppose that the sequence (Yij)∞j=1 is first generated from its marginal distribution, and N_i is then generated from its conditional distribution conditioned on (Yij)∞j=1. If Y_{i1}, Y_{i2},... are i.i.d. and if $P(N_i = k|Y_{i1}, Y_{i2},...) = P(N_i = k|Y_{i1},..., Y_{ik})$, $k = 1, 2,...$, the likelihood for what we observe is

∏i=1Mf(Yi1,...,YiNi)P(Ni|Yi1,...,YiNi).

However, that although (Yij)∞j=1 are exchangeable, the observed variables $Y_{i1},..., Y_{i\,Ni}$ may not have this property.

Example

In the analysis of recurrent events during follow-up periods of fixed lengths *ci*, individuals (clusters) with a tendency to shorter gaps contribute more events to the analysis than individuals with a tendency to longer gaps. Now

$N_i = k \Leftrightarrow Y_{i1} + ... + Y_{i,k-1} < c_i \le Y_{i1} + ... + Y_{ik}$,

and the observation Y_{ik} is right-censored.

As a result of the design, Kaplan-Meier estimates are biased estimates of the marginal survival function. Exchangeability condition holds for $Y_{i1},..., Y_{i,k-1}$.

latent variable models

A third unobservable random variable ξ_i is assumed to be simultaneously influencing both the cluster size N_i and the outcomes Y_{i1}, Y_{i2}, ... The observed data likelihood contribution of the *i*th cluster is obtained by integrating the latent variable ξ_i and $Y_{i,Ni+1}$, $Y_{i,Ni+2}$, ... out of the full likelihood expression. If N_i and Y_{i1}, Y_{i2}, ... are conditionally independent and Y_{i1}, Y_{i2}, ... conditionally i.i.d, then we get the likelihood

∏i=1M[∫p(Ni;ξ*i*)∏j=1Nif(Yij;ξ*i*)dQ(ξ*i*)].

This is a model where exchangeability is met as well.

Example

Consider the association between the disease status of teeth, from a sample of individuals, and explanatory variables of interest. Disease status of teeth from the same person are correlated, and the individuals with poor dental status are likely to have fewer teeth. Poor dental health or hygiene can be thought to be the latent variable influencing both the disease status and the number of teeth.

It is observed that introduction of treatments on the female mice in Example 1, may conceptually change it to a latent variable model. As explained by Dunson et al. treatments may have an effect on fetal weight with or without an effect on fetal losses. Treatment may be acting on some unidentified latent variable, which influences both fetal weight and fetal losses. They argue that in settings like this, it is important to model the cluster size and the outcomes jointly, although the probability distribution of the cluster size is rarely of direct interest.

Nonparametric models

As studied earlier, under appropriate assumptions parametric models can be used. In the nonparametric approach, the general aim is to make inference on the distributions of $Y_{i1},\ldots, Y_{iNi}$ with an unspecified data generating mechanism.

Bickel and Lehmann introduced the general idea that one should first define measures (functionals) of different interesting characteristics of the population and then use the corresponding sample statistics as estimators.

For example, if $Y_1,\ldots, Y_M$ is a random sample from an unknown univariate distribution F, then for the sample mean Y'=1MΣMi=1Yi and the sample variance S2=1MΣMi=1(Yi–Y')², the corresponding functionals are the mean functional $\mu(F) = \int x dF(x)$ and the variance functional $\sigma^2(F) = \int(x - \mu(F))^{2dF}(x)$, respectively.

Under general assumptions on F, two functionals $\mu_1(F)$ and $\mu_2(F)$ may recover the same value (e.g. the mean functional and the median functional in the nonparametric model of symmetric distribution) but the statistical properties (e.g. efficiency and robustness) of the corresponding estimates may be completely different. The functional approach has now been generally adapted in the robust community. The approach seems particularly attractive in the framework of informative cluster size as it avoids much of the inevitable complexities in the parametric approach.

3.3 REJECTION SAMPLING

To visualize the motivation behind rejection sampling, imagine graphing the density function of a random variable onto a large rectangular board and throwing darts at it. Assume that the darts are uniformly distributed around the board. Now remove all of the darts that are outside the area under the curve. The remaining darts will be distributed uniformly within the area under the curve, and the x-positions of these darts will be distributed according to the random variable's density. This is because there is the most room for the darts to land where the curve is highest and thus the probability density is greatest.

The visualization as just described is equivalent to a particular form of rejection sampling where the proposal distribution is uniform (hence its graph is a rectangle). The general form of rejection sampling assumes that the board is not necessarily rectangular but is shaped according to some distribution that we know how to sample from (for example, using inversion sampling), and which is at least as high at every point as the distribution we want to sample from, so that the former completely encloses the latter. Otherwise, there will be parts of the curved area we want to sample from that can never be reached. Rejection sampling works as follows:

- Sample a point on the x-axis from the proposal distribution.
- Draw a vertical line at this x-position, up to the curve of the proposal distribution.
- Sample uniformly along this line from 0 to the maximum of the probability density function. If the sampled value is greater than the value of the desired distribution at this vertical line, return to first step.

This algorithm can be used to sample from the area under any curve, regardless of whether the function integrates to 1. In fact, scaling a function by a constant has no effect on the sampled x-positions. Thus, the algorithm can be used to sample from a distribution whose normalizing constant is unknown, which is common in computational statistics.

If you have a function you are trying to sample from, whose functional form is well known, basically accept the sample by generating a uniform random number at any x and accepting it if the value is below the value of the function at that x. This is illustrated in the diagram below:

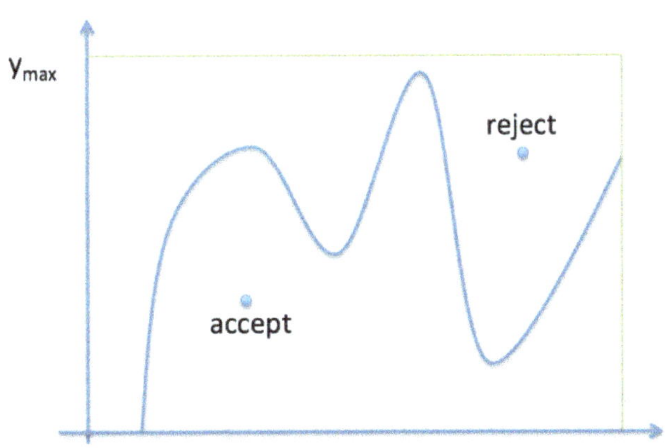

3.3.1 The process

- Draw xx uniformly from [xmin,xmax]
- Draw y uniformly from [xy max]
- If y < f(x), accept the sample
- Otherwise reject it
- Repeat

This works as more samples will be accepted in the regions of x-space where the function *ff* is higher: indeed they will be accepted in the ratio of the height of the function at any given xx to ymax.

The reason this all works is the frequentist interpretation of probability in each x sliver As we have more samples the accept-to-total ratio reflects the probability mass in that sliver better.

Example

The following code produces samples that follow the distribution *P(x)=e-x*P(x)=e−x for *x*=[0,10]x=[0,10] and generates a histogram of the sampled distribution.

```
P = lambda x: np.exp(-x)
# domain limits
xmin = 0 # the lower limit of our domain
xmax = 10 # the upper limit of our domain
# range limit (supremum) for y
ymax = 1
#you might have to do an optimization to find this.
N = 10000 # the total of samples we wish to generate
accepted = 0 # the number of accepted samples
samples = np.zeros(N)
count = 0 # the total count of proposals
# generation loop
while (accepted < N):
    # pick a uniform number on [xmin, xmax) (e.g. 0...10)
    x = np.random.uniform(xmin, xmax)
    # pick a uniform number on [0, ymax)
    y = np.random.uniform(0,ymax)
```

```
        # Do the accept/reject comparison
        if y < P(x):
            samples[accepted] = x
            accepted += 1
        count +=1
print("Count",count, "Accepted", accepted)
# get the histogram info
hinfo = np.histogram(samples,30)
# plot the histogram
plt.hist(samples,bins=30, label=u'Samples');
# plot our (normalized) function
xvals=np.linspace(xmin, xmax, 1000)
plt.plot(xvals, hinfo[0][0]*P(xvals), 'r', label=u'P(x)')
# turn on the legend
plt.legend()
Count 100294 Accepted 10000
<matplotlib.legend.Legend at 0x114063908>
```

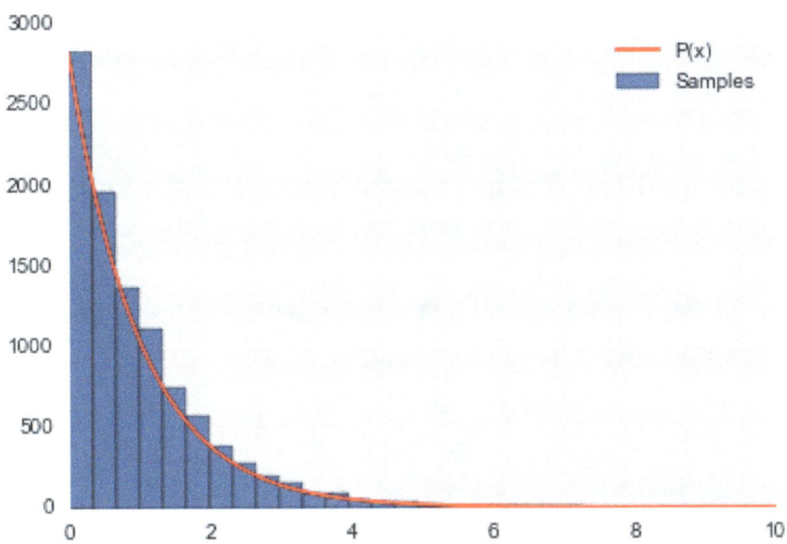

Notice that y_{max} was just assumed here. In general we might have to do a maximization. This has a cost. We want to keep this cost low, or we might be spending some time there.

3.3.2 Rejection Sampling with Steroids

The simple rejection sampling method has fundamental problems. For our simple example, it's quite easy to determine the supremum. In practice, while you may know how to quickly (i.e. constant time) evaluate your function everywhere on the domain of interest, finding a bound very close to the supremum may not be a feasible calculation. In addition, even if you find a tight bound for the supremum, basic rejection sampling will still be very inefficient as you will reject many samples (especially in low density regions).

Furthermore, if you support is infinitely large, you are not going to be able to reject from an infinitely long box in finite time. This is a hard problem to solve and we will need other techniques to address this problem of low acceptance probability.

However, it is possible to do a more efficient job while still taking advantage of the simplicity of rejection sampling. Our modified technique will introduce a proposal density g(x)g(x). This notion of a proposal density is one used in many sampling techniques, in different ways, but its importance will always lie in figuring ways to increase the acceptance rate.

The proposal density will have the following characteristics:

- g(x) is easy to sample from and (calculate the pdf)
- Some M between 1 and ∞ exists so that Mg(x)>f(x) in your entire domain of interest
- Ideally g(x) will be somewhat close to *ff* so that you'll sample more in high density regions and much less in low density regions

Its probably obvious that an optimal value for M is the supremum over your domain of interest of f/g. At that *xx* you will accept stuff with probability 1. In general you want M as close to 1 as possible, since the probability of acceptance is 1/M.

You can see that this is the case by finding the proportion of samples from g(x) that are accepted at each x and then averaging over x:

∫dxg(x)prop(x)=∫dxg(x)f(x)Mg(x)=1M∫dxf(x)=1M

Once you've picked a proposal distribution g, your modified rejection sampling technique is as follows:

- Draw *xx* from your proposal distribution *g*(*x*)g(x)
- Draw *yy* uniformly from [0,1]
- If *yy* < f(xx)/*Mg*(*x*)Mg(x), accept the sample
- Otherwise reject it
- Repeat

The entire process is illustrated in the diagram below:

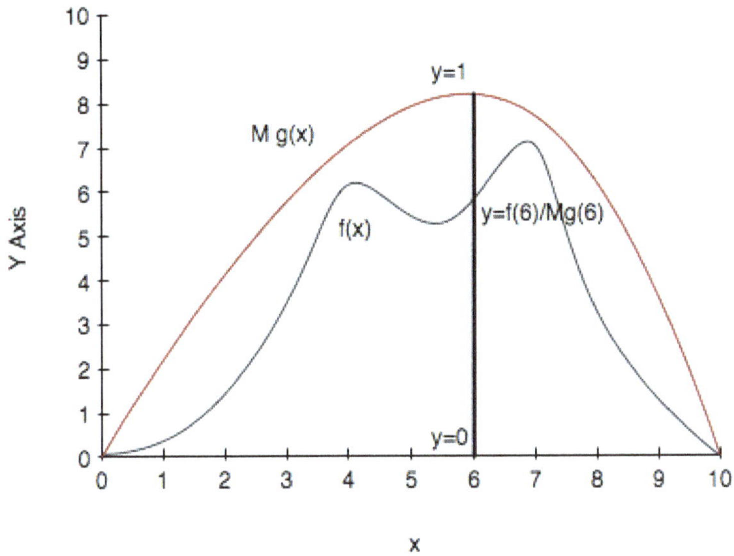

Example

The following code produces samples that follow the distribution P(x)=e-x for x=[0,10] and generates a histogram of the sampled distribution.

```
p = lambda x: np.exp(-x)  # our distribution
g = lambda x: 1/(x+1)  # our proposal pdf (choosing M to be 1)
invCDFg = lambda x: np.log(x +1) # generates our proposal using inverse sampling
# domain limits
xmin = 0 # the lower limit of our domain
xmax = 10 # the upper limit of our domain
# range limits for inverse sampling
umin = invCDFg(xmin)
umax = invCDFg(xmax)
N = 10000 # the total of samples we wish to generate
accepted = 0 # the number of accepted samples
samples = np.zeros(N)
count = 0 # the total count of proposals
# generation loop
while (accepted < N):
```

```
    # Sample from g using inverse sampling
    u = np.random.uniform(umin, umax)
    xproposal = np.exp(u) - 1

    # pick a uniform number on [0, 1)
    y = np.random.uniform(0,1)
    # Do the accept/reject comparison
    if y < p(xproposal)/g(xproposal):
        samples[accepted] = xproposal
        accepted += 1
    count +=1
print("Count", count, "Accepted", accepted)
# get the histogram info
hinfo = np.histogram(samples,50)
# plot the histogram
plt.hist(samples,bins=50, label=u'Samples');
# plot our (normalized) function
xvals=np.linspace(xmin, xmax, 1000)
plt.plot(xvals, hinfo[0][0]*p(xvals), 'r', label=u'p(x)')
plt.plot(xvals, hinfo[0][0]*g(xvals), 'k', label=u'g(x)')
# turn on the legend
plt.legend()
Count 24359 Accepted 10000
<matplotlib.legend.Legend at 0x11748c2b0>
```

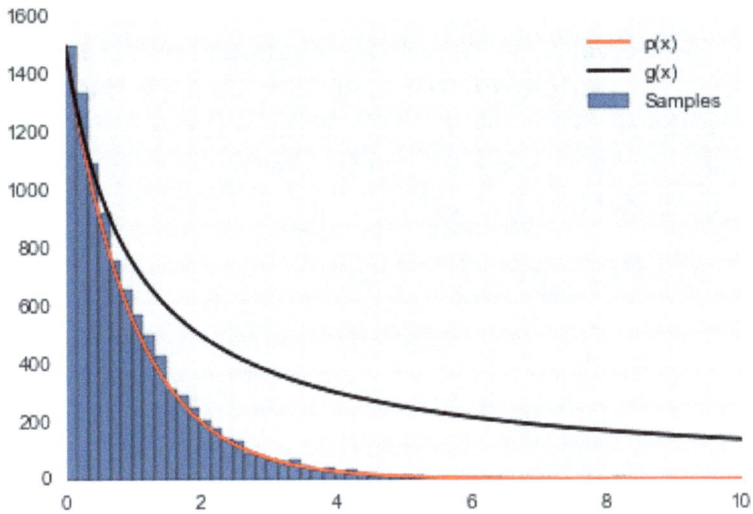

Fig Sample

3.3.3 Rejection sampling of a random discrete distribution

This next example shows how rejection sampling can be used to sample from any arbitrary distribution, continuous or not, and with or without an analytic probability density function.

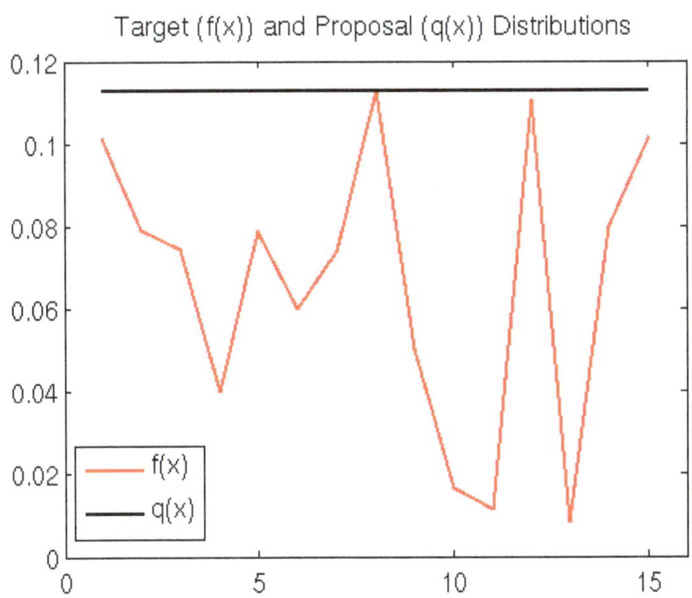

Fig: Random Discrete Target Distribution and Proposal that Bounds It.

The figure above shows a random ***discrete*** probability density function $f(x)$ generated on the interval (0,15). We will use rejection sampling as described above to sample from $f(x)$. Our proposal/envelope distribution is the uniform discrete distribution on the same interval (i.e. any of the integers from 1-15 are equally probable) multiplied by a constant c that is determined such that the maximum value of $f(x)$ lies under (or equal to) $cq(x)$.

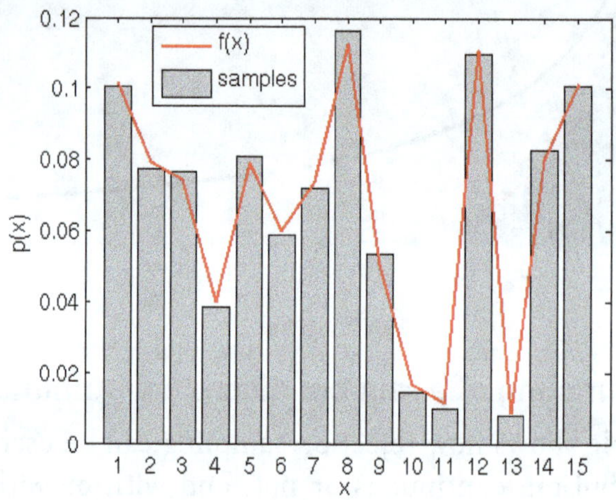

Fig: Rejection Samples For Discrete Distribution on interval [1 15]

Plotted above is the target distribution along with the discrete samples obtained using the rejection sampling. The MATLAB code used to sample from the target distribution and display the plot above is here:

```
rand('seed',12345)
randn('seed',12345)
fLength = 15;
% CREATE A RANDOM DISTRIBUTION ON THE INTERVAL [1 fLength]
f = rand(1,fLength); f = f/sum(f);
figure; h = plot(f,'r','Linewidth',2);
hold on;
l = plot([1 fLength],[max(f) max(f)],'k','Linewidth',2);
legend([h,l],{'f(x)','q(x)'},'Location','Southwest');
xlim([0 fLength + 1])
xlabel('x');
ylabel('p(x)');
title('Target (f(x)) and Proposal (q(x)) Distributions');
```

```
% OUR PROPOSAL IS THE DISCRETE UNIFORM ON THE INTERVAL [1 fLength]
% SO OUR CONSTANT IS
c = max(f/(1/fLength));
nSamples = 10000;
i = 1;
while i < nSamples
  proposal = unidrnd(fLength);
  q = c*1/fLength; % ENVELOPE DISTRIBUTION
  if rand < f(proposal)/q
    samps(i) = proposal;
    i = i + 1;
  end
end
% DISPLAY THE SAMPLES AND COMPARE TO THE TARGET DISTRIBUTION
bins = 1:fLength;
counts = histc(samps,bins);
figure
b = bar(1:fLength,counts/sum(counts),'FaceColor',[.8 .8 .8])
hold on;
h = plot(f,'r','Linewidth',2)
legend([h,b],{'f(x)','samples'});
xlabel('x'); ylabel('p(x)');
xlim([0 fLength + 1]);
```

3.3.4 Rejection sampling from unit circle to estimate π

Though the ratio-based acceptance-rejection criterion introduced above is a common choice for drawing samples from complex distributions, it is not the only criterion we could use. For instance we could use a different set of criteria to generate some geometrically-bounded distribution. If we wanted to generate points uniformly within the unit circle (i.e. a circle centered at $(y, x) = 0$ and with radius $r = 1$), we could do so by sampling Cartesian spatial coordinates x and y uniformly from the interval (-1,1)–which samples form a square centered at (0,0)– and reject those points that lie outside of the radius $r = \sqrt{x^2 + y^2} = 1$

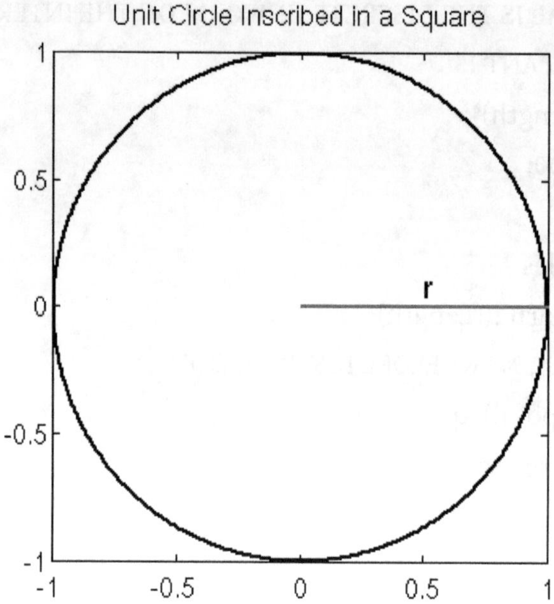

Fig: Unit Circle Inscribed in Square

Something clever that we can do with such a set of samples is to approximate the value π: Because a square that inscribes the unit circle has area:

$$A_{square} = (2r)^2 = 4r^2$$

and the unit circle has the area:

$$A_{circle} = \pi r^2$$

We can use the ratio of their areas to approximate π:

$$\pi = 4\frac{A_{circle}}{A_{square}}$$

The figure below shows the rejection sampling process and the resulting estimate of π from the samples. One-hundred thousand 2D points are sampled uniformly from the interval (-1,1). Those points that lie within the unit circle are plotted as blue dots. Those points that lie outside of the unit circle are plotted as red x's. If we take four times the ratio of the area in blue to the entire area, we get a very close approximation to 3.14 for π.

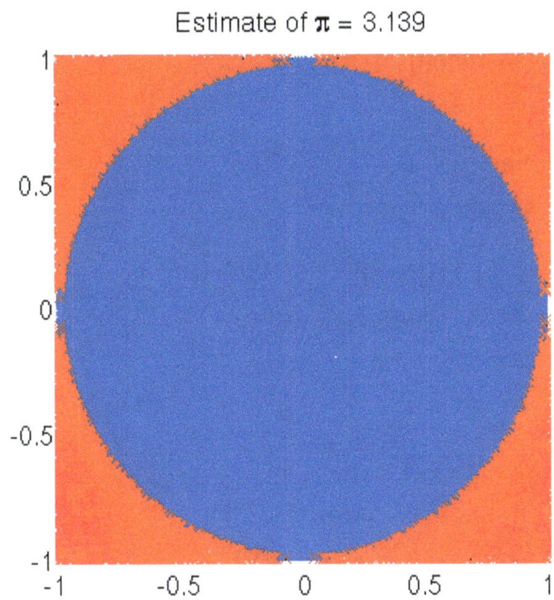

Rejection Criterion

The MATLAB code used to generate the example figures is below:

```
% DISPLAY A CIRCLE INSCRIBED IN A SQUARE
figure;
a = 0:.01:2*pi;
x = cos(a); y = sin(a);
hold on
plot(x,y,'k','Linewidth',2)
t = text(0.5, 0.05,'r');
l = line([0 1],[0 0],'Linewidth',2);
axis equal
box on
xlim([-1 1])
ylim([-1 1])
title('Unit Circle Inscribed in a Square')
pause;
rand('seed',12345)
randn('seed',12345)
delete(l); delete(t);
```

```
% DRAW SAMPLES FROM PROPOSAL DISTRIBUTION
samples = 2*rand(2,100000) - 1;
% REJECTION
reject = sum(samples.^2) > 1;
% DISPLAY REJECTION CRITERION
scatter(samples(1,~reject),samples(2,~reject),'b.')
scatter(samples(1,reject),samples(2,reject),'rx')
hold off
xlim([-1 1])
ylim([-1 1])
piHat = mean(sum(samples.*samples)<1)*4;
title(['Estimate of \pi = ',num2str(piHat)]);
```

3.3.5 Features

Rejection sampling is a simple way to generate samples from complex distributions. However, Rejection sampling also has a number of weaknesses:

- Finding a proposal distribution that can cover the support of the target distribution is a non-trivial task.
- Additionally, as the dimensionality of the target distribution increases, the proportion of points that are rejected also increases. This curse of dimensionality makes rejection sampling an inefficient technique for sampling multi-dimensional distributions, as the majority of the points proposed are not accepted as valid samples.
- Some of these problems are solved by changing the form of the proposal distribution to "hug" the target distribution as we gain knowledge of the target from observing accepted samples. Such a process is called *Adaptive Rejection Sampling*, which will be covered in another post.

3.3.6 Drawbacks

Rejection sampling can lead to a lot of unwanted samples being taken if the function being sampled is highly concentrated in a certain region, for example a function that has a spike at some location. For many distributions, this problem can be solved using an adaptive extension. In addition, as the dimensions of the problem get larger, the ratio of the embedded volume to the "corners" of the embedding volume tends towards zero, thus a lot of rejections can take place before a useful sample is generated, thus making the algorithm inefficient and impractical. See curse of dimensionality. In high dimensions, it is necessary to use a different approach, typically a Markov chain Monte Carlo method such as Metropolis sampling or Gibbs sampling.

3.3.7 Adaptive Rejection Sampling

For many distributions, finding a proposal distribution that includes the given distribution without a lot of wasted space is difficult. An extension of rejection sampling that can be used to overcome this difficulty and efficiently sample from a wide variety of distributions is known as adaptive rejection sampling (ARS).

There are three basic ideas to this technique as ultimately introduced by Gilks:

- If it helps, define your envelope distribution in log space (e.g. log-probability or log-density) instead. That is, work with h(x)=logg(x){\displaystyle h\left(x\right)=\mathrm {log} \;g\left(x\right)}h(x0 = log g(x) instead of g(x) {\displaystyle g\left(x\right)}g(x) directly. Often, distributions that have algebraically messy density functions have reasonably simpler log density functions.
- Instead of a single uniform envelope density function, use a piecewise linear density function as your envelope instead.
    - Each time you have to reject a sample, you can use the value of f(x) {\displaystyle f\left(x\right)}f(x) that you evaluated, to improve the piecewise approximation h(x){\displaystyle h\left(x\right)}h(x). This therefore reduces the chance that your next attempt will be rejected. Asymptotically, the probability of needing to reject your sample should converge to zero, and in practice, often very rapidly.
    - As proposed, any time we choose a point that is rejected, we tighten the envelope with another line segment that is tangent to the curve at the point with the same x-coordinate as the chosen point.
    - A piecewise linear model of the proposal log distribution results in a set of piecewise exponential distributions. Exponential distributions are well behaved and well understood. The logarithm of an exponential distribution is a straight line, and hence this method essentially involves enclosing the logarithm of the density in a series of line segments. This is the source of the log-concave restriction: if a distribution is log-concave, then its logarithm is concave, meaning that a line segment tangent to the curve will always pass over the curve.

If not working in log space, a piecewise linear density function can also be sampled via triangle distributions

- We can take even further advantage of the (log) concavity requirement, to potentially avoid the cost of evaluatingf(x){\displaystyle f\left(x\right)} f(x) when your sample *is* accepted.
  - Just like we can construct a piecewise linear upper bound (the "envelope" function) using the values of h(x){\displaystyle h\left(x\right)}h(x) that we had to evaluate in the current chain of rejections, we can also construct a piecewise linear lower bound (the "squeezing" function) using these values as well.
  - Before evaluating (the potentially expensive) f(x){\displaystyle f\left(x\right)}f(x) to see if your sample will be accepted, we may *already know* if it will be accepted by comparing against the (ideally cheaper) gl(x) {\displaystyle g_{l}\left(x\right)}gl(x)hl(x){\displaystyle h_{l}\left(x\right)} squeezing function that have available.
  - This squeezing step is optional, even when suggested by Gilks. At best it saves you from only one extra evaluation of your (messy and/or expensive) target density. However, presumably for particularly expensive density functions (and assuming the rapid convergence of the rejection rate toward zero) this can make a sizable difference in ultimate runtime.

The method essentially involves successively determining an envelope of straight-line segments that approximates the logarithm better and better while still remaining above the curve, starting with a fixed number of segments. Sampling from a truncated exponential random variable is straight foward. Just take the log of a uniform random variable.

In standard ARS, the probability of adding a new nodes vanishes to zero as the number of iterations increases. However, there is always a positive probability of adding a new node. For this reason, the number of nodes grows with the iterations. Two variants of the classical ARS scheme have been proposed to speed up the method, keeping fixed the number of nodes or finding a better addition statistical test.

Unfortunately, ARS can only be applied from sampling from log-concave target densities. For this reason, several extensions of ARS have been proposed in literature for tackling non-log-concave target distributions. Furthermore, different combinations of ARS and the Metropolis-Hastings method have been designed in order to obtain a universal sampler that builds a self-tuning proposal densities. This class of method is often called as Adaptive Rejection Metropolis Sampling (ARMS) algorithms. The resulting adaptive techniques can be always applied but the generated samples are correlated in this case.

3.4 CONDITIONAL DISTRIBUTIONS

From conditional CDF and conditional PDF of random variable conditioned on some events defined in terms of the same random variable, it is observed that

$$F_X(x/B) = \frac{P[\{X \leq x\} \cap B]}{P(B)} \qquad P(B) \neq 0$$

and

$$f_X(x/B) = \frac{d}{dx} F_X(x/B)$$

We can define these quantities for two random variables. We start with the *conditional probability mass functions* of two random variables.

3.4.1 Conditional Probability Mass Functions

Suppose X and Y are two discrete jointly random variable with the joint PMF $p_{X,Y}(x,y)$. The conditional PMF of Y given $X = x$ is defined as

$$p_{Y/X}(y/x) = P(\{Y = y\}/\{X = x\})$$
$$= \frac{P(\{X = x\} \cap \{Y = y\})}{P\{X = x\}}$$
$$= \frac{p_{X,Y}(x,y)}{p_X(x)} \quad \text{provided } p_X(x) \neq 0$$

Similarly we can define the conditional probability mass function

$$p_{X/Y}(x/y)$$

Remarks

The conditional PMF satisfies the properties of the probability mass functions.

From the definition of conditional probability mass functions, we can define two *independent random variables.* Two discrete random variables X and Y are said to be *independent* if and only if

$$\forall (x,y) \in R_X \times R_Y$$
$$p_{Y/X}(y/x) = p_Y(y)$$

so that

$$p_{X,Y}(x,y) = p_X(x)p_Y(y)$$

3.4.2 Bayes' rule for discrete random variables

Suppose X and Y are two discrete jointly random variables. Given $p_X(x)$ and $p_{Y/X}(y/x)$ we can determine the a posteriori probability mass function $p_{X/Y}(x/y)$ by using the Bayes' rule as follows:

$$
\begin{aligned}
p_{X/Y}(x/y) &= P(\{X=x\}/\{Y=y\}) \\
&= \frac{P(\{X=x\}\cap\{Y=y\})}{P\{Y=y\}} \\
&= \frac{p_{X,Y}(x,y)}{p_Y(y)} \\
&= \frac{p_{X,Y}(x,y)}{\sum_{x'\in R_X} p_{X,Y}(x',y)} \qquad \text{(Using the total probability law)}
\end{aligned}
$$

Example

Consider the random variables X and Y with the joint probability mass function as presented in the following table

X Y	0	1	2	$P_Y(Y)$
0	0.25	0.1	0.15	0.5
1	0.14	0.35	0.01	0.5
$p_X(x)$	0.39	0.45		

The marginal probabilities are as shown in the last column and the last row

$$
\begin{aligned}
p_{Y/X}(0/1) &= \frac{p_{X,Y}(0,1)}{p_X(1)} \\
&= \frac{0.14}{0.39}
\end{aligned}
$$

3.4.3 Conditional Probability Distribution function

Consider two continuous jointly random variables X and Y with the joint probability distribution function $F_{X,Y}(x,y)$. We are interested to find the conditional distribution of one of the random variables on the condition of a particular value of the other random variable.

We cannot define the conditional distribution of the random variable Y on the condition of the event $\{X=x\}$ by the relation

$$F_{Y/X}(y/x) = P(Y \le y / X = x)$$
$$= \frac{P(Y \le y, X = x)}{P(X = x)}$$

as $P(X = x) = 0$ in the above expression. The conditional distribution function is defined in the *limiting sense* as follows:

$$F_{Y/X}(y/x) = lim_{\Delta x \to 0} P(Y \le y / x < X \le x + \Delta x)$$
$$= lim_{\Delta x \to 0} \frac{P(Y \le y, x < X \le x + \Delta x)}{P(x < X \le x + \Delta x)}$$
$$= lim_{\Delta x \to 0} \frac{\int_{\infty}^{y} f_{X,Y}(x,u)\Delta x du}{f_X(x)\Delta x}$$
$$= \frac{\int_{\infty}^{y} f_{X,Y}(x,u) du}{f_X(x)}$$

3.4.4 Conditional Probability Density Function

$f_{Y/X}(y/X = x) = f_{Y/X}(y/x)$ is called conditional density of Y given X.

Let us define the conditional distribution function .

The conditional density is defined in the limiting sense as follows

$$f_{Y/X}(y/X = x) = \lim_{\Delta y \to 0} (F_{Y/X}(y + \Delta y / X = x) - F_{Y/X}(y / X = x) \ / \Delta y$$
$$= \lim_{\Delta y \to 0, \Delta x \to 0} (F_{Y/X}(y + \Delta y / x < X \le x + \Delta x) - F_{Y/X}(y / x < X \le x + \Delta x) \ / \Delta y \qquad (1)$$

Because $(X = x) = \lim_{\Delta x \to 0} (x < X \le x + \Delta x)$

The right hand side in equation (1) is

$$\lim_{\Delta y \to 0, \Delta x \to 0} (F_{Y/X}(y + \Delta y / x < X < x + \Delta x) - F_{Y/X}(y / x < X < x + \Delta x)) / \Delta y$$
$$= \lim_{\Delta y \to 0, \Delta x \to 0} (P(y < Y \le y + \Delta y / x < X \le x + \Delta x)) / \Delta y$$
$$= \lim_{\Delta y \to 0, \Delta x \to 0} (P(y < Y \le y + \Delta y, x < X \le x + \Delta x)) / P(x < X \le x + \Delta x)\Delta y$$
$$= \lim_{\Delta y \to 0, \Delta x \to 0} f_{X,Y}(x, y)\Delta x \Delta y / f_X(x)\Delta x \Delta y$$
$$= f_{X,Y}(x, y) / f_X(x)$$
$$\therefore f_{Y/X}(y/x) = f_{X,Y}(x, y) / f_X(x)$$

Similarly we have

$$\therefore f_{X/Y}(x/y) = f_{X,Y}(x,y)/f_Y(y)$$

Two random variables are statistically independent if for all $(x, y) \in \mathbb{R}^2$,

$$f_{Y/X}(y/x) = f_Y(y)$$

or equivalently

$$f_{X,Y}(x,y) = f_X(x) f_Y(y)$$

3.4.5 Bayes' Rule for Continuous Random Variables:

From above expressions, we get the Bayes' rule for two continuous joint random varibles

$$f_{X/Y}(x/y) = \frac{f_{X,Y}(x,y)}{f_Y(y)}$$

$$\therefore f_{X/Y}(x/y) = \frac{f_X(x) f_{Y/X}(y/x)}{f_Y(y)}$$

$$= \frac{f_{X,Y}(x,y)}{\int_{-\infty}^{\infty} f_{X,Y}(x,y)dx}$$

$$= \frac{f_{Y/X}(y/x) f_X(x)}{\int_{-\infty}^{\infty} f_X(u) f_{Y/X}(y/x)du}$$

Given the joint density function we can find out the conditional density function.

Example:

For random variables X and Y, the joint probability density function is given by

$$f_{X,Y}(x,y) = \frac{1+xy}{4} \quad |x| \le 1, \ |y| \le 1$$

$$= 0 \ \text{ otherwise}$$

Find the marginal density $f_X(x), f_Y(y)$ and $f_{Y/X}(y/x)$. Are X and Y independent?

$$f_X(x) = \int_{-1}^{1} \frac{1+xy}{4} dy$$

$$= \frac{1}{2}$$

Similarly

$$f_Y(y) = \frac{1}{2} \qquad -1 \le y \le 1$$

and

$$f_{Y/X}(y/x) = \frac{f_{X,Y}(x,y)}{f_X(x)}$$

$$= \frac{1+xy}{2} \ne f_Y(y)$$

Hence, X and Y are not independent.

3.4.6 Bayes' Rule for Mixed Random Variables

Let X be a discrete random variable with probability mass function $p_X(x)$ and Y be a continuous random variable defined on the same sample space with the conditional probability density function $f_{Y/X}(y/x)$. In practical problems we may have to estimate the conditional PMF of X given the observed value $Y.=y$ We can define this conditional PMF also in the limiting sense

$$p_{X/Y}(x/y) = \lim_{\Delta y \to 0} P(X = x / y < Y \le y + \Delta y)$$

$$= \lim_{\Delta y \to 0} \frac{P(X = x, y < Y \le y + \Delta y)}{P(y < Y \le y + \Delta y)}$$

$$= \lim_{\Delta y \to 0} \frac{p_X(x) f_{Y/X}(y/x) \Delta y}{f_Y(y) \Delta y}$$

$$= \frac{p_X(x) f_{Y/X}(y/x)}{f_Y(y)}$$

$$= \frac{p_X(x) f_{Y/X}(y/x)}{\sum_x p_X(x) f_{Y/X}(y/x)}$$

Example

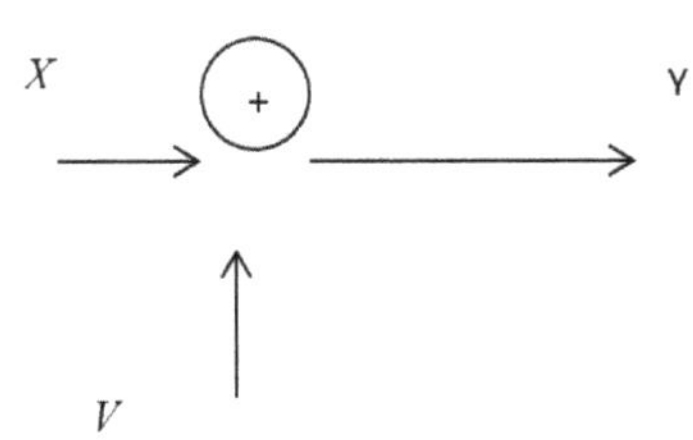

X is a binary random variable with

$$X = \begin{cases} 1 \text{ with probability } p \\ -1 \text{ with probability } 1\text{-}p \end{cases}$$

V is the Gaussian noise with mean 0 and variance $\sigma.^2$

Then

$$p_{X/Y}(x=1/y) = \frac{p_X(x)f_{Y/X}(y/x)}{\sum_x p_X(x)f_{Y/X}(y/x)}$$

$$= \frac{pe^{-(y-1)^2/2\sigma^2}}{pe^{-(y-1)^2/2\sigma^2} + (1-p)e^{-(y+1)^2/2\sigma^2}}$$

3.4.7 Independent Random Variables

Let X and Y be two random variables characterized by the joint distribution function

$F_{X,Y}(x,y) = P\{X \le x, Y \le y\}$ and the corresponding joint density function $f_{X,Y}(x,y) = \frac{\partial^2}{\partial x \partial y} F_{X,Y}(x,y)$

Then X and Y are independent if $\forall (x,y) \in \mathbb{R}^2$, $\{X \le x\}$ and $\{Y \le y\}$ are independent events. Thus,

$$\begin{aligned} F_{X,Y}(x,y) &= P\{X \le x, Y \le y\} \\ &= P\{X \le x\}P\{Y \le y\} \\ &= F_X(x)F_Y(y) \end{aligned}$$

$$\begin{aligned} \therefore f_{X,Y}(x,y) &= \frac{\partial^2 F_{X,Y}(x,y)}{\partial x \partial y} \\ &= f_X(x)f_Y(y) \end{aligned}$$

and equivalently

$$f_{Y/X}(y) = f_Y(y)$$

3.4.8 Marginal and Conditional Distributions of Multivariate Normal Distribution

Assume an n-dimensional random vector

$$\mathbf{x} = \begin{bmatrix} \mathbf{x}_1 \\ \mathbf{x}_2 \end{bmatrix}$$

has a normal distribution $N(\mathbf{x}, \mu, \Sigma)$ with

$$\mu = \begin{bmatrix} \mu_1 \\ \mu_2 \end{bmatrix} \quad \text{and} \quad \Sigma = \begin{bmatrix} \Sigma_{11} & \Sigma_{12} \\ \Sigma_{21} & \Sigma_{22} \end{bmatrix}$$

where x1 and x2 are two subvectors of respective dimensions p and q with p+q=n. Note that $\Sigma = \Sigma^T$, and $\Sigma_{21} = \Sigma_{21}^T$.

Theorem:

Part a: The marginal distributions of x1 and x2 are also normal with mean vector μi and covariance matrix Σ (i=1,2), respectively.

Part b The conditional distribution of xi given xj is also normal with mean vector

$$\mu_{i|j} = \mu_i + \Sigma_{ij}\Sigma_{jj}^{-1}(\mathbf{x}_j - \mu_j)$$

and covariance matrix $\Sigma_{i|j} = \Sigma_{jj} - \Sigma_{ij}^T \Sigma_{ii}^{-1} \Sigma_{ij}$

Proof: The joint density of $\mathbf{x}$ is:

$$f(\mathbf{x}) = f(\mathbf{x}_1, \mathbf{x}_2) = \frac{1}{(2\pi)^{n/2}|\Sigma|^{1/2}} exp[-\frac{1}{2}(\mathbf{x}-\mu)^T\Sigma^{-1}(\mathbf{x}-\mu)] = \frac{1}{(2\pi)^{n/2}|\Sigma|^{1/2}} exp[-\frac{1}{2}Q(\mathbf{x}_1, \mathbf{x}_2)]$$

where Q is defined as

$$\begin{aligned} Q(\mathbf{x}_1, \mathbf{x}_2) &= (\mathbf{x} - \mu)^T \Sigma^{-1} (\mathbf{x} - \mu) \\ &= [(\mathbf{x}_1 - \mu_1)^T, (\mathbf{x} - \mu_2)^T] \begin{bmatrix} \Sigma^{11} & \Sigma^{12} \\ \Sigma^{21} & \Sigma^{22} \end{bmatrix} \begin{bmatrix} \mathbf{x}_1 - \mu_1 \\ \mathbf{x}_2 - \mu_2 \end{bmatrix} \\ &= (\mathbf{x}_1 - \mu_1)^T \Sigma^{11} (\mathbf{x}_1 - \mu_1) + 2(\mathbf{x}_1 - \mu_1)^T \Sigma^{12} (\mathbf{x}_2 - \mu_2) + (\mathbf{x}_2 - \mu_2)^T \Sigma^{22} (\mathbf{x}_2 - \mu_2) \end{aligned}$$

Here we have assumed $\Sigma^{-1} = \begin{bmatrix} \Sigma_{11} & \Sigma_{12} \\ \Sigma_{21} & \Sigma_{22} \end{bmatrix}^{-1} = \begin{bmatrix} \Sigma^{11} & \Sigma^{12} \\ \Sigma^{21} & \Sigma^{22} \end{bmatrix}$

According to theorem, we have

$$\Sigma^{11} = (\Sigma_{11} - \Sigma_{12}\Sigma_{22}^{-1}\Sigma_{12}^T)^{-1} = \Sigma_{11}^{-1} + \Sigma_{11}^{-1}\Sigma_{12}(\Sigma_{22} - A_{12}^T\Sigma_{11}^{-1}\Sigma_{12})^{-1}\Sigma_{12}^T\Sigma_{11}^{-1}$$
$$\Sigma_{33} = (\Sigma^{33} - \Sigma^{I3}_{\perp}\Sigma^{II}_{-I}\Sigma^{I3})_{-I} = \Sigma^{33}_{-I} + \Sigma^{33}_{-I}\Sigma^{I3}_{\perp}(\Sigma^{II} - \Sigma^{I3}\Sigma^{33}_{-I}\Sigma^{I3}_{\perp})_{-I}\Sigma^{I3}\Sigma^{33}_{-I}$$

$$\Sigma^{12} = -\Sigma_{11}^{-1}\Sigma_{12}(\Sigma_{22} - \Sigma_{12}^T\Sigma_{11}^{-1}\Sigma_{12})^{-1} = (\Sigma^{21})^T$$

Substituting the second expression for Σ^{11}, first expression for Σ^{22}, and Σ^{12} into Q(x1,x2) to get:

$$
\begin{aligned}
Q(\mathbf{x}_1,\mathbf{x}_2) = & (\mathbf{x}_1-\mu_1)^T[\Sigma_{11}^{-1}+\Sigma_{11}^{-1}\Sigma_{12}(\Sigma_{22}-A_{12}^T\Sigma_{11}^{-1}\Sigma_{12})^{-1}\Sigma_{12}^T\Sigma_{11}^{-1}](\mathbf{x}_1-\mu_1) \\
& -2(\mathbf{x}_1-\mu_1)^T[\Sigma_{11}^{-1}\Sigma_{12}(\Sigma_{22}-\Sigma_{12}^T\Sigma_{11}^{-1}\Sigma_{12})^{-1}](\mathbf{x}_2-\mu_2) \\
& +(\mathbf{x}_2-\mu_2)^T[(\Sigma_{22}-\Sigma_{12}^T\Sigma_{11}^{-1}\Sigma_{12})^{-1}](\mathbf{x}_2-\mu_2) \\
= & (\mathbf{x}_1-\mu_1)^T\Sigma_{11}^{-1}(\mathbf{x}_1-\mu_1) \\
& +(\mathbf{x}_1-\mu_1)^T\Sigma_{11}^{-1}\Sigma_{12}(\Sigma_{22}-A_{12}^T\Sigma_{11}^{-1}\Sigma_{12})^{-1}\Sigma_{12}^T\Sigma_{11}^{-1}](\mathbf{x}_1-\mu_1) \\
& -2(\mathbf{x}_1-\mu_1)^T[\Sigma_{11}^{-1}\Sigma_{12}(\Sigma_{22}-\Sigma_{12}^T\Sigma_{11}^{-1}\Sigma_{12})^{-1}](\mathbf{x}_2-\mu_2) \\
& +(\mathbf{x}_2-\mu_2)^T[(\Sigma_{22}-\Sigma_{12}^T\Sigma_{11}^{-1}\Sigma_{12})^{-1}](\mathbf{x}_2-\mu_2) \\
= & (\mathbf{x}_1-\mu_1)^T\Sigma_{11}^{-1}(\mathbf{x}_1-\mu_1) \\
& +[(\mathbf{x}_2-\mu_2)-\Sigma_{12}^T\Sigma_{11}^{-1}(\mathbf{x}_1-\mu_1)]^T(\Sigma_{22}-\Sigma_{12}^T\Sigma_{11}^{-1}\Sigma_{12})^{-1}[(\mathbf{x}_2-\mu_2)-\Sigma_{12}^T\Sigma_{11}^{-1}(\mathbf{x}_1-\mu_1)]
\end{aligned}
$$

The last equal sign is due to the following equations for any vectors u and v and a symmetric matrix $A = A^T$:

$$
\begin{aligned}
& u^TAu - 2u^TAv + v^TAv = u^TAu - u^TAv - u^TAv + v^TAv \\
= & u^TA(u-v) - (u-v)^TAv = u^TA(u-v) - v^TA(u-v) \\
= & (u-v)^TA(u-v) = (v-u)^TA(v-u)
\end{aligned}
$$

We define

$$
\begin{aligned}
b &\triangleq \mu_2 + \Sigma_{12}^T\Sigma_{11}^{-1}(\mathbf{x}_1-\mu_1) \\
A &\triangleq \Sigma_{22} - \Sigma_{12}^T\Sigma_{11}^{-1}\Sigma_{12}
\end{aligned}
$$

and

$$\begin{cases} Q_1(\mathbf{x}_1) & \triangleq (\mathbf{x}_1-\mu_1)^T\Sigma_{11}^{-1}(\mathbf{x}_1-\mu_1) \\ Q_2(\mathbf{x}_1,\mathbf{x}_2) & \triangleq [(\mathbf{x}_2-\mu_2)-\Sigma_{12}^T\Sigma_{11}^{-1}(\mathbf{x}_1-\mu_1)]^T(\Sigma_{22}-\Sigma_{12}^T\Sigma_{11}^{-1}\Sigma_{12})^{-1}[(\mathbf{x}_2-\mu_2)-\Sigma_{12}^T\Sigma_{11}^{-1}(\mathbf{x}_1-\mu_1)] \\ & = (\mathbf{x}_2-b)^TA^{-1}(\mathbf{x}_2-b) \end{cases}$$

and get $Q(\mathbf{x}_1,\mathbf{x}_2) = Q_1(\mathbf{x}_1)+Q_2(\mathbf{x}_1,\mathbf{x}_2)$

Now the joint distribution can be written as:

$$\begin{aligned} f(\mathbf{x}) &= f(\mathbf{x}_1,\mathbf{x}_2) = \frac{1}{(2\pi)^{n/2}|\Sigma|^{1/2}}exp[-\frac{1}{2}Q(\mathbf{x}_1,\mathbf{x}_2)] \\ &= \frac{1}{(2\pi)^{n/2}|\Sigma_{11}|^{1/2}|\Sigma_{22}-\Sigma_{12}^T\Sigma_{11}^{-1}\Sigma_{12}|^{1/2}}exp[-\frac{1}{2}Q(\mathbf{x}_1,\mathbf{x}_2)] \\ &= \frac{1}{(2\pi)^{p/2}|\Sigma_{11}|^{1/2}}exp[-\frac{1}{2}(\mathbf{x}_1-\mu_1)^T\Sigma_{11}^{-1}(\mathbf{x}_1-\mu_1)]\frac{1}{(2\pi)^{q/2}|A|^{1/2}}exp[-\frac{1}{2}(\mathbf{x}_2-b)^TA^{-1}(\mathbf{x}_2-b)] \\ &= N(\mathbf{x}_1,\mu_1,\Sigma_{11})\ N(\mathbf{x}_2,b,A) \end{aligned}$$

The third equal sign is due to above theorem: $|\Sigma| = |\Sigma_{11}||\Sigma_{22}-\Sigma_{12}^T\Sigma_{11}^{-1}\Sigma_{12}|$

The marginal distribution of x1is

$$f_1(\mathbf{x}_1) = \int f(\mathbf{x}_1,\mathbf{x}_2)d\mathbf{x}_2 = \frac{1}{(2\pi)^{p/2}|\Sigma_{11}|^{1/2}}exp[-\frac{1}{2}(\mathbf{x}_1-\mu_1)^T\Sigma_{11}^{-1}(\mathbf{x}_1-\mu_1)]$$

and the conditional distribution of x2 given x1is

$$f_{2|1}(\mathbf{x}_2|\mathbf{x}_1) = \frac{f(\mathbf{x}_1,\mathbf{x}_2)}{f(\mathbf{x}_1)} = \frac{1}{(2\pi)^{q/2}|A|^{1/2}}exp[-\frac{1}{2}(\mathbf{x}_2-b)^TA^{-1}(\mathbf{x}_2-b)]$$

with

$$b = \mu_2+\Sigma_{12}^T\Sigma_{11}^{-1}(\mathbf{x}_1-\mu_1)$$

$$A = \Sigma_{22}-\Sigma_{12}^T\Sigma_{11}^{-1}\Sigma_{12}$$

REFERENCES

Ackley, D., Hinton, G. E., and Sejnowski, T. J. (1985). A learning algorithm for Boltzmann machines. Cogn. Sci. 9, 147–169. doi: 10.1207/s15516709cog0901_7

Albert, R., and Barabasi, A. L. (2002). Statistical mechanics of complex networks. Rev. Mod. Phys. 74, 47–97. doi: 10.1103/RevModPhys.74.47

Botvinick, M. M., Niv, Y., and Barto, A. C. (2009). Hierarchically organized behavior and its neural foundations: a reinforcement learning perspective. Cognition 113, 262–280. doi: 10.1016/j.cognition.2008.08.011

Bowers, J. S. (2009). On the biological plausibility of grandmother cells: implications for neural network theories in psychology and neuroscience. Psychol. Rev. 116, 220–251. doi: 10.1037/a0014462

Bressler, S. L., and Menon, V. (2010). Large-scale brain networks in cognition: emerging methods and principles. Trends Cogn. Sci. 14, 277–290. doi: 10.1016/j.tics.2010.04.004

Buckner, R. L., Andrews-Hanna, J. R., and Schacter, D. L. (2008). The brain's default network: anatomy, function and relevance to disease. Ann. N Y Acad. Sci. 1124, 1–38. doi: 10.1196/annals.1440.011

Buesing, L., Bill, J., Nessler, B., and Maass, W. (2011). Neural dynamics as sampling: a model for stochastic computation in recurrent networks of spiking neurons. PLoS Comput. Biol. 7:e1002211. doi: 10.1371/journal.pcbi.1002211

Bullmore, E., and Sporns, O. (2009). Complex brain networks: graph theoretical analysis of structural and functional systems. Nat. Rev. Neurosci. 10, 186–198. doi: 10.1038/nrn2575

Cappelletti, M., Didino, D., Stoianov, I., and Zorzi, M. (2014). Number skills are maintained in healthy ageing. Cogn. Psychol. 69, 25–45. doi: 10.1016/j.cogpsych.2013.11.004

Casarotti, M., Lisi, M., Umiltà, C., and Zorzi, M. (2012). Paying attention through eye movements: a computational investigation of the premotor theory of spatial attention. J. Cogn. Neurosci. 24, 1519–1531. doi: 10.1162/jocn_a_00231

Clark, A. (2013). Whatever next? Predictive brains, situated agents and the future of cognitive science. Behav. Brain Sci. 36, 181–204. doi: 10.1017/S0140525X12000477

Corbetta, M., and Shulman, G. L. (2002). Control of goal-directed and stimulus-driven attention in the brain. Nat. Rev. Neurosci. 3, 201–215. doi: 10.1038/nrn755

Cox, D. D., and Dean, T. (2014). Neural networks and neuroscience-inspired computer vision. Curr. Biol. 24, R921–R929. doi: 10.1016/j.cub.2014.08.026

De Filippo De Grazia, M., Cutini, S., Lisi, M., and Zorzi, M. (2012). Space coding for sensorimotor transformations can emerge through unsupervised learning. Cogn. Process. 13, S141–S146. doi: 10.1007/s10339-012-0478-4

Deco, G., Jirsa, V. K., and McIntosh, A. R. (2013). Resting brains never rest: computational insights into potential cognitive architectures. Trends Neurosci. 36, 268–274. doi: 10.1016/j.tins.2013.03.001

Dehaene, S., and Cohen, L. (2007). Cultural recycling of cortical maps. Neuron 56, 384–398. doi: 10.1016/j.neuron.2007.10.004

Dehaene, S., Meyniel, F., Wacongne, C., Wang, L., and Pallier, C. (2015). The neural representation of sequences: from transition probabilities to algebraic patterns and linguistic trees. Neuron 88, 2–19. doi: 10.1016/j.neuron.2015.09.019

Deneve, S. (2008). Bayesian spiking neurons I: inference. Neural Comput. 20, 91–117. doi: 10.1162/neco.2008.20.1.91

Di Bono, M. G., and Zorzi, M. (2013). Deep generative learning of location-invariant visual word recognition. Front. Psychol. 4:635. doi: 10.3389/fpsyg.2013.00635

Elman, J. L., Bates, E., Johnson, M., Karmiloff-smith, A., Parisi, D., and Plunkett, K. (1996). Rethinking Innateness: A Connectionist Perspective on Development. Cambridge, MA: MIT Press.

Engel, A. K., Fries, P., and Singer, W. (2001). Dynamic predictions: oscillations and synchrony in top-down processing. Nat. Rev. Neurosci. 2, 704–716. doi: 10.1038/35094565

Farah, M. J. (2004). Visual Agnosia. Cambridge, MA: MIT Press.

Feigin, V. L., Forouzanfar, M. H., Krishnamurthi, R., Mensah, G. A., Connor, M., Bennett, D. A., et al. (2014). Global and regional burden of stroke during 1990–2010: findings from the Global Burden of Disease Study 2010. Lancet 383, 245–255. doi: 10.1016/s0140-6736(13)61953-4

Felleman, D. J., and Van Essen, D. C. (1991). Distributed hierarchical processing in the primate cerebral cortex. Cereb. Cortex 1, 1–47. doi: 10.1093/cercor/1.1.1

Fiser, J., Berkes, P., Orbán, G., and Lengyel, M. (2010). Statistically optimal perception and learning: from behavior to neural representations. Trends Cogn. Sci. 14, 119–130. doi: 10.1016/j.tics.2010.01.003

Friston, K. J. (2010). The free-energy principle: a unified brain theory? Nat. Rev. Neurosci. 11, 127–138. doi: 10.1038/nrn2787

Gao, J., Barzel, B., and Barabási, A.-L. (2016). Universal resilience patterns in complex networks. Nature 530, 307–312. doi: 10.1038/nature16948

Gerstner, W., Sprekeler, H., and Deco, G. (2012). Theory and simulation in neuroscience. Science 338, 60–65. doi: 10.1126/science.1227356

Ghahramani, Z. (2015). Probabilistic machine learning and artificial intelligence. Nature 521, 452–459. doi: 10.1038/nature14541

Gilbert, C. D., and Sigman, M. (2007). Brain states: top-down influences in sensory processing. Neuron 54, 677–696. doi: 10.1016/j.neuron.2007.05.019

Gläscher, J., Daw, N. D., Dayan, P., and O'Doherty, J. P. (2010). States versus rewards: dissociable neural prediction error signals underlying model-based and model-free reinforcement learning. Neuron 66, 585–595. doi: 10.1016/j.neuron.2010.04.016

Greicius, M. D., Krasnow, B., Reiss, A. L., and Menon, V. (2003). Functional connectivity in the resting brain: a network analysis of the default mode hypothesis. Proc. Natl. Acad. Sci. U S A 100, 253–258. doi: 10.1073/pnas.0135058100

Griffiths, T. L., Kemp, C., and Tenenbaum, J. B. (2008). "Bayesian models of cognition," in Cambridge Handbook of Computational Cognitive Modeling, ed. R. Sun (Cambridge, MA: Cambridge University Press), 59–100.

Hinton, G. E. (2002). Training products of experts by minimizing contrastive divergence. Neural Comput. 14, 1771–1800. doi: 10.1162/089976602760128018

Hinton, G. E. (2007). Learning multiple layers of representation. Trends Cogn. Sci. 11, 428–434. doi: 10.1016/j.tics.2007.09.004

Hinton, G. E., Dayan, P., Frey, B., and Neal, R. M. (1995). The "wake-sleep" algorithm for unsupervised neural networks. Science 268, 1158–1161. doi: 10.1126/science.7761831

Hinton, G. E., and Salakhutdinov, R. (2006). Reducing the dimensionality of data with neural networks. Science 313, 504–507. doi: 10.1126/science.1127647

Hinton, G. E., and Shallice, T. (1991). Lesioning an attractor network: investigations of acquired dyslexia. Psychol. Rev. 98, 74–95. doi: 10.1037/0033-295x.98.1.74

Humphreys, G. W., and Forde, E. M. (2001). Hierarchies, similarity and interactivity in object recognition: "category-specific" neuropsychological deficits. Behav. Brain Sci. 24, 453–476; discussion 476–509.

Itti, L., and Baldi, P. (2009). Bayesian surprise attracts human attention. Vision Res. 49, 1295–1306. doi: 10.1016/j.visres.2008.09.007

Jirsa, V. K., Sporns, O., Breakspear, M., Deco, G., and McIntosh, A. R. (2010). Towards the virtual brain: network modeling of the intact and the damaged brain. Arch. Ital. Biol. 148, 189–205.

Joanisse, M., and Seidenberg, M. S. (1999). Impairments in verb morphology after brain injury: a connectionist model. Proc. Natl. Acad. Sci. U S A 96, 7592–7597. doi: 10.1073/pnas.96.13.7592

Jordan, M. I., and Sejnowski, T. J. (2001). Graphical Models: Foundations of Neural Computation. Cambridge, MA: MIT Press.

Kelso, J. A. S. (2012). Multistability and metastability: understanding dynamic coordination in the brain. Philos. Trans. R. Soc. Lond. B Biol. Sci. 367, 906–918. doi: 10.1098/rstb.2011.0351

Khaligh-Razavi, S. M., and Kriegeskorte, N. (2014). Deep supervised, but not unsupervised, models may explain IT cortical representation. PLoS Comput. Biol. 10:e1003915. doi: 10.1371/journal.pcbi.1003915

Kirkpatrick, S., Gelatt, C. Jr., and Vecchi, M. (1983). Optimization by simmulated annealing. Science 220, 671–680. doi: 10.1126/science.220.4598.671

Koller, D., and Friedman, N. (2009). Probabilistic Graphical Models: Principles and Techniques. Cambridge, MA: The MIT Press.

Lake, B. M., Salakhutdinov, R., and Tenenbaum, J. B. (2015). Humal-level concept learning through probabilistic program induction. Science 350, 1332–1338. doi: 10.1126/science.aab3050

Le, Q. V., Ranzato, M. A., Monga, R., Devin, M., Chen, K., Corrado, G. S., et al. (2012). "Building high-level features using large scale unsupervised learning," in Proceedings of the 29th International Conference on Machine Learning (Edinburgh, Scotland, UK).

LeCun, Y., Bengio, Y., and Hinton, G. E. (2015). Deep learning. Nature 521, 436–444. doi: 10.1038/nature14539

Lee, T. S., and Mumford, D. (2003). Hierarchical bayesian inference in the visual cortex. J. Opt. Soc. Am. A Opt. Image Sci. Vis. 20, 1434–1448. doi: 10.1364/josaa.20.001434

Ma, W. J., Beck, J. M., Latham, P. E., and Pouget, A. (2006). Bayesian inference with probabilistic population codes. Nat. Neurosci. 9, 1432–1438. doi: 10.1038/nn1790

Manford, M., and Andermann, F. (1998). Complex visual hallucinations. Clinical and neurobiological insights. Brain 121, 1819–1840. doi: 10.1093/brain/121.10.1819

Mathers, C., Fat, D. M., and Boerma, T. J. (2008). The Global Burden of Disease: 2004 Update. Geneva, Switzerland: World Health Organization.

Mavritsaki, E., Heinke, D., Allen, H., Deco, G., and Humphreys, G. W. (2011). Bridging the gap between physiology and behavior: evidence from the sSoTS model of human visual attention. Psychol. Rev. 118, 3–41. doi: 10.1037/a0021868

McClelland, J. L. (2013). Integrating probabilistic models of perception and interactive neural networks: a historical and tutorial review. Front. Psychol. 4:503. doi: 10.3389/fpsyg.2013.00503

McClelland, J. L., McNaughton, B., and O'Reilly, R. C. (1995). Why there are complementary learning systems in the hippocampus and neocortex: insights from the successes and failures of connectionist models of learning and memory. Psychol. Rev. 102, 419–457. doi: 10.1037/0033-295x.102.3.419

Medaglia, J. D., Lynall, M.-E., and Bassett, D. S. (2015). Cognitive network neuroscience. J. Cogn. Neurosci. 27, 1471–1491. doi: 10.1162/jocn_a_00810

Mnih, V., Kavukcuoglu, K., Silver, D., Rusu, A. A., Veness, J., Bellemare, M. G., et al. (2015). Human-level control through deep reinforcement learning. Nature 518, 529–533. doi: 10.1038/nature14236

Nessler, B., Pfeiffer, M., Buesing, L., and Maass, W. (2013). Bayesian computation emerges in generic cortical microcircuits through spike-timing-dependent plasticity. PLoS Comput. Biol. 9:e1003037. doi: 10.1371/journal.pcbi.1003037

Newman, M. (2010). Networks: An Introduction. New York, NY: Oxford University Press.

Ngiam, J., Khosla, A., Kim, M., Nam, J., Lee, H., and Ng, A. Y. (2011). "Multimodal deep learning," in Proceedings of the 28th International Conference on Machine Learning (ICML-11), Bellevue, WA, 689–696.

O'Reilly, R. C., and Munakata, Y. (2000). Computational Exploration in Cognitive Neuroscience. Cambridge, MA: MIT Press.

Park, H.-J., and Friston, K. J. (2013). Structural and functional brain networks: from connections to cognition. Science 342:1238411. doi: 10.1126/science.1238411

Pecevski, D., Buesing, L., and Maass, W. (2011). Probabilistic inference in general graphical models through sampling in stochastic networks of spiking neurons. PLoS Comput. Biol. 7:e1002294. doi: 10.1371/journal.pcbi.1002294

Plaut, D. C., and Behrmann, M. (2011). Complementary neural representations for faces and words: a computational exploration. Cogn. Neuropsychol. 28, 251–275. doi: 10.1080/02643294.2011.609812

Plaut, D. C., and Shallice, T. (1993). Deep dyslexia: a case study of connectionist neuropsychology. Cogn. Neuropsychol. 10, 377–500. doi: 10.1080/02643299308253469

Pouget, A., and Driver, J. (2000). Relating unilateral neglect to the neural coding of space. Curr. Opin. Neurobiol. 10, 242–249. doi: 10.1016/s0959-4388(00)00077-5

Raichle, M. E. (2015). The restless brain: how intrinsic activity organizes brain function. Philos. Trans. R. Soc. Lond. B Biol. Sci. 370:20140172. doi: 10.1098/rstb.2014.0172

Raina, R., Madhavan, A., and Ng, A. Y. (2009). "Large-scale deep unsupervised learning using graphics processors," in International Conference on Machine Learning, (New York, NY: ACM Press), 873–880.

Rao, R. P. N. (2004). Bayesian computation in recurrent neural circuits. Neural Comput. 16, 1–38. doi: 10.1162/08997660460733976

Reichert, D. P., Series, P., and Storkey, A. (2013). Charles bonnet syndrome: evidence for a generative model in the cortex? PLoS Comput. Biol. 9:e1003134. doi: 10.1371/journal.pcbi.1003134

Roitman, J. D., Brannon, E. M., and Platt, M. L. (2007). Monotonic coding of numerosity in macaque lateral intraparietal area. PLoS Biol. 5:e208. doi: 10.1371/journal.pbio.0050208

Rotzer, S., Kucian, K., Martin, E., von Aster, M., Klaver, P., and Loenneker, T. (2008). Optimized voxel-based morphometry in children with developmental dyscalculia. Neuroimage 39, 417–422. doi: 10.1016/j.neuroimage.2007.08.045

Rumelhart, D. E., and McClelland, J. L. (1986). Parallel Distributed Processing: Explorations in the Microstructure of Cognition, Vol. 1: Foundations. Cambridge, MA: MIT Press.

Sillito, A. M., Cudeiro, J., and Jones, H. E. (2006). Always returning: feedback and sensory processing in visual cortex and thalamus. Trends Neurosci. 29, 307–316. doi: 10.1016/j.tins.2006.05.001

Silver, D., Huang, A., Maddison, C. J., Guez, A., Sifre, L., van den Driessche, G., et al. (2016). Mastering the game of Go with deep neural networks and tree search. Nature 529, 484–489. doi: 10.1038/nature16961

Snodgrass, J. G., and Vanderwart, M. (1980). A standardized set of 260 pictures: norms for name agreement, image agreement, familiarity and visual complexity. J. Exp. Psychol. Hum. Learn. 6, 174–215. doi: 10.1037/0278-7393.6.2.174

Stoianov, I., and Zorzi, M. (2012). Emergence of a "visual number sense" in hierarchical generative models. Nat. Neurosci. 15, 194–196. doi: 10.1038/nn.2996

Stoianov, I., and Zorzi, M. (2013). "Developmental trajectories of numerosity perception," in Poster Presented at the Workshop: Interactions Between Space, Time and Number: 20 Years of Research (Paris).

Stoianov, I., Zorzi, M., and Umiltà, C. (2004). The role of semantic and symbolic representations in arithmetic processing: insights from simulated dyscalculia in a connectionist model. Cortex 40, 194–196. doi: 10.1016/s0010-9452(08)70948-1

Sutskever, I., Hinton, G. E., and Taylor, G. (2008). The recurrent temporal restricted Boltzmann machine. Adv. Neural Inf. Process. Syst. 20, 1601–1608.

Tenenbaum, J. B., Kemp, C., Griffiths, T. L., and Goodman, N. D. (2011). How to grow a mind: statistics, structure and abstraction. Science 331, 1279–1285. doi: 10.1126/science.1192788

Testolin, A., Stoianov, I., De Filippo De Grazia, M., and Zorzi, M. (2013). Deep unsupervised learning on a desktop PC: a primer for cognitive scientists. Front. Psychol. 4:251. doi: 10.3389/fpsyg.2013.00251

Testolin, A., Stoianov, I., Sperduti, A., and Zorzi, M. (2016). Learning orthographic structure with sequential generative neural networks. Cogn. Sci. 40, 579–606. doi: 10.1111/cogs.12258

Testolin, A., Stoianov, I., and Zorzi, M. (under review). Human-like letter perception emerges from unsupervised deep learning and recycling of natural image statistics.

Varela, F., Lachaux, J. P., Rodriguez, E., and Martinerie, J. (2001). The brainweb: phase synchronization and large-scale integration. Nat. Rev. Neurosci. 2, 229–239. doi: 10.1038/35067550

Zorzi, M., Stoianov, I., and Umiltà, C. (2005). "Computational modeling of numerical cognition," in Handbook of Mathematical Cognition, ed. J. Campbell (New York, NY: Psychology Press), 67–84.

Zorzi, M., Testolin, A., and Stoianov, I. (2013). Modeling language and cognition with deep unsupervised learning: a tutorial overview. Front. Psychol. 4:515. doi: 10.3389/fpsyg.2013.00515

4 Chapter
PATTERNS OF INFERENCE

4.1 CAUSAL DEPENDENCE

4.1.1 Introduction

Probabilistic programs encode knowledge about the world in the form of causal models, and it is useful to understand how their function relates to their structure by thinking about some of the intuitive properties of causal relations. Causal relations are local, modular, and directed. They are modular in the sense that any two arbitrary events in the world are most likely causally unrelated, or independent. If they are related, or dependent, the relation is only very weak and liable to be ignored in our mental models. Causal structure is local in the sense that many events that are related are not related directly: They are connected only through causal chains of several steps, a series of intermediate and more local dependencies. And the basic dependencies are directed: when we say that A causes B, it means something different than saying that B causes A. The causal influence flows only one way along a causal relation where we expect that manipulating the cause will change the effect, but not vice versa while an information can flow both ways by learning about either event will give us information about the other.

Let's examine this notion of "causal dependence" a little more carefully. What does it mean to believe that A depends causally on B? Viewing cognition through the lens of probabilistic programs, the most basic notions of causal dependence are in terms of the structure of the program and the flow of evaluation (or "control") in its execution. We say that expression A causally depends on expression B if it is necessary to evaluate B in order to evaluate A.

Note that this causal dependence order is weaker than a notion of ordering in time where one expression might happen to be evaluated before another in time (for instance the first of two arguments to a function before the second), but without the second expression requiring the first. Such notion of causal dependence is roughly the same as the notion of control flow dependence in the programming language literature.

Example

(define samples

(mh-query 200 100

Here, cough depends causally on both lung-disease and cold, while fever depends causally on cold but not lung-disease. We can see that cough depends causally on smokes but only indirectly: although cough does not call smokes directly, in order to evaluate whether a patient coughs, we first have to evaluate the expression lung-disease that must itself evaluate smokes. The causal dependence structure is not always immediately clear from examining a program, particularly where there are complex functions calls; a useful way of diagnosing causal dependence, which is even sometimes taken as the definition, is by intervention on the program as shown on sidebar.

There are several special situations that are worth mentioning. In some cases, whether expression A requires expression B will depend on the value of some third expression C.

For example, here is a particular way of writing a noisy-logical AND gate:

(define C (flip))

(define B (flip))

(define A (if C (if B (flip 0.85) false) false))

A always requires C, but only evaluates B if C returns true. Under the above definition of causal dependence A depends on B (as well as C). However, one could imagine a more fine-grained notion of causal dependence that would be useful here: we could say that A depends causally on B only in certain contexts (just those where C happens to return true and thus A calls B).

Another nuance is that an expression that occurs inside a function body may get evaluated several times in a program execution. In such cases it is useful to speak of causal dependence between specific evaluations of two expressions.

4.1.2 Lewis Theory

Similar to many contemporary counterfactual theories, Lewis's theory employs a possible world semantics for counterfactuals. Such semantics describes truth conditions for counterfactuals in terms of similarity relations between possible worlds. Lewis famously espouses a realism about possible worlds, according to which non-actual possible worlds are real concrete entities on a par with the actual world. However, most contemporary philosophers would seek to deploy the explanatorily fruitful possible worlds framework while distancing themselves from full-blown realism about possible worlds themselves. For example, many would propose to understand possible worlds as maximally consistent sets of propositions; or even to treat them instrumentally as useful theoretical entities having no independent reality.

The central notion of a possible world semantics for counterfactuals is a relation of comparative similarity between worlds. One world is said to be closer to actuality than another if the first resembles the actual world more than the second does. Shortly we shall consider the respects of similarity that Lewis says are important for the counterfactuals linked to causation. For now we simply note two formal constraints he imposes on this similarity relation. First, the relation of similarity produces a weak ordering of worlds so that any two worlds can be ordered with respect to their closeness to the actual world, with allowance being made for ties in closeness. Secondly, the actual world is closest to actuality, resembling itself more than any other world resembles it.

With relation to such similarity relation, the truth condition for the counterfactual "If A were (or had been) the case, C would be (or have been) the case" will be as follows:

(1) "If A were the case, C would be the case" is true in the actual world if and only if:

- There are no possible A-worlds
- Some A-world where C holds is closer to the actual world than is any A-world where C does not hold.

Ignoring the first case where the counterfactual is vacuously true. The fundamental idea of this analysis is that the counterfactual "If A were the case, C would be the case" is true just in case it takes less of a departure from actuality to make the antecedent true along with the consequent than to make the antecedent true without the consequent. In terms of counterfactuals, Lewis defines a notion of causal dependence between events, which plays a central role in his theory of causation.

(2) Where c and e are two distinct possible events, e causally depends on c if and only if, if c were to occur e would occur; and if c were not to occur e would not occur.

Such condition states that whether e occurs or not depends on whether c occurs or not. Where c and e are actual occurrence events, this truth condition can be simplified somewhat. For in this case it follows from the second formal condition on the comparative similarity relation that the counterfactual "If c were to occur e would occur" is automatically true: this formal condition implies that a counterfactual with true antecedent and true consequent is itself true. Consequently, the truth condition for causal dependence becomes:

(3) Where c and e are two distinct actual events, e causally depends on c if and only if, if c were not to occur e would not occur.

The right hand side of this condition is, of course, Hume's second definition of causation. As stated, Lewis's official definition of causation differs from it, as he defines causation not in terms of causal dependence directly, but in terms of chains of causal dependence. Hence it is plausible to think that causation is conceptually linked with counterfactuals in the way specified by this definition of causal dependence. One reason is that the idea of a cause is conceptually linked with the idea of something that makes a difference and this idea in turn is best understood in terms of counterfactuals. In Lewis's words: "We think of a cause as something that makes a difference, and the difference it makes must be a difference from what would have happened without it. Had it been absent, its effects some of them, at least, and usually all — would have been absent as well."

There are three important things to note about the definition of causal dependence. First, it takes the primary relation of causal dependence to be events. Lewis's own theory of events construes events as classes of possible spatiotemporal regions. However, very different conceptions of events are compatible with the basic definition. Indeed, it even seems possible to formulate it in terms of facts rather than events.

Also, definition requires the causally dependent events to be distinct from each other. Distinctness means that the events are not identical, neither is part of the other, and neither implies the other. This qualification is important if spurious non-causal dependences are to be ruled out. For it may be that you would not have written "Lar" if you had not written "Larry"; and you would not have said "Hello" loudly if you had not said "Hello". But neither dependence counts as a causal dependence since the paired events are not distinct from each other in the required sense.

Further the counterfactuals that are employed in the analysis are to be understood according to what Lewis calls the standard interpretation. There are several possible ways of interpreting counterfactuals; and some interpretations give rise to spurious non-causal dependences between events. For example, suppose that the events c and e are effects of a common cause d. It is tempting to reason that there must be a causal dependence between c and e by engaging in the following piece of counterfactual reasoning: if c had not occurred, then it would have to have been the case that d did not occur, in which case e would not have occurred. But Lewis says these counterfactuals, which he calls backtracking counterfactuals, are not to be used in the assessment of causal dependence. The right counterfactuals to be used are non-backtracking counterfactuals that typically hold the past fixed up until the time at which the counterfactual antecedent is supposed to obtain.

4.1.3 Temporal Asymmetry of Causal Dependence

Now we will study about direction of the causal relation and know the reason as why this direction typically aligned with temporal direction from past to future. As per Lewis, the direction of causation is the direction of causal dependence which is typically true as events causally depend on earlier events but not on later events. He emphasises the contingency of the latter fact because he regards backwards or time-reversed causation as a conceptual possibility that cannot be ruled out a priori. Accordingly, he dismisses any analysis of counterfactuals that would deliver the temporal asymmetry by conceptual fiat.

Lewis's explanation of the temporal asymmetry of counterfactual dependence is based on a de facto asymmetry about the actual world. He defines a determinant for an event as any set of conditions jointly sufficient, given the laws of nature, for the event's occurrence. It is noted that determinants of an event may be causes or traces of the event. He claims it is contingently true that events typically have very few earlier determinants but very many later determinants. As an illustration, he cites Popper's example of a spherical wavefront expanding outwards from a point source. This is a process where each sample of the wave postdetermines what happens at the point at which the wave is emitted. He says the reverse process in which a spherical wave contracts inward with each sample of wave predetermining what happens at the point the wave is absorbed would obey the laws of nature but seldom happens in actual fact.

Lewis combines the de facto asymmetry of over determination with his analysis of the comparative similarity relation. According to this analysis, there are several respccts of similarity to be taken into account in evaluating non-backtracking counterfactuals: similarity with respect to laws of nature and also similarity with respect to particular matters of fact. Worlds are more similar to the actual world the fewer miracles or violations of the actual laws of nature they contain. Again, worlds are more similar to the actual world the greater the spatio-temporal region of perfect match of particular fact they have with the actual world. If the actual world is governed by deterministic laws, these rules will clash in assessing which counterfactual worlds are more similar to the actual world. For a world that makes a counterfactual antecedent true must differ from the actual world either in allowing some violation of the actual laws, or in differing from the actual world in particular matters of fact.

Lewis's analysis allows a trade off between these competing respects of similarity in such cases. It implies that worlds with an extensive region of perfect match of particular fact can be considered very similar to the actual world provided that the match in particular facts with the actual world is achieved at the cost of a small, local miracle, but not at the cost of a big, diverse miracle. Taken by itself, this account contains no built-in time asymmetry. That comes only when it is combined with the asymmetry of over determination.

To see how the two parts combine, consider the famous example of Nixon and the Nuclear Holocaust. An early objection to Lewis's account of counter factuals was that, counter intuitively, it makes this counterfactual false:

If Nixon had pressed the button, there would have been a nuclear war. The argument is that a world in which Nixon pressed the button, but some minute violation of the laws then prevented a nuclear war, is much more like the actual world than one in which Nixon pressed the button and a nuclear war took place. As per Lewis, it does not accord with the account of the similarity relation while on basis of this account, button-pressing world diverges from actual world by virtue of a miracle is more like the actual world than a button-pressing world that converges with the actual world by virtue of a miracle. For in view of the asymmetry of over determination, the divergence miracle that allows Nixon to press the button need only be a small, local miracle, but the convergence miracle required to wipe out the traces of Nixon's pressing the button must be a very big, diverse miracle. Also, if the asymmetry of over determination went in the opposite temporal direction, the very same standards of similarity would dictate the opposite verdict.

In general, then, the symmetric analysis of similarity, combined with the defacto asymmetry of over determination, implies that worlds that accommodate counterfactual changes by preserving the actual past and allowing for divergence miracles are more similar to the actual world than worlds that accommodate such changes by allowing for convergence miracles that preserve the actual future. This fact in turn implies that, where the asymmetry of over determination obtains, the present counterfactually depends on the past, but not on the future.

4.1.4 Detecting Dependence through Intervention

Causal dependence structure is not always immediately clear from examining a program, particularly where there are complex functions calls. Another way to detect causal dependence is more operational, in terms of "difference making"; If we manipulate A, does B tend to change? By manipulate here we don't mean an assumption in the sense of condition. Instead we mean actually edit, or intervene on, the program in order to make an expression have a particular value independent of its (former) causes. If setting A to different values in this way changes the distribution of values of B, then B causally depends on A.

```
var BdoA = function(Aval) {
 return Infer({method: 'enumerate'}, function() {
  var C = flip()
  var A = Aval //we directly set A to the target value
  var B = A ? flip(.1) : flip(.4)
  return {B: B} }) }
viz(BdoA(true))
viz(BdoA(false))
```

This method is known in the causal Bayesian network literature as the "do operator" or graph surgery. It is also the basis for interesting theories of counterfactual reasoning by Pearl and colleagues. For example, this code represents whether a patient is likely to have a cold or a cough a priori, without conditions or observations:

```
var medicalDist = Infer({method: 'enumerate'}, function() {
 var smokes = flip(.2)
 var lungDisease = flip(0.001) || (smokes && flip(0.1))
 var cold = flip(0.02)
 var cough = (cold && flip(0.5)) || (lungDisease && flip(0.5)) || flip(0.001)
 var fever = (cold && flip(0.3)) || flip(0.01)
 var chestPain = (lungDisease && flip(0.2)) || flip(0.01)
 var shortnessOfBreath = (lungDisease && flip(0.2)) || flip(0.01)
 return {cough: cough, cold: cold} })
viz.marginals(medicalDist)
```

Imagine we now give our hypothetical patient a cold—for example, by exposing him to a strong cocktail of cold viruses. We should not model this as an observation (e.g. by conditioning on having a cold), because we have taken direct action to change the normal causal structure. Instead we implement intervention by directly editing the program: try to first do var cold = true, then do var cold = false:

```
var medicalDist = Infer({method: 'enumerate'}, function() {
 var smokes = flip(.2)
 var lungDisease = flip(0.001) || (smokes && flip(0.1))
 var cold = true // we intervene to make cold true
 var cough = (cold && flip(0.5)) || (lungDisease && flip(0.5)) || flip(0.001)
```

```
var fever = (cold && flip(0.3)) || flip(0.01)
var chestPain = (lungDisease && flip(0.2)) || flip(0.01)
var shortnessOfBreath = (lungDisease && flip(0.2)) || flip(0.01)
return {cough: cough, cold: cold} })
viz.marginals(medicalDist)
```

You should see that the distribution on cough changes: coughing becomes more likely if we know that a patient has been given a cold by external intervention. But the reverse is not true: Try forcing the patient to have a cough by writing var cough = true: the distribution on cold is unaffected. We have captured a familiar fact: treating the symptoms of a disease directly doesn't cure the disease, but treating the disease does relieve the symptoms.

Verify in the program above that the method of manipulation works also to identify causal relations that are only indirect: for example, force a patient to smoke and show that it increases their probability of coughing, but not vice versa.

If we are given a program representing a causal model, and the model is simple enough, it is straightforward to read off causal dependencies from the program code itself. However, the notion of causation as difference-making may be easier to compute in much larger, more complex models which does not require an analysis of the program code. As long as we can modify the definitions in the program and can run the resulting model, we can compute whether two events or functions are causally related by the difference-making criterion.

4.2 BAYESIAN NETWORKS AND CAUSALITY

A Bayesian network, is a model or probabilistic directed acyclic graphical model that represents a set of random variables and their conditional dependencies via a directed acyclic graph (DAG). For example, a Bayesian network could represent the probabilistic relationships between diseases and symptoms. Given symptoms, the network can be used to compute the probabilities of the presence of various diseases. A PGM is a graph that encodes the causal relationships between events.

For example, you might construct this graph to model a chain of causes resulting in someone getting a college scholarship:

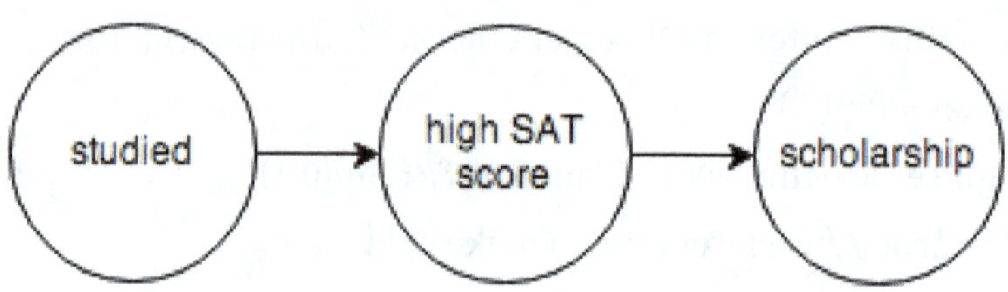

Or relationship between diseases and their symptoms:

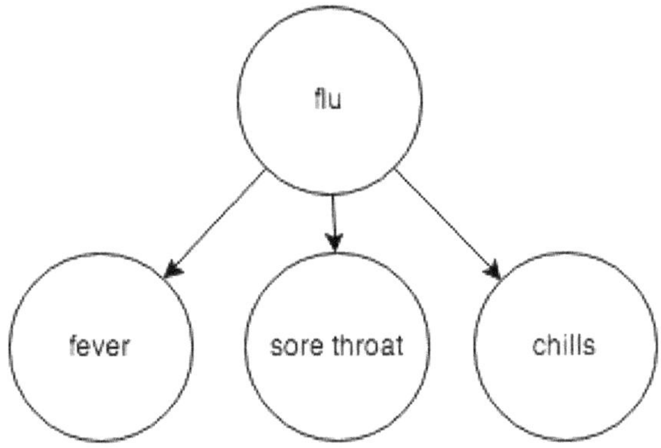

Fig: Relationship between diseases and symptoms

Or events surrounding a traffic jam:

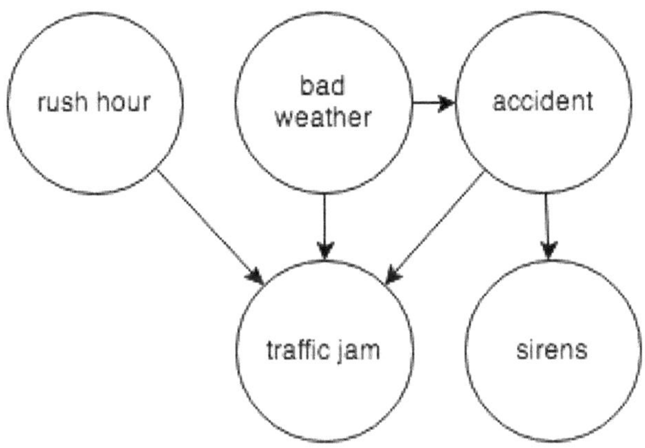

In this, every node represents a random variable, and the arrows represent dependence relations between them. You can think of a node with incoming arrows as a probability distribution parameterized on some set of inputs; in other words, a function from some set of inputs to a probability distribution.

PGMs with directed edges and no cycles are specifically called Bayesian networks, and that's the kind of PGM I'm going to focus on. It's easy to translate a Bayesian network into code using this toy probability library.

```
val rushHour: Distribution[Boolean] = tf(0.2)
val badWeather: Distribution[Boolean] = tf(0.05)
```

In this hypothetical world, 20% of the time it's rush hour, and 5% of the time there's bad weather. For nodes with incoming arrows, we return a different distribution depending on the particular value its in-neighbor takes.

```
def accident(badWeather: Boolean): Distribution[Boolean] = {
 badWeather match {
  case true => tf(0.3)
  case false => tf(0.1)
 }
}
```

If the weather is bad, we're 30% likely to see an accident, but otherwise accidents occur only 10% of the time.

```
def sirens(accident: Boolean): Distribution[Boolean] = {
 accident match {
  case true => tf(0.9)
  case false => tf(0.2)
 }
}
```

Now let's tackle traffic Jam. It's going to have 3 Boolean inputs, and we'll need to return a different probability distribution depending on which of the inputs are true. Let's say that if any two of of the inputs are true, there's a 95% chance of a traffic jam, and that traffic jams are less likely if only one of them is true, and somewhat unlikely if none are.

```
def trafficJam(rushHour: Boolean,
        badWeather: Boolean,
        accident: Boolean): Distribution[Boolean] = {
 (rushHour, badWeather, accident) match {
  case (true, true, _) => tf(0.95)
  case (true, _, true) => tf(0.95)
  case (_, true, true) => tf(0.95)
  case (true, false, false) => tf(0.5)
  case (false, true, false) => tf(0.3)
  case (false, false, true) => tf(0.6)
  case (false, false, false) => tf(0.1)
 }
}
```

If you've done any Scala or Haskell programming, you've probably noticed that these are all functions of typeA => Distribution[B]—and yeah, you better believe we're gonna flatMap that shit. Now produce the joint probability distribution for all these events.

```
case class Traffic(
  rushHour: Boolean,
  badWeather: Boolean,
  accident: Boolean,
  sirens: Boolean,
  trafficJam: Boolean)
val traffic: Distribution[Traffic] = for {
  r <- rushHour
  w <- badWeather
  a <- accident(w)
  s <- sirens(a)
  t <- trafficJam(r, w, a)
} yield Traffic(r, w, a, s, t)
```

Now we can query this distribution to see what affects what. Finding chances of traffic jam as:

```
scala> traffic.given(_.badWeather).pr(_.trafficJam)
res0: Double = 0.5658
```

Then you hear sirens.

```
scala> traffic.given(_.badWeather).given(_.sirens).pr(_.trafficJam)
res1: Double = 0.6718
```

Here, sirens increases the thought that there's an accident, which will in turn affect the traffic. Now let's look at things the other way around. Say you're sitting in traffic and you want to know whether there's an accident up ahead.

```
scala> traffic.given(_.trafficJam).pr(_.accident)
res2: Double = 0.3183
```

Also, it's raining, so you decide to factor that in:

```
scala> traffic.given(_.trafficJam).given(_.badWeather).pr(_.accident)
res3: Double = 0.4912
```

Makes sense, bad weather increases the chance of an accident. Suppose instead the weather is fine, but it is rush hour:

```
scala> traffic.given(_.trafficJam).given(_.rushHour).pr(_.accident)
res4: Double = 0.1807
```

It is good as it gave knowledge that during rush hour, there are likelihood that there's an accident, but there's no direct causal link in our model between rush hour and accidents.

4.2.1 Belief propagation

The neat thing about Bayesian networks is that they completely explain which nodes can be correlated and which are independent. By following a few simple rules, you can read this information right off the graph.

Rule 0. In the graph below, A and B can be correlated:

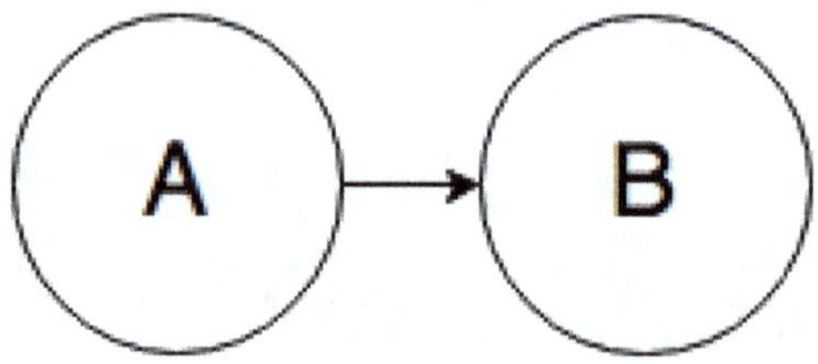

Fig: Graph

It's almost too simple to mention, but knowing the value of A will change your belief about the value of B. What's slightly less obvious is that knowing the value of B will change your belief about the value of A. For example, if rain causes the sidewalk to be wet, then seeing a wet sidewalk changes your belief about whether it rained.

Rule 1. In the graph below, A and B can be correlated:

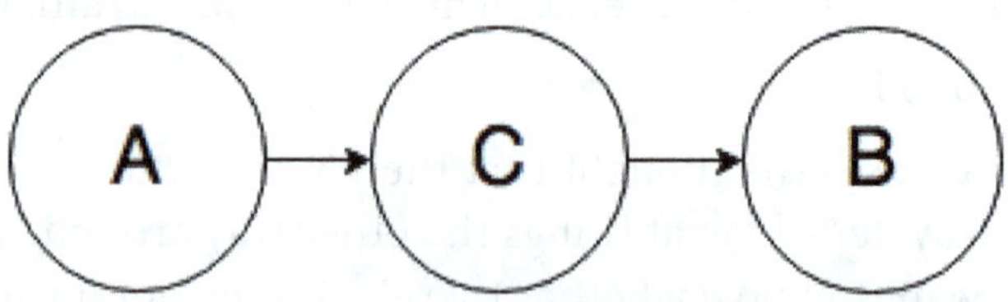

Fig: Graph

Knowing the value of A will change your belief about the value of B. Furthermore, knowing the value of B will also change your belief about the value of A. Intuitively, if someone got a scholarship (B), that raises your belief about whether they studied for their SATs (A), even if there's an intermediate cause in the mix, say a high SAT score (C). So far, it seems like belief can propagate through arrows in either direction.

Rule 2. In the graph below, A and B can be correlated:

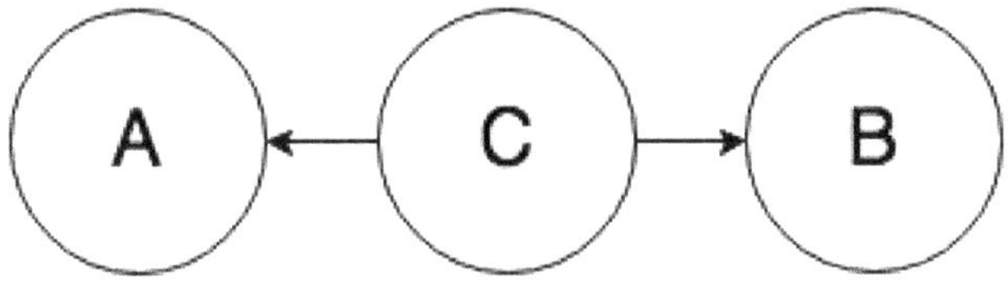

Fig: Graph

Knowing the value of A influences your belief about the value of C, which directly affects the value of B. For example, knowing that someone has a fever (A) increases your belief that they have the flu (C), which in turn increases your belief that they have a sore throat (B). So what's the point of arrows if belief can propagate across them in either direction? Glad you asked.

Rule 3. In the graph below, A and B must be independent:

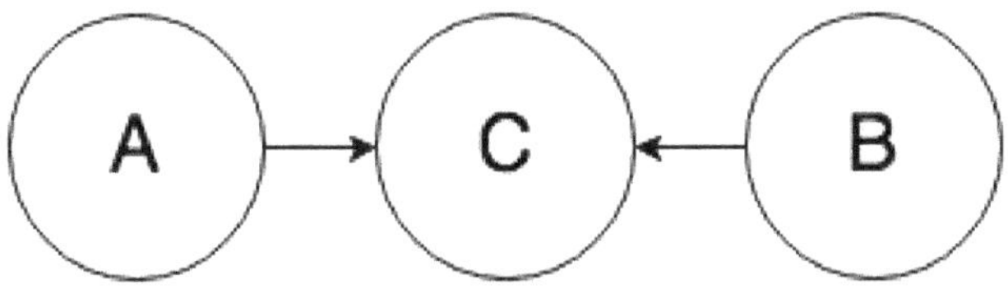

Fig: A and B independent in graph

To give you the intuition, whether the weather is bad (A) should have no influence over whether it's currently rush hour (B), even though they both cause traffic jams (C). So we have two cases where belief can propagate through a node, and one case where it can't. But something interesting happens when the value of the middle node, C, is known—the situation completely reverses.

Belief Propagation with Observed Nodes

Rule 1a. In the graph below, if C is known, A and B must be independent.

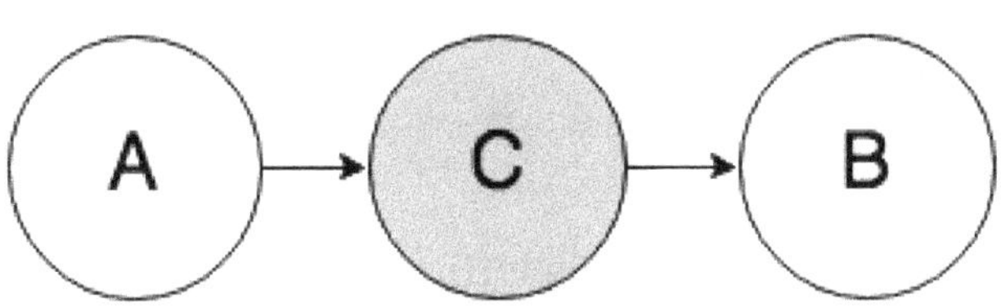

Fig: Graph

Knowing C "blocks" belief from propagating from A to B. If you know that someone got a high SAT score (C), whether they studied for their SATs (A) doesn't tell you anything new about whether they got a scholarship (B). In the reverse case, if you know that someone got a high SAT score, then knowing whether or not they got a scholarship should not change your belief about whether or not they studied.

Rule 2a. In the graph below, if C is known, A and B must be independent.

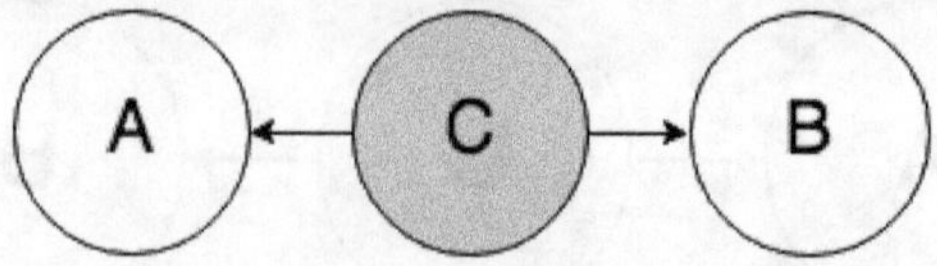

Fig: Graph

Again, knowledge of the middle node blocks belief from propagating through it. If you know someone has the flu (C), knowing that they have a sore throat (A) does not affect your belief that they have a fever (B); knowing that they have the flu already tells you everything you need to know about their body temperature.

Rule 3a. In the graph below, if C is known, A and B can be correlated.

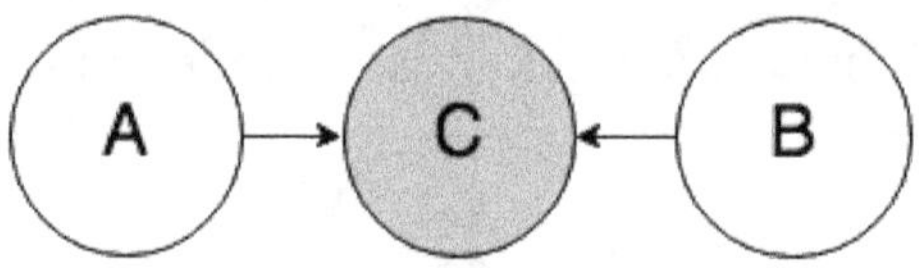

Fig: Correlation Graph

It is an interesting case as its belief would not be able to propagate through node C like this, but if its value is known, the node becomes "activated" and belief can flow through. The intuition here is that if I already know that there's a traffic jam (C), then knowing that it's rush hour (A) should *decrease* my belief that the weather is bad (B). Rush hour "explains away" the traffic jam, making bad weather seem less likely.

Rule 3b. In the graph below, if D is known, A and B can be correlated.

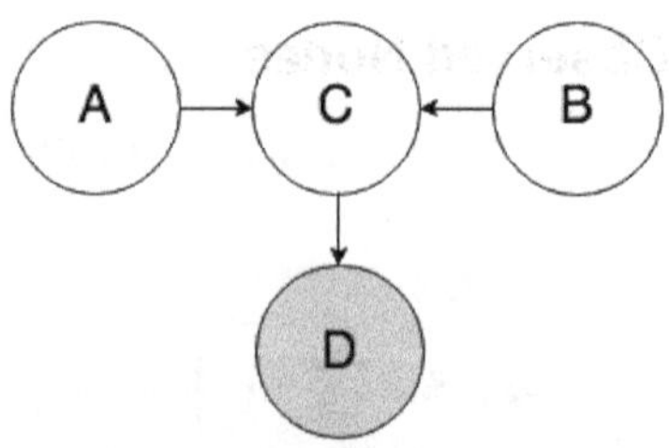

Fig: Correlation Graph

This rule is a variation on Rule 3a. If we know D, then we also know something about C, which partially activates C and allows belief to flow through it from A to B. For example, if I observe someone wearing a college sweatshirt (D), that increases my belief that they went to college (C). If I find out that they got a high SAT score (A), that can decrease my belief that they played sports (B).

These rules are collectively known as the Bayes-Ball algorithm.

Flipping of Coin

It is known that flipping of coin are independent of one another, so if you flip a coin 10 times and it comes with heads each time, then the probability that it will come up heads on the next flip ill remain 50%. Further, if a coin is flipped 100 times and it comes up heads 85 times, then it is observed that this is astronomically unlikely under the assumption which can be concluded as that the coin's bias is actually 85%, where next flip will have chance of 85% with head to appear that shows that next flip was *not* independent of the other flips.

There's a subtle difference between the two that becomes clear when you draw out the graph.

Here's the first case:

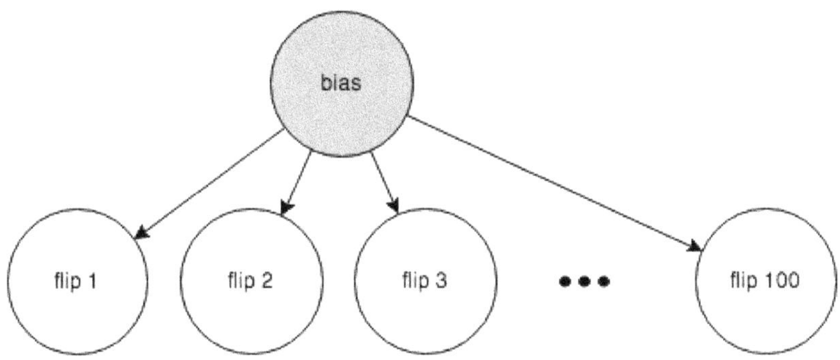

Fig: Coin Flip

The bias is known (50%), so belief is blocked from propagating between the individual flips (Rule 2a). Here's the second case:

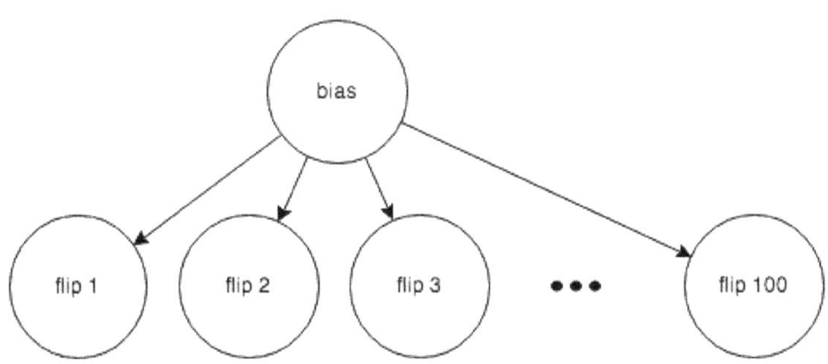

Fig: Coin Flip

Here, the bias is unknown, so belief is allowed to flow through the "bias" node (Rule 2).

So both are right! They just make subtly different assumptions. The Bayesian network below represents the blood types of several members of a family. The shaded nodes indicate nodes we can't observe. But as long as we know how they interact with the observable nodes, we can make inferences about how the observable nodes interact with each other.

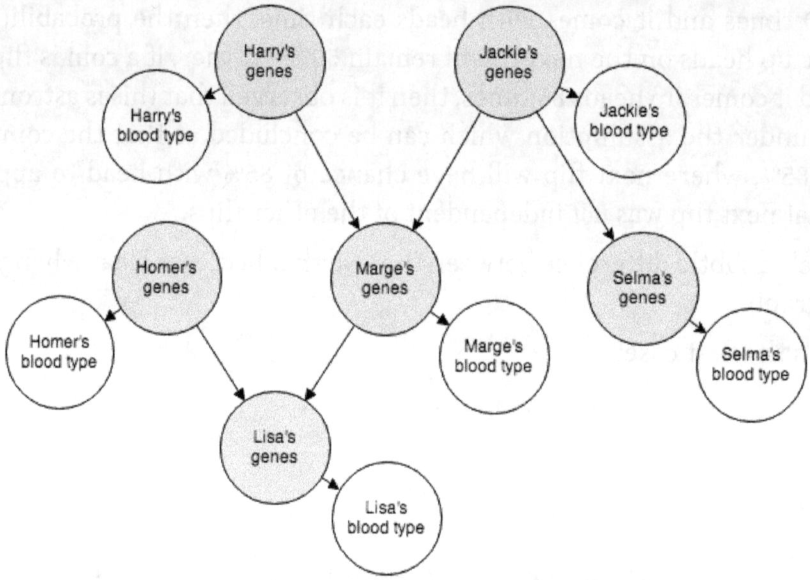

Fig: Bayesian network

Consider a code to represent genotypes and phenotypes (blood types):

```
Sealed trait BloodGene
Case object A_ extends BloodGene
Case object B_ extends BloodGene
Case object O_ extends BloodGene
Sealed trait BloodType
Case object A extends BloodType
Case object B extends BloodType
Case object AB extends BloodType
Case object O extends BloodType
```

For arrows linking each person's genes to their blood type, we need a function that determines BloodType given two BloodGenes. This happens to be a deterministic function, but I'm implementing it as a stochastic function anyway.

```
def typeFromGene(g: (BloodGene, BloodGene)): Distribution[BloodType] = {
g match {
  Case (A_, B_) => always(AB)
  Case (B_, A_) => always(AB)
```

```
      Case (A_, _) => always(A)
      Case (_, A_) => always(A)
      Case (B_, _) => always(B)
      Case (_, B_) => always(B)
      Case (O_, O_) => always(O)
    }
  }
```

For the arrows linking parents' genes to their children's genes, we can implement this function that chooses one gene from each parent at random:

```
def childFromParents(p1: (BloodGene, BloodGene),
 p2: (BloodGene, BloodGene)): Distribution[(BloodGene, BloodGene)] = {
  val (p1a, p1b) = p1
  val (p2a, p2b) = p2
  discreteUniform(for {
    p1 <- List(p1a, p1b)
    p2 <- List(p2a, p2b)
  } yield (p1, p2))
}
```

Finally, for the people whose parents are not specified, we supply a prior on each of the 3 genes refecting theirprevalence in the general population.

```
val bloodGenePrior: Distribution[(BloodGene, BloodGene)] = {
  val geneFrequencies = discrete(A_ -> 0.26, B_ -> 0.08, O_ -> 0.66)
  for {
    g1 <- geneFrequencies
    g2 <- geneFrequencies
  } yield (g1, g2)
}
```

Now writing everything and making it clear translation of Bayesian network in a code.

```
case class BloodTrial(lisa: BloodType, homer: BloodType, marge: BloodType,
                selma: BloodType, jackie: BloodType, harry: BloodType)
val bloodType: Distribution[BloodTrial] = for {
```

```
  gHomer <- bloodGenePrior
  gHarry <- bloodGenePrior
  gJackie <- bloodGenePrior
  gSelma <- childFromParents(gHarry, gJackie)
  gMarge <- childFromParents(gHarry, gJackie)
  gLisa <- childFromParents(gHomer, gMarge)
  bLisa <- typeFromGene(gLisa)
  bHomer <- typeFromGene(gHomer)
  bMarge <- typeFromGene(gMarge)
  bSelma <- typeFromGene(gSelma)
  bJackie <- typeFromGene(gJackie)
  bHarry <- typeFromGene(gHarry)
} yield BloodTrial(bLisa, bHomer, bMarge, bSelma, bJackie, bHarry)
```

Output:

```
scala> bloodType.map(_.marge).hist
 A 40.40%
 B 11.19%
AB  4.25%
 O 44.16%
scala> bloodType.given(_.lisa == B).map(_.marge).hist
 A 12.65%
 B 42.98%
AB 13.32%
 O 31.05%
scala> bloodType.given(_.lisa == AB).map(_.marge).hist
 A 45.71%
 B 37.40%
AB 16.89%
```

Now let's look at Lisa and her Selma:

```
scala> bloodType.map(_.lisa).hist
 A 41.79%
```

```
B 11.24%
AB  3.94%
O 43.03%
scala> bloodType.given(_.selma == A).map(_.lisa).hist
A 52.82%
B  7.47%
AB  4.90%
O 34.81%
scala> bloodType.given(_.selma == B).map(_.lisa).hist
A 26.84%
B 27.22%
AB  9.08%
O 36.86%
```

Homer and Marge should not affect each other, unless Lisa's blood type is known:

```
scala> bloodType.map(_.homer).hist
A 40.34%
B 10.74%
AB  4.21%
O 44.71%
scala> bloodType.given(_.marge == A).map(_.homer).hist
A 40.60%
B 10.83%
AB  3.91%
O 44.66%
scala> bloodType.given(_.lisa == B).map(_.homer).hist
A 11.91%
B 42.84%
AB 13.77%
O 31.48%
scala> bloodType.given(_.lisa == B).given(_.marge == A).map(_.homer).hist
```

B 73.99%

AB 26.01%

This is Rule 3b in effect where Harry and Jackie are correlated if their grandchild's blood type is known:

```
scala> bloodType.given(_.lisa == AB).map(_.harry).hist
A 43.83%
B 23.51%
AB 10.90%
O 21.76%
scala> bloodType.given(_.lisa == AB).given(_.jackie == O).map(_.harry).hist
A 45.01%
B 37.73%
AB 17.26%
```

4.2.2 Causal Fallacies

If you observe that two events A and B are correlated, you cannot determine the direction of causality from observational data on these two events alone. Any of:

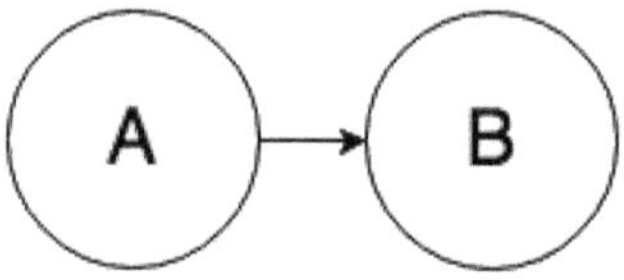

("A causes B") or

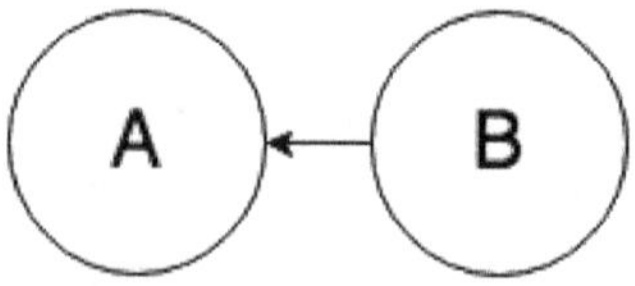

("B causes A") or

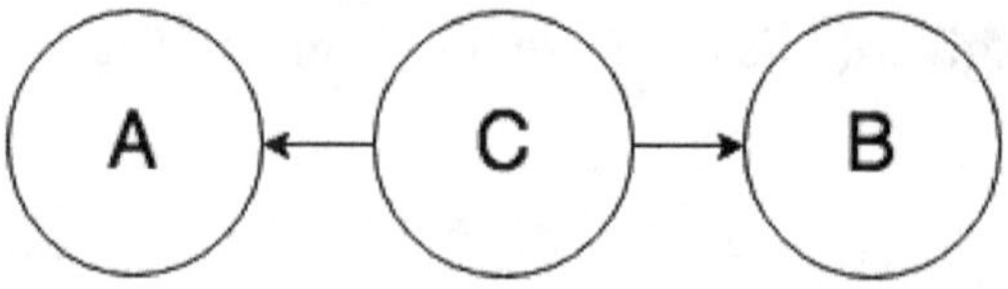

("A and B have a common cause") could explain the observed correlation. But there's also this possibility:

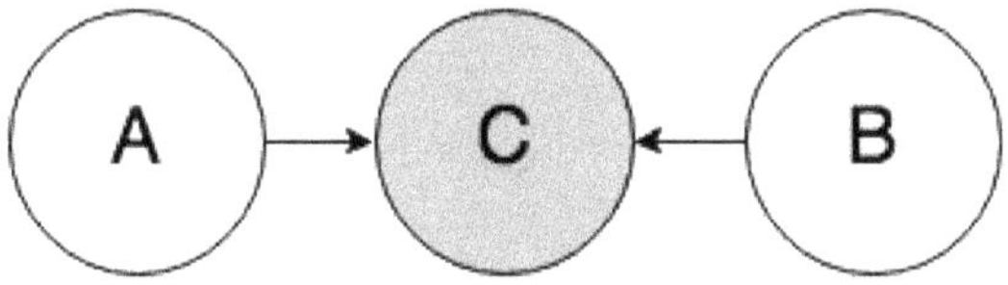

where C is known. This is just a biased sample—you might conclude that academic ability interferes with athletic ability after observing that they are inversely correlated, until you realize you only surveyed college students, and that academic and athletic scholarships are quite common. But it's neat that graphical models unify these causal fallacies.

To go further, you could come up with causal graphs that predict a correlation between A and B, but where the causal link between A and B is non-trivial. For example, the graph below allows A and B to be correlated, but neither directly causes the other, they don't have a common cause, and although there is a biased sample, it appears to only directly affect B.

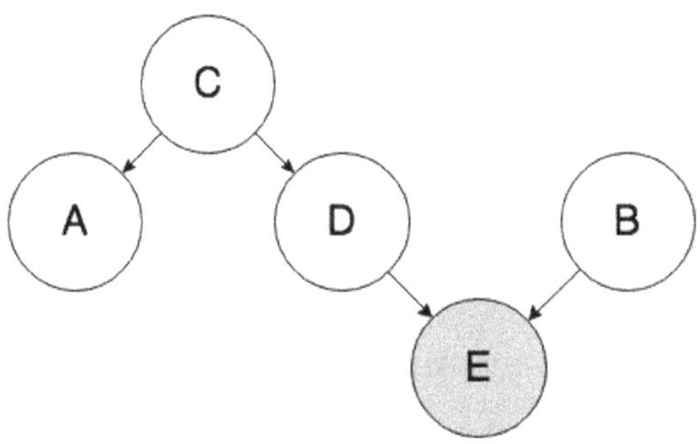

Fig: correlated graph

Determining causality

It is observed that when some events and their frequencies are there, then finding which of possible graphs could be correctly drawn. Well, the great thing about Bayesian networks is that they *make testable predictions*. In particular, for a given graph, if the independence relations that we now know how to read off it do not bear themselves out empirically, we can eliminate that graph as a possibility. We can also use common sense to rule out graphs that make unphysical predictions, for example, the sidewalk being wet causes it to rain, and effects preceding their causes in general.

To take an example, the graph

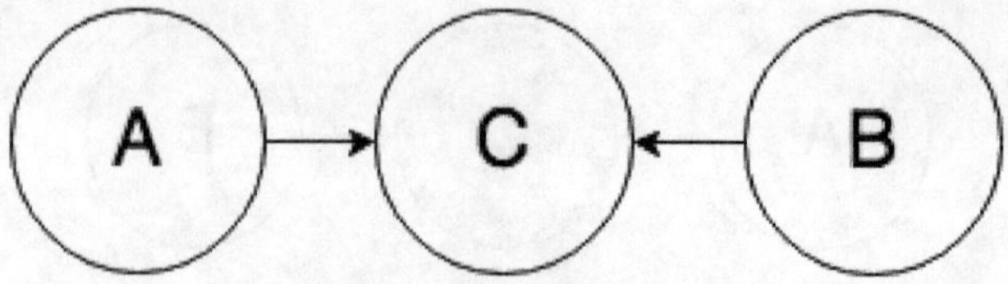

Fig Graph

predicts that A and B are independent, unless C is known.

If we observe that, say, P(A=true|B=true)>P(A=true), then we can rule out that graph as a possible model.

Usually we can use observations like this to narrow down the set of possible graphs. With only 2 events to observe, there's no way to distinguish A→B and A←B just from the data.

With 3 events that are all dependent, you can't distinguish between $A \to B \to C$A→B→C and $A \leftarrow B \leftarrow C$A←B←C and $A \leftarrow B \to C$A←B→C. However, you can distinguish $A \to B \to C$A→B→C from $B \to A \to C$B→A→C, since in the first case, AA and CC are independent when you control for BB.

By converging the set of possible graphs enough to be able to infer what arrows there are and what direction they point in, there you will know, from where you've inferred causality from mere correlation.

In practice, though, this rarely happens, especially if you have more than like 5 nodes in your graph. There are simply too many possible graphs to consider, and the very connected ones don't make any predictions at all that might help us falsify them. But if you can step in and control things a bit, you can simplify the interactions and make the problem tractable again.

Controlled Experiments

Suppose you're trying to decide whether playing a musical instrument results in higher SAT scores. In your empirical observations you're careful to identify socio-economic status as a possible confounding factor. Consider with 2 possible graphs:

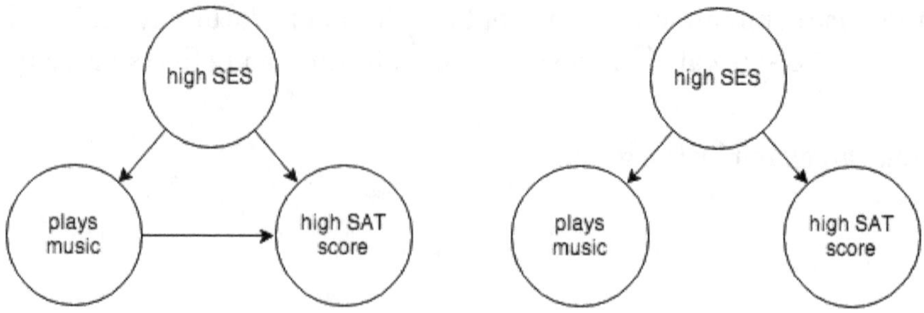

You want to know whether the arrow from "plays music" to "high SAT score" exists or not. One thing you can try is to control for socio-economic status:

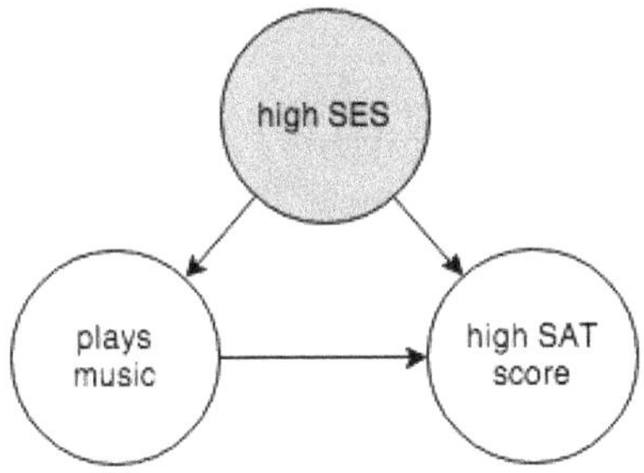

This prevents belief from propagating through the "high SES" node. If "plays music" and "high SAT score" are still correlated after controlling for socio-economic status, then you can eliminate the graph on the right and conclude that there is a causal link between the two events.

(Technically we don't know which way the arrow should point, but that's where common sense steps in.) If "plays music" and "high SAT score" are independent when controlling for socio economic status, then you have to reject the graph on the left and accept that there is no direct causal link between the events.

Socio-economic status might not be the only confounding factor, though. There are a whole host of possible confounding factors, and we can't rule out the possibility that we missed one. So what we really have is this:

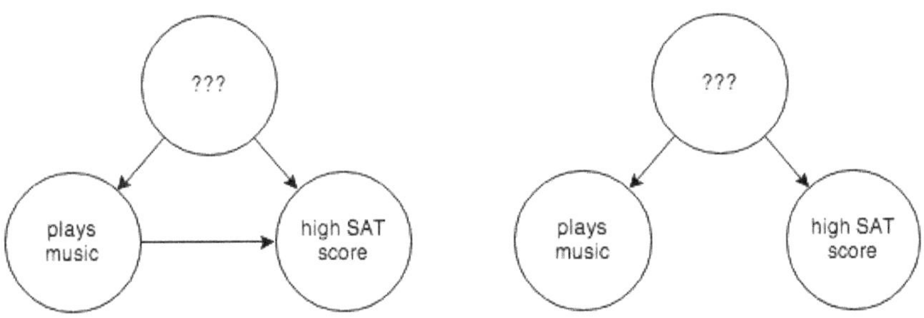

You can't control for things you can't observe. So in this case you have to step in and rewire things a bit:

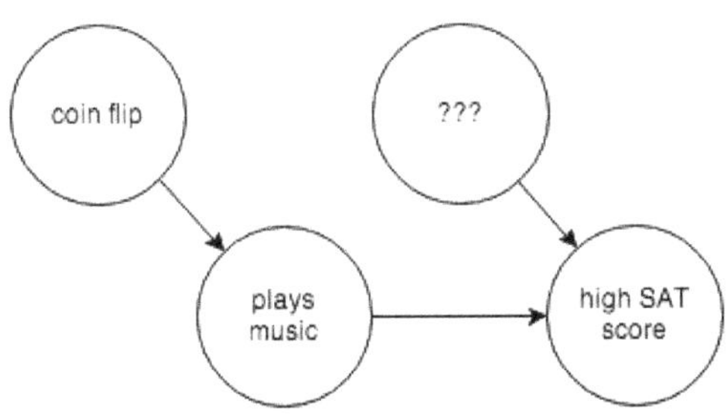

By forcing "plays music" to be determined randomly and independent of anything else, you break the causal link between it and any other confounding factors. Then it's easy to determine whether the arrow between "plays music" and "high SAT score" really exists.

But often this is not practical. Further, it is required to determine whether smoking causes lung cancer directly or if instead there are some environmental factors that happen to cause both. For this, consider following possible graphs:

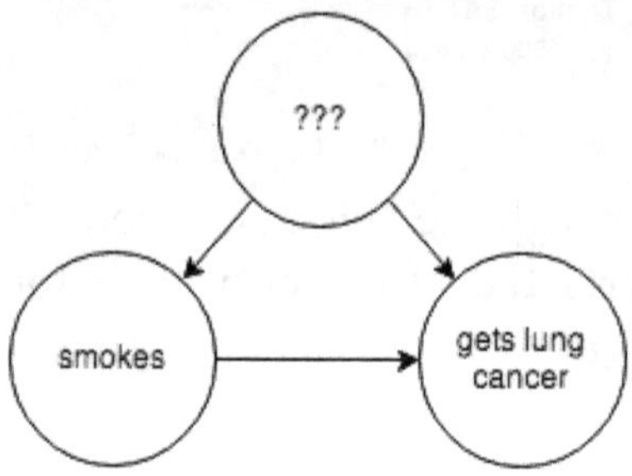

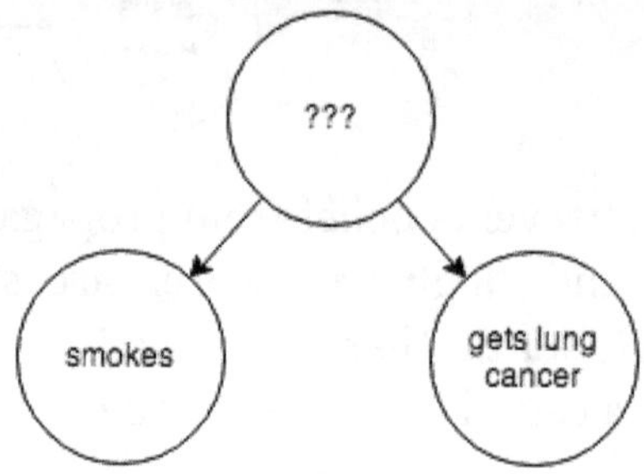

You can't step in and force some people to smoke or not smoke. In this example, if you are able to hypothesize some observable intermediate cause, such as the presence of tar in someone's lungs:

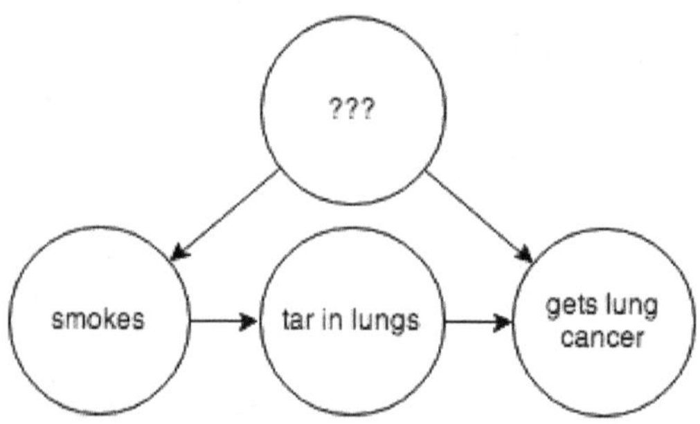

then through a series of formal manipulations, you can arrive at a graph that, weirdly enough, looks like this:

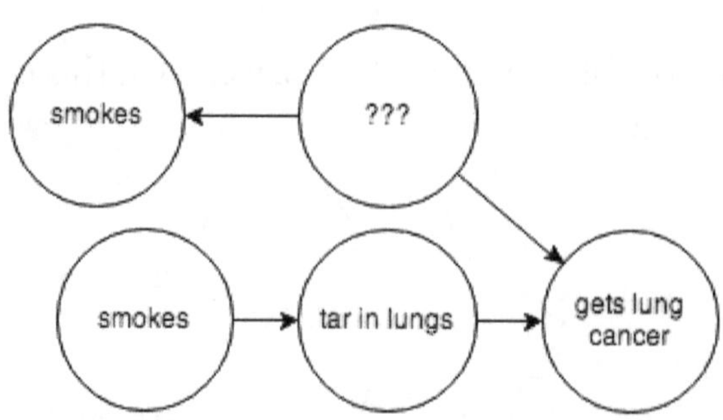

The two "smokes" nodes have the same probability distribution but are independent from one another. Using the "smokes" node on the bottom, we can now ask this graph about the probability of someone getting cancer, as if their decision to smoke was independent of any other factors. In other words, we can now determine *what would have happened* if we had been able to force our subjects to smoke or not smoke in a controlled experiment.

Since this node represents unknown causes in our model, we're not going to be able to observe it or its effects on other nodes. Fortunately, due to the magic of the Bayes-Ball rules, we can replace it with an arrow that goes directly from "smokes" to "cancer", without changing the meaning of the graph. So our two graphs become:

Now all of our nodes and arrows are observable, and we can go ahead and code this up.

Suppose we observe that 50% of the population smokes. We'll have:

```
def smokes: Distribution[Boolean] = tf(0.5)
```

We can also encode observations of the frequencies at which smokers and non-smokers have tar in their lungs:

```
def tar(smokes: Boolean): Distribution[Boolean] = {
  smokes match {
    case true => tf(0.95)
    case false => tf(0.05)
  }
}
```

And the last one, observed frequencies of cancer, broken out by whether someone smokes or has tar in their lungs:

```
def cancer(smokes: Boolean, tar: Boolean): Distribution[Boolean] = {
  (smokes, tar) match {
    case (false, false) => tf(0.1)
    case (true, false) => tf(0.9)
    case (false, true) => tf(0.05)
    case (true, true) => tf(0.85)
  }
}
```

Again, these numbers represent simple observed frequencies. We could actually do this in practice if we had experimental data.

Attempting to do in two ways: the first way encoding the original graph, and the second way encoding the manipulated graph that separates "smokes" from external influences.

```
case class SmokingTrial(smokes: Boolean, tar: Boolean, cancer: Boolean)
def smoking1: Distribution[SmokingTrial] = {
 for {
  s <- smokes
  t <- tar(s)
  c <- cancer(s, t)
 } yield SmokingTrial(s, t, c)
}
def smoking2: Distribution[SmokingTrial] = {
 for {
  s1 <- smokes
  s2 <- smokes
  t <- tar(s1)
  c <- cancer(s2, t)
 } yield SmokingTrial(s1, t, c)
}
```

Output:

```
scala> smoking1.pr(_.cancer)
res0: Double = 0.4723
scala> smoking1.given(_.smokes).pr(_.cancer)
res1: Double = 0.8576
scala> smoking2.pr(_.cancer)
res2: Double = 0.4759
scala> smoking2.given(_.smokes).pr(_.cancer)
res3: Double = 0.4577
```

As per such numbers, smoking actually prevents cancer, even though empirically, smokers have a higher incidence of cancer as compared with population.

4.3 STATISTICAL DEPENDENCE

As observed, correlation does not imply causation as it is different kind of dependence among events or functions that are statistical dependence. If A and B are statistically dependent, then learning information about A tells us something about B and vice versa. Now using the condition to make assumption about A changes the value as expected for B. Statistical dependence is a symmetric relation between events referring to how information flows between them when we observe or reason about them. The fact that we need to be warned against confusing statistical and causal dependence suggests they are related, and indeed, they are. In general, if A causes B, then A and B will be statistically dependent.

Diagnosing statistical dependence using condition is similar to diagnosing causal dependence through intervention. We condition on various values of the possible statistical dependent, here A, and see whether it changes the distribution on the target, here B:

```
var BcondA = function(Aval) {
 return Infer({method: 'enumerate'}, function() {
  var C = flip()
  var A = flip()
  var B = A ? flip(.1) : flip(.4)
  condition(A == Aval) //condition on new information about A
  return {B: B}
 })
}
viz(BcondA(true))
viz(BcondA(false))
```

Because the two distributions on B (when we have different information about A) are different, we can conclude that B statistically depends on A. Do the same procedure for testing if A statistically depends on B. How is this similar (and different) from the causal dependence between these two? As an exercise, make a version of the above medical example to test the statistical dependence between cough and cold. Verify that statistical dependence holds symmetrically for events that are connected by an indirect causal chain, such as smokes and coughs.

Correlation is not just a symmetrized version of causality. Two events may be statistically dependent even if there is no causal chain running between them, as long as they have a common cause (direct or indirect). That is, two expressions in a Web PPL program can be statistically dependent if one calls the other, directly or indirectly, or if they both at some point in their evaluation histories refer to some other expression. Here is an example of statistical dependence generated by a common cause:

```
var BcondA = function(Aval) {
  return Infer({method: 'enumerate'}, function() {
    var C = flip();
    var A = C ? flip(.5) : flip(.9);
    var B = C ? flip(.1) : flip(.4);
    condition(A == Aval);
    return {B: B};
  })
}
viz(BcondA(true))
viz(BcondA(false))
```

Situations like this are extremely common. In the medical example above, cough and fever are not causally dependent but they are statistically dependent, because they both depend on cold; likewise for chestPain and shortnessOfBreath which both depend on lungDisease. Here we can read off these facts from the program definitions, but more generally all of these relations can be diagnosed by reasoning using Infer.

Successful learning and reasoning with causal models typically depends on exploiting the close coupling between causation and correlation. Causal relations are typically unobservable, while correlations are observable from data. Noticing patterns of correlation is thus often the beginning of causal learning, or discovering what causes what. On the other hand, with a causal model already in place, reasoning about the statistical dependencies implied by the model allows us to predict many aspects of the world not directly observed from those aspects we do observe.

4.4 CONDITIONAL DEPENDENCE

In probability theory, conditional dependence is a relationship between two or more events that are dependent when a third event occurs. For example, if A and B are two events that individually affect the happening of a third event C, and do not directly affect each other, then initially (when the event C has not occurred)

$P(A|B) = P(A)$ or $P(B|A) = P(B)$

where A and B are independent

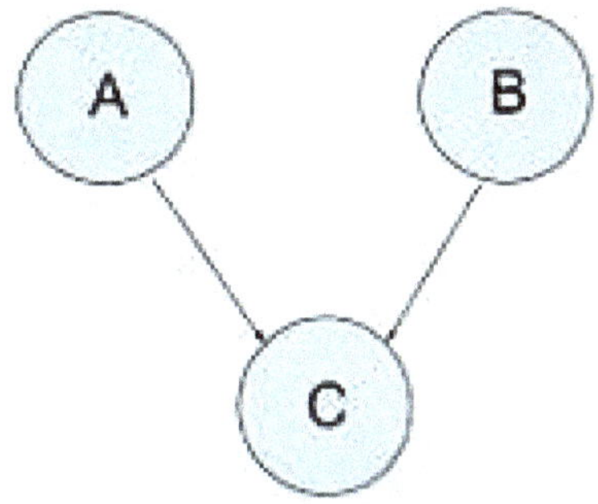

Fig: Bayesian Network

Eventually the event C occurs and when event A occurs, probability of occurrence of event B decreases (event B occur first will decrease the probability of occurrence of A). Hence, now the two events A and B become conditionally dependent because their probability of occurrence is dependent on either event's occurrence.

Further, we can say that as A and B both were probable causes of C, given C has occurred, occurrence of either of A or B alone could explain away the happening of C.

$P(B|C) > P(B|C,A)$

In essence probability comes from a person's information content about occurrence of an event. For example, if event A will be 'I have a new car' and event B is 'I have a new watch' and event C be 'I am happy', then on assuming that event C takes place which shows 'I am happy', then when a third person sees the new watch, he/she will attribute this reason to happiness. Hence, as per the view, probability of event A ('I have a new car') to have been the cause of event C ('I am happy') will decrease as event C has been explained away by the event B.

Conditional dependence is different from conditional independence. In conditional independence two events (which may be dependent or not) become independent given the occurrence of a third event.

Consider an opposite situations of two dependent nodes becoming independent, by taking large network:

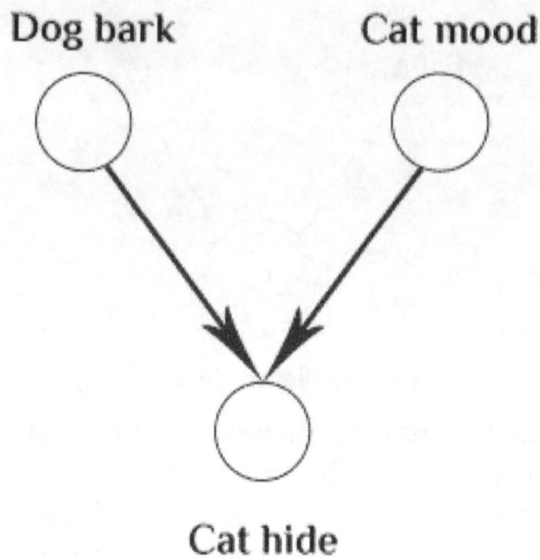

In this, assume the mood the cat's as independent of dog's decision to start barking. In such case, the cat's decision to hide is dependent on dog's behavior and current mood. Now building the joint sample space of the network by showing Dog bark and Cat mood nodes as:

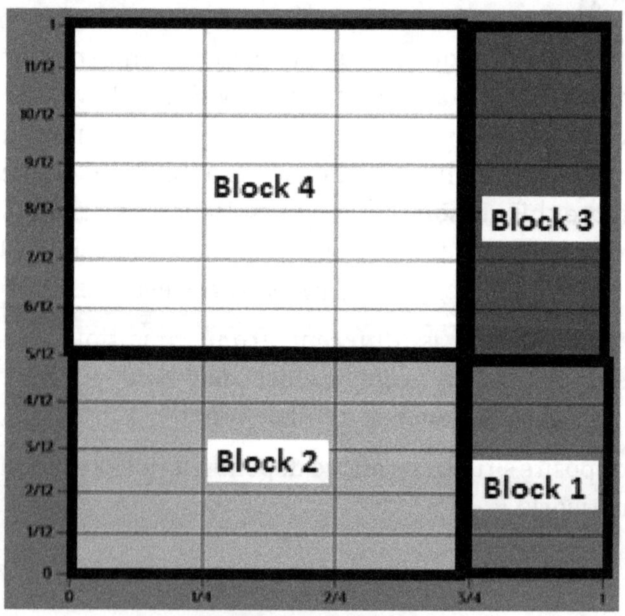

Fig:Sample Space

In this, the Block 2 rectangles shows that the Dog barks event while Block 3 rectangles shows the Cat stressed event. On considering the pattern of independence, distribute the Cat hides event over the current sample space in a relatively sensible way:

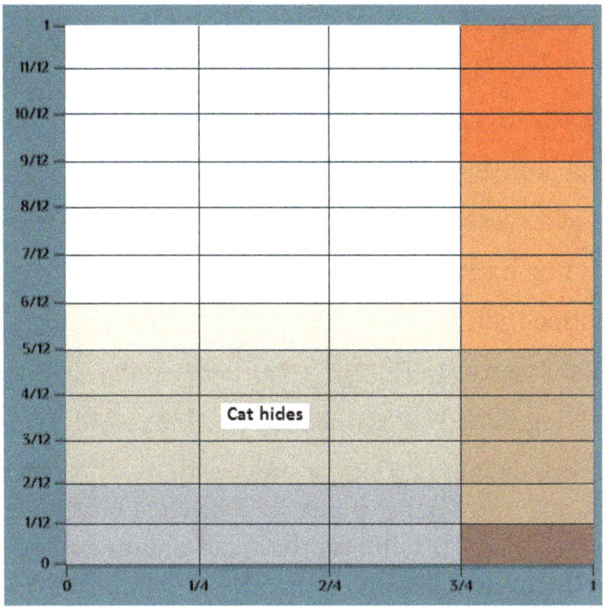

Here, the rectangles shows Cat hides that are disproportionately spread over Dog barks and Cat stressed rectangles. It's precisely this dis-proportionality that will make the parent nodes conditionally dependent, given their child.

On observing the Cat hide node, it is observed that cat's currently under the couch which shows posterior sample space having 20 Cat hides rectangles as:

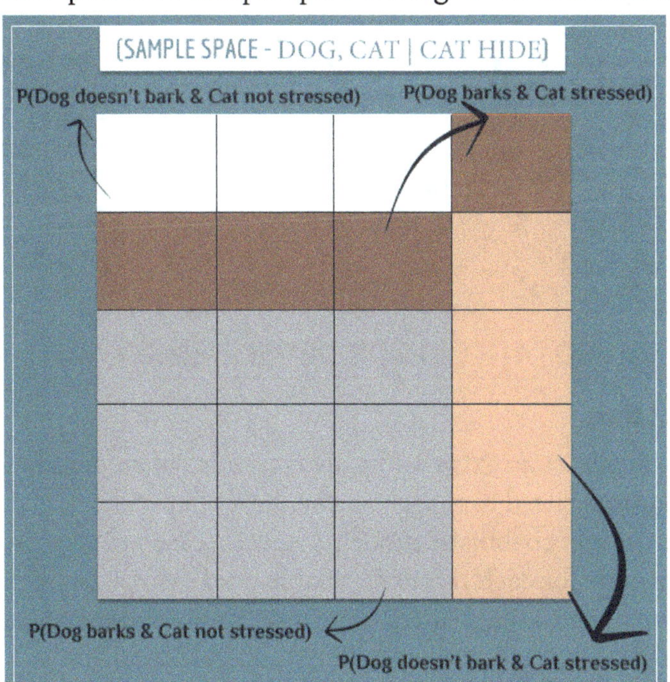

Now considering posterior probabilities of two main events:

P(Dog barks) = 13/20

P(Cat stressed) = 8/20 = 2/5

Conditional probabilities:

P(Dog barks | Cat stressed) = 4/8 = 1/2

P(Cat stressed | Dog barks) = 4/13

Specifically, notice that:

P(Dog barks | Cat stressed) ≠ P(Dog barks)

P(Cat stressed | Dog barks) ≠ P(Cat stressed)

It shows that the events are no longer independent. The idea behind this is that both parent nodes are potential explanations of the child node, so there's some competition between them. It's limited because one event's occurrence doesn't exclude the other. It simply makes it less likely.

For example, P(Dog barks | Cat stressed) = 1/2, which is less than P(Dog barks) = 13/20.

Such phenomenon shows explaining away as normally more likely one explanation becomes less likely the other explanations will be and vice versa. By the way, most frequently used notation for conditional dependence is very similar to notation for conditional independence:

(CONDITIONAL DEPENDENCE)

Dog bark $\not\perp\!\!\!\perp$ Cat mood | Cat hide

4.5 GRAPHICAL NOTATIONS FOR DEPENDENCE

4.5.1 Introduction

Graphical models are an extremely important idea in modern machine learning: a graphical diagram is used to represent the direct dependence structure between random choices in a probabilistic model. A special case are Bayesian networks, in which there is a node for each random variable (and expression in our terms) and a link between two nodes if there is a direct conditional dependence between them (a direct causal dependence in our terms). The sets of nodes and links define a directed acyclic graph (hence the term graphical model), a data structure over which many efficient algorithms can be defined. Each node has a conditional probability table

(CPT), which represents the conditional probability distribution of that node, given its parents. The joint probability distribution over random variables is given by the product of the conditional distributions for each variable in the graph.

The figure below defines a Bayesian network for the medical diagnosis example. The graph contains a node for each random variable assignment (define statement) in our church program, with links to that node from each variable that appears in the assignment expression. There is a CPT for each node, with a column for each value of the random variable, and a row for each combination of values for its parents.

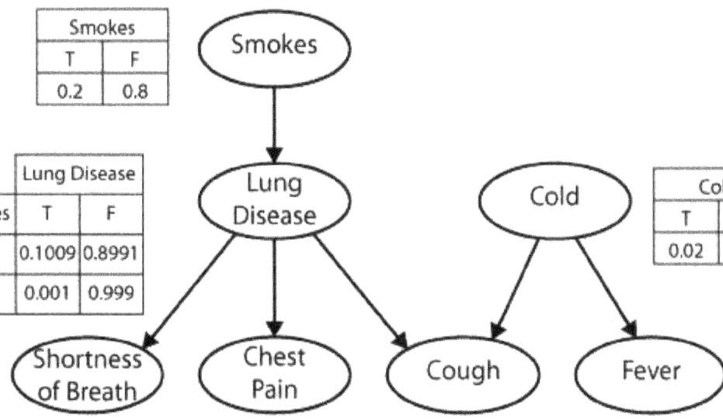

Smokes	
T	F
0.2	0.8

	Lung Disease	
Smokes	T	F
T	0.1009	0.8991
F	0.001	0.999

Cold	
T	F
0.02	0.98

	Shortness of Breath	
Lung Disease	T	F
T	0.208	0.792
F	0.01	0.99

	Chest Pain	
Lung Disease	T	F
T	0.208	0.792
F	0.01	0.99

		Cough	
Lung Disease	Cold	T	F
T	T	0.7525	0.2475
T	F	0.505	0.495
F	T	0.505	0.495
F	F	0.01	0.99

	Fever	
Cold	T	F
T	0.307	0.693
F	0.01	0.99

Simple generative models will have a corresponding graphical model that captures all of the dependencies (and independencies) of the model, without capturing the precise form of these functions. For example, while the graphical model shown above faithfully represents the probability distribution encoded by the church program, it captures the noisy-OR form of the causal dependencies only implicitly. As a result, the CPTs provide a less compact representation of the conditional probabilities than the church model. For instance, the CPT for cough specifies 4 parameters - one for each pair of values of lung-disease and cold.

In contrast, the define statement for cold in church specifies only 3 parameters: the base rate of cough, and the strength with which lung-disease and cold cause cough. This difference becomes more pronounced for noisy-OR relations with many causes - the size of the CPT for a node will be exponential in the number of parents, while the number of terms in the noisy-OR expression in church for that node will be linear in the number of causal dependencies. As we will see, this has important implications for the ability to learn the values of the parameters from data.

More complicated generative models, which can be expressed as probabilistic programs, often don't have such a graphical model.

4.5.2 From Priori Dependence to Conditional Dependence

The relationships between causal structure and correlation structure, or statistical dependence, become particularly interesting and subtle when we look at the effects of further observations or assumptions. Events that are statistically dependent a priori (sometimes called marginally dependent) may become independent when we condition on some other observation; this is often called screening off, or sometimes context-specific independence. Also, events that are statistically independent a priori (marginally independent) may become dependent when we condition on other observations; this is known as explaining away. The dynamics of screening off and explaining away are extremely important for understanding patterns of inference - reasoning and learning - in probabilistic models.

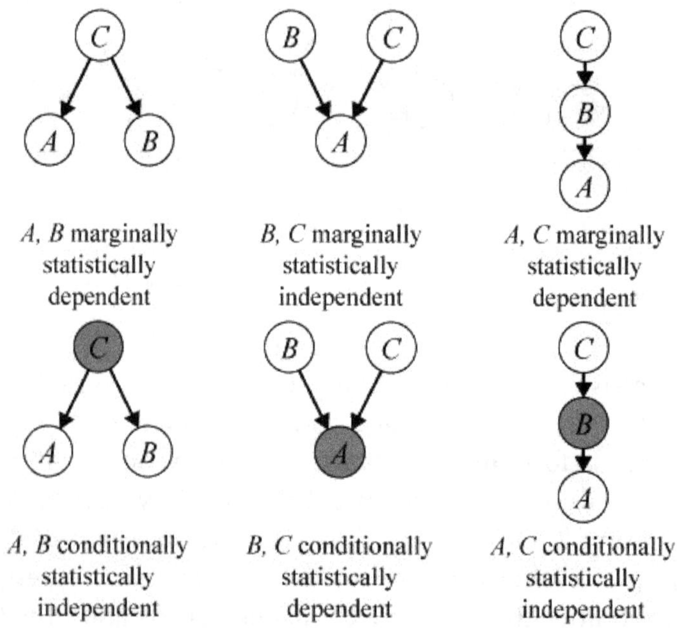

Screening off

Screening off are patterns of statistical inference that is quite common in both scientific and intuitive reasoning. If the statistical dependence between two events A and B is only indirect, mediated strictly by one or more other events C, then conditioning on (observing) C should render A and B statistically independent. This can occur if A and B are connected by one or more causal chains, and all such chains run through the set of events C, or if C comprises one or more common causes of A and B. As an example in our simple medical scenario, smokes is correlated with (statistically dependent on) several symptoms, cough, chest-pain, and shortness-of-breath, due to the causal chain between them mediated by lung-disease. We can see this easily by conditioning on these symptoms and querying smokes:

```
(define samples
 (mh-query 200 100
  (define smokes (flip 0.2))
  (define lung-disease (or (flip 0.001) (and smokes (flip 0.1))))
  (define cold (flip 0.02))
  (define cough (or (and cold (flip 0.5)) (and lung-disease (flip 0.5)) (flip 0.001)))
  (define fever (or (and cold (flip 0.3)) (flip 0.01)))
  (define chest-pain (or (and lung-disease (flip 0.2)) (flip 0.01)))
  (define shortness-of-breath (or (and lung-disease (flip 0.2)) (flip 0.01)))
   smokes
   (and cough chest-pain shortness-of-breath)
 )
)
(hist samples "smokes")
```

The conditional probability of smokes is much higher than the base rate, 0.2, because observing all these symptoms gives strong evidence for smoking. See how much evidence the different symptoms contribute by dropping them out of the conditioning set. For instance, condition the above query on or just cough; you should observe the probability of smokes decrease as fewer symptoms are observed.

Now, suppose we condition also on knowledge about the function that mediates these causal links: lung-disease. Is there still an informational dependence between these various symptoms and smokes, conditioned on knowing that lung-disease is true or false? In the query below, try adding and removing various symptoms but maintaining the observation lung-disease:

```
(define samples
 (mh-query 500 100
  (define smokes (flip 0.2))
  (define lung-disease (or (flip 0.001) (and smokes (flip 0.1))))
  (define cold (flip 0.02))
  (define cough (or (and cold (flip 0.5)) (and lung-disease (flip 0.5)) (flip 0.001)))
```

```
   (define fever (or (and cold (flip 0.3)) (flip 0.01)))
   (define chest-pain (or (and lung-disease (flip 0.2)) (flip 0.01)))
   (define shortness-of-breath (or (and lung-disease (flip 0.2)) (flip 0.01)))
   smokes
   (and lung-disease
      (and cough chest-pain shortness-of-breath)
   )
  )
)
(hist samples "smokes")
```

Try the same experiment of varying the symptom patterns for cough, chest-pain, shortness-of-breath while maintaining the observation:

```
(define samples
  (mh-query 500 100
   (define smokes (flip 0.2))
   (define lung-disease (or (flip 0.001) (and smokes (flip 0.1))))
   (define cold (flip 0.02))
   (define cough (or (and cold (flip 0.5)) (and lung-disease (flip 0.5)) (flip 0.001)))
   (define fever (or (and cold (flip 0.3)) (flip 0.01)))
   (define chest-pain (or (and lung-disease (flip 0.2)) (flip 0.01)))
   (define shortness-of-breath (or (and lung-disease (flip 0.2)) (flip 0.01)))
   smokes
   (and (not lung-disease)
      (and cough chest-pain shortness-of-breath)
   )
  )
)
(hist samples "smokes")
```

You should see an effect of whether or not the patient has lung disease on conditional inferences about smoking -- a person is judged to be substantially more likely to be a smoker if they have lung disease than otherwise -- but there is no separate effects of chest pain, shortness of breath or cough, over and above the evidence provided by knowing whether the patient has lung-disease. We say that the intermediate variable lung disease screens off the root cause from the more distant effects.

Screening off is a purely statistical phenomenon. For example, consider the the causal chain model, where A directly causes C, which in turn directly causes B. Here, when we observe C – the event that mediates an *indirect*causal relation between A and B – A and B are still causally dependent in our model of the world: it is just our beliefs about the states of A and B that become uncorrelated. There is also an analogous causal phenomenon. If we can actually manipulate or *intervene* on the causal system, and set the value of C to some known value, then A and B become both statistically and causally independent (by intervening on C, we break the causal link between A and C).

Explaining away

Explaining away are complementary pattern of statistical inference which is somewhat more subtle than screening off. If two events A and B are statistically independent, but they are both causes of one or more other events C, then conditioning on C can render A and B statistically dependent. As with screening off, we are only talking about inducing statistical dependence here, not causal dependence: when we observe C, A and B remain causally independent in our model of the world; it is just our states of knowledge about A and B that become correlated.

Here is a concrete example in our medical scenario. Having a cold and having lung disease are a priori independent both causally and statistically. But because they are both causes of coughing if we observe cough then cold and lung-disease become statistically dependent. That is, learning something about whether a patient has cold or lung-disease will, in the presence of their common effect cough, convey information about the other condition. We say that cold and lung-cancer are marginally (or a priori) independent, but conditionally dependent given cough. To show, observe how the probabilities of cold and lung-disease change when we observe cough is true:

```
(define samples
 (mh-query 500 100
  (define smokes (flip 0.2))
  (define lung-disease (or (flip 0.001) (and smokes (flip 0.1))))
  (define cold (flip 0.02))
  (define cough (or (and cold (flip 0.5)) (and lung-disease (flip 0.5)) (flip 0.001)))
  (define fever (or (and cold (flip 0.3)) (flip 0.01)))
```

```
    (define chest-pain (or (and lung-disease (flip 0.2)) (flip 0.01)))
    (define shortness-of-breath (or (and lung-disease (flip 0.2)) (flip 0.01)))
   (list cold lung-disease)
   cough
  )
 )
 (hist (map first samples) "cold")
 (hist (map second samples) "lung-disease")
 (hist samples "cold, lung-disease")
```

Both cold and lung disease are now far more likely that their baseline probability: the probability of having a cold increases from 2% to around 40%; the probability of having lung disease increases from 1 in a 1000 to a few percent. Given a cough, cold is the much more likely explanation simply because it was much more probable a priori.

Now suppose we learn that the patient does not have a cold.

```
(define samples
  (mh-query 500 100
    (define smokes (flip 0.2))
    (define lung-disease (or (flip 0.001) (and smokes (flip 0.1))))
    (define cold (flip 0.02))
    (define cough (or (and cold (flip 0.5)) (and lung-disease (flip 0.5)) (flip 0.001)))
    (define fever (or (and cold (flip 0.3)) (flip 0.01)))
    (define chest-pain (or (and lung-disease (flip 0.2)) (flip 0.01)))
    (define shortness-of-breath (or (and lung-disease (flip 0.2)) (flip 0.01)))
   (list cold lung-disease)
   (and cough (not cold))
  )
)
(hist (map first samples) "cold")
(hist (map second samples) "lung-disease")
(hist samples "cold, lung-disease")
```

The probability of having lung disease increases dramatically. If instead we had observed that the patient does have a cold, the probability of lung cancer returns to its very low base rate of 1 in a 1000.

```
(define samples
 (mh-query 500 100
  (define smokes (flip 0.2))
  (define lung-disease (or (flip 0.001) (and smokes (flip 0.1))))
  (define cold (flip 0.02))
  (define cough (or (and cold (flip 0.5)) (and lung-disease (flip 0.5)) (flip 0.001)))
  (define fever (or (and cold (flip 0.3)) (flip 0.01)))
  (define chest-pain (or (and lung-disease (flip 0.2)) (flip 0.01)))
  (define shortness-of-breath (or (and lung-disease (flip 0.2)) (flip 0.01)))
  (list cold lung-disease)
  (and cough cold)
 )
)
(hist (map first samples) "cold")
(hist (map second samples) "lung-disease")
(hist samples "cold, lung-disease")
```

This is the conditional statistical dependence between lung disease and cold, given cough: Learning that the patient does in fact have a cold "explains away" the observed cough, so the alternative of lung disease decreases to a much lower value - roughly back to its 1 in a 1000 in the general population. If on the other hand, we had learned that the patient does not have a cold, so the most likely alternative to lung disease is not in fact available to "explain away" the observed cough, that raises the conditional probability of lung disease dramatically. As an exercise, check that if we remove the observation of coughing, the observation of having a cold or not having a hold has no influence on our belief about lung disease; this effect is purely conditional on the observation of a common effect of these two causes.

Consider (in the above example) a patient with a cough who also smokes, you will find that cold and lung disease are roughly equally likely explanations. Or add the observation that the patient has chest pain, so lung disease becomes an even more probable condition than having a cold. These are the settings where explaining away effects will be strongest. Modify the above program to observe that the patient either has a cold or does not have a cold, in addition to having a cough, smoking, and perhaps having chest-pain. It is observed that how far up or down knowledge about whether the patient has a cold can push the conditional belief in having lung disease.

Explaining away effects can be more indirect. Instead of observing the truth value of cold, a direct alternative cause of cough, we might simply observe another symptom that provides evidence for cold, such as fever. Compare these conditioners with the above church program to see an "explaining away" conditional dependence in belief between fever and lung-disease.

(and smokes chest-pain cough) with (and smokes chest-pain cough fever) or

(and smokes chest-pain cough (not fever))

In this case, finding out that the patient either does or does not have a fever makes a crucial difference in whether we think that the patient has lung disease even though fever itself is not at all diagnostic of lung disease, and there is no causal connection between them. We can express the general phenomenon of explaining away with the following schematic Church query:

```
(query
 (define a ...)
 (define b ...)
 ...
 (define data (... a... b...))
 b
 (and (equal? data some-value) (equal? a some-other-value)))
```

We have defined two independent variables a and b both of which are used to define the value of our data. If we condition on the data and a the posterior distribution on b will now be dependent on a: observing additional information about a changes our conclusions about b.

The most typical pattern of explaining away we see in causal reasoning is a kind of anti-correlation: the probabilities of two possible causes for the same effect increase when the effect is observed, but they are conditionally anti-correlated, so that observing additional evidence in favor of one cause should lower our degree of belief in the other cause. However, the coupling in belief states induced by conditioning on common effects is not always an anti-correlation. That depends on the nature of the interaction between the causes.

4.6 NON-MONOTONIC REASONING

One reason explaining away is an important phenomenon in probabilistic inference is that it is an example of non-monotonic reasoning. In formal logic, a theory is said to be monotonic if adding an assumption (or formula) to the theory never reduces the set of consequences of the previous assumptions. Most traditional logics (e.g. First Order) are monotonic, but human reasoning does not seem to be. For instance, if tweety is a bird, then he can fly while if tweety is an ostrich, then the conclusion is that he will fly. Over the years many non-monotonic logics have been introduced to model aspects of human reasoning. One of the first ways in which probabilistic reasoning with Bayesian networks was recognized as important for AI was that it could perspicuously capture these patterns of reasoning.

Another way to think about monotonicity is by considering the trajectory of our belief in a specific proposition, as we gain additional relevant information. In traditional logic, there are only three states of belief: true, false, and unknown (when neither a proposition nor its negation can be proven). As we learn more about the world, maintaining logical consistency requires that our belief in any proposition only move from unknown to true or false. That is our "confidence" in any conclusion only increases (and only does so in one giant leap from unknown to true or false).

In a probabilistic approach, by contrast, there is a spectrum of degrees of belief. We can think of confidence as a measure of how far our beliefs are from a uniform distribution, or how close to the extremes of 0 or 1. In probabilistic inference, unlike in traditional logic, our confidence in a proposition can both increase and decrease. As we will see in the next example, even fairly simple probabilistic models can induce complex explaining-away dynamics that lead our degree of belief in a proposition to reverse directions multiple times as the conditioning set expands.

Example: Trait Attribution

Often we have to make inferences about different types of entities and their interactions, and a highly interactive set of relations between the entities leads to very challenging explaining away problems. Inference is computationally difficult in these situations but the inferences come very naturally to people, suggesting these are important problems that our brains have specialized somewhat to.

A familiar example comes from reasoning about the causes of students' patterns of success and failure in the classroom. Imagine yourself in the position of an interested outside observer -- a parent, another teacher, a guidance counselor or college admissions officer in thinking about these conditional inferences.

```
(define samples
 (mh-query 1000 10
```

```
(define exam-fair (flip .8))
(define does-homework (flip .8))
(define pass? (flip (if exam-fair
                    (if does-homework 0.9 0.6)
                    (if does-homework 0.4 0.2))))
(list does-homework exam-fair)
(not pass?)))
(hist samples "Joint: Student Does Homework?, Exam Fair?")
(hist (map first samples) "Student Does Homework")
(hist (map second samples) "Exam Fair")
```

Now what if you have evidence from several students and several exams? We first re-write the above model to allow many students and exams:

```
(define samples
 (mh-query 1000 10
  (define exam-fair-prior .8)
  (define does-homework-prior .8)
  (define exam-fair? (mem (lambda (exam) (flip exam-fair-prior))))
   (define does-homework? (mem (lambda (student) (flip does-homework-
prior))))
  (define (pass? student exam) (flip (if (exam-fair? exam)
                          (if (does-homework? student) 0.9 0.6)
                          (if (does-homework? student) 0.4 0.2))))
  (list (does-homework? 'bill) (exam-fair? 'exam1))
(not (pass? 'bill 'exam1))))
hist samples "Joint: Bill Does His Homework?, Exam 1 Fair?")
(hist (map first samples) "Bill Does His Homework?")
(hist (map second samples) "Exam 1 Fair?")
```

Initially we observe that Bill failed exam 1. A priori, we assume that most students do their homework and most exams are fair, but given this one observation it becomes somewhat likely that either the student didn't study or the exam was unfair.

Observed that how conditional inferences about Bill and exam 1 change as you add in more data about this student or this exam, or additional students and exams. Paste each of the data sets below into the above Church box, as a substitute for the current conditioner (not (pass 'bill 'exam1)).

Considering the dynamics of inference result at each stage, it is seen that what does each new piece of large data set contributes to intuition about Bill and exam 1.

```
(and (not (pass? 'bill 'exam1)) (not (pass? 'bill 'exam2)))

(and (not (pass? 'bill 'exam1))
  (not (pass? 'mary 'exam1))
  (not (pass? 'tim 'exam1)))

(and (not (pass? 'bill 'exam1)) (not (pass? 'bill 'exam2))
  (not (pass? 'mary 'exam1))
  (not (pass? 'tim 'exam1)))

(and (not (pass? 'bill 'exam1))
  (not (pass? 'mary 'exam1)) (pass? 'mary 'exam2) (pass? 'mary 'exam3) (pass? 'mary 'exam4) (pass? 'mary 'exam5)
  (not (pass? 'tim 'exam1)) (pass? 'tim 'exam2) (pass? 'tim 'exam3) (pass? 'tim 'exam4) (pass? 'tim 'exam5))

(and (not (pass? 'bill 'exam1))
  (pass? 'mary 'exam1)
  (pass? 'tim 'exam1))

(and (not (pass? 'bill 'exam1))
  (pass? 'mary 'exam1) (pass? 'mary 'exam2) (pass? 'mary 'exam3) (pass? 'mary 'exam4) (pass? 'mary 'exam5)
  (pass? 'tim 'exam1) (pass? 'tim 'exam2) (pass? 'tim 'exam3) (pass? 'tim 'exam4) (pass? 'tim 'exam5))

(and (not (pass? 'bill 'exam1)) (not (pass? 'bill 'exam2))
  (pass? 'mary 'exam1) (pass? 'mary 'exam2) (pass? 'mary 'exam3) (pass? 'mary 'exam4) (pass? 'mary 'exam5)
  (pass? 'tim 'exam1) (pass? 'tim 'exam2) (pass? 'tim 'exam3) (pass? 'tim 'exam4) (pass? 'tim 'exam5))

(and (not (pass? 'bill 'exam1)) (not (pass? 'bill 'exam2)) (pass? 'bill 'exam3) (pass? 'bill 'exam4) (pass? 'bill 'exam5)
```

(not (pass? 'mary 'exam1)) (not (pass? 'mary 'exam2)) (not (pass? 'mary 'exam3)) (not (pass? 'mary 'exam4)) (not (pass? 'mary 'exam5))

(not (pass? 'tim 'exam1)) (not (pass? 'tim 'exam2)) (not (pass? 'tim 'exam3)) (not (pass? 'tim 'exam4)) (not (pass? 'tim 'exam5)))

Example of Blickets and Blocking

It was noticed that children's causal learning abilities using blicket detector which is a toy box that lights up when certain blocks, blickets are put on top. Children are shown a set of evidence and then asked which blocks are blickets. When a block A makes detector go off, it is probably a blicket. Ambiguous patterns are particularly interesting. Imagine that blocks A and B are put on the detector together, making the detector go off; it is likely that A is a blicket. Now B is put on the detector alone, making the detector go off; it is now less plausible that A is a blocket. This is called backward blocking, and it is an example of explaining away.

On capturing the particular set with model in which each block has a persistent blicketness property, and the causal power of the block to make the machine go off depends on whether it is a blicket.

```
(define samples
 (mh-query 100 100
(define blicket (mem (lambda (block) (flip 0.2))))
  (define (power block) (if (blicket block) 0.9 0.05))
(define (machine blocks)
   (if (null? blocks)
     (flip 0.05)
     (or (flip (power (first blocks)))
       (machine (rest blocks)))))
(blicket 'A)
(machine (list 'A 'B))))
hist samples "Is A a blicket?")
```

Visual Perception of Surface Lightness and Color

Visual perception is full of rich conditional inference phenomena, including both screening off and explaining away. Some very impressive demonstrations have been constructed using the perception of surface structure by mid-level vision researchers. Most striking is when conditional inference appears to violate or alter the apparently modular structure of visual processing. Neuroscientists have developed an understanding of the primate visual system in which processing for different aspects of visual stimuli related to color, shape, motion, stereo that appears to be at least local in different brain regions. This view is consistent with findings by cognitive psychologists that at least in early vision, these different stimulus dimensions are not integrated but processed in a somewhat modular fashion.

Yet vision is at heart about constructing a unified and coherent percept of a three-dimensional scene from the patterns of light falling on our retinas. That is, vision is causal inference on a grand scale. Its output is a rich description of the objects, surface properties and relations in the world that are not themselves directly grasped by the brain but that are the true causes of the retinal stimulus. Solving this problem requires integration of many appearance features across an image, and this results in the potential for massive effects of explaining away and screening off.

In vision, the luminance of a surface depends on two factors, the illumination of the surface and its reflectance. The actual luminance is the product of the two factors. Thus luminance is inherently ambiguous. The visual system has to determine what proportion of the luminance is due to reflectance and what proportion is due to the illumination of the scene.

The illusion results from the fact that in the image above both the square labeled A and the square labeled B are actually the same shade of gray. This can be seen in the figure below where they are connected by solid gray bars on either side.

What is happening here is that the presence of the cylinder is providing evidence that the illumination of square B is actually less than that of square A. Thus we perceive square B as having higher reflectance since its luminance is identical to square A and we believe there is less light hitting it. The following program implements a simple version of this scenario "before" we see the shadow cast by the cylinder.

```
(define noisy=
  (lambda (target value variance)
    (= 0 (gaussian (- target value) variance))))
 (define samples
  (mh-query
   100 100
(define reflectance (gaussian 1 1))
   (define illumination (gaussian 3 0.5))
   (define luminance (* reflectance illumination))
reflectance
(noisy= 3.0 luminance 0.1)
  ))
(truehist samples 10 "Reflectance")
```

Here we have introduced a third kind of primitive random procedure, gaussian which outputs real numbers, in addition to flip (which outputs binary truth values) and beta (which outputs numbers in the interval [0,1]). gaussian implements the well-known Gaussian or normal distribution. It takes two parameters: a mean, μ, and a variance, σ^2.

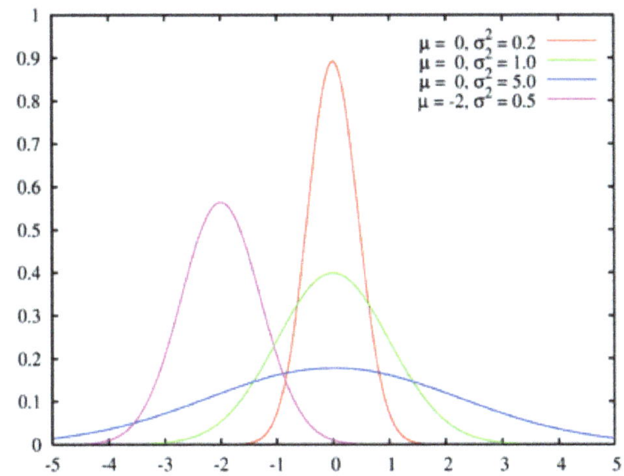

Now let's condition on the presence of the cylinder:

```
(define noisy=
  (lambda (target value variance)
   (= 0 (gaussian (- target value) variance))))
 (define samples
  (mh-query
   100 100
(define reflectance (gaussian 1 1))
   (define illumination (gaussian 3 0.5))
   (define luminance (* reflectance illumination))
reflectance
(and (noisy= 3.0 luminance 0.1) (noisy= 0.5 illumination 0.1))
  ))
 (truehist samples 10 "Reflectance")
```

Conditional inference takes into account all the different paths through the generative process that could have generated the data. Two variables on different causal paths can thus become dependent once we condition on the way the data came out. The important point is that the variables reflectance and illumination are conditionally independent in the generative model, but after we condition on luminance they become dependent: changing one of them affects the probability of the other. This phenomenon has important consequences for cognitive science modeling. Although our model of our knowledge of the world and language have a certain kind of modularity implied by conditional independence, as soon as we start using the model to do conditional inference on some data, formerly modularly isolated variables can become dependent.

4.7 MODULARITY

4.7.1 Introduction

Modularity is widely used in technological and organizational systems. Product systems are deemed modular, when decomposed in number of components which can be mixed and matched in variety of configurations. The components are able to connect, interact, or exchange resources (such as energy or data) in some way, by adhering to a standardized interface. Unlike a tightly integrated product whereby each component is designed to work specifically with other particular components in a tightly coupled system, modular products are systems of components that are loosely coupled.

Considering Language of New Media, there are five principles of new media which can be understood not as absolute laws but rather as general tendencies of culture undergoing computerization which includes:

- Numerical representation
- Modularity
- Automation
- Variability
- Transcoding

Modularity in new media shows new media as being composed of many separate self-sufficient modules which acts independently or together in synchronisation to complete the new media object. Organizational systems are said to become increasingly modular when they begin to substitute loosely coupled forms for tightly integrated, hierarchical structures. Also, when the firm utilizes contract manufacturing rather than in-house manufacturing, it is using an organizational component that is more independent than building such capabilities in-house: the firm can switch between contract manufacturers that perform different functions, and the contract manufacturer can similarly work for different firms.

As firms in a given industry begin to substitute loose coupling with organizational components that lie outside of firm boundaries for activities that were once conducted in-house, the entire production system becomes increasingly modular. The firms themselves become more specialized components. Using loosely coupled structures enables firms to achieve greater flexibility in both scope and scale. The firm can switch easily between different providers of these activities compared to building the capabilities for all activities in house, thus responding to different market needs more quickly. However, these flexibility gains come with a price. Therefore, the organization must assess the flexibility gains achievable, and any accompanying loss of performance, with each of these forms.

Modularization in firms leads to disaggregation of traditional form of hierarchical governance. The firm is decomposed in relatively small autonomous organizational units to reduce complexity. Modularization leads to structure where modules integrate strongly interdependent tasks, while interdependencies among modules are weak. In connection, dissemination of modular organizational forms has been facilitated by widespread efforts of big firms to re-engineer, refocus and restructure. These efforts usually involve a strong process-orientation: the complete service-provision process of the business is split up into partial processes, which can then be handled autonomously by cross-functional teams within organizational units (modules). The co-ordination of the modules is often carried out by using internal market mechanisms, in particular by the implementation of profit centers.

On the whole, modularization allows more flexible and quicker reaction to change general or market conditions. Building on such principles, different forms of modularization of firms are possible. However, it is crucial to note that modularization is not an independent and self-contained organizational concept, but rather consists of several basic ideas, which are integral parts of other organizational concepts. These central ideas can be found in every firm. Accordingly, it is not sensible to characterize a firm as modular or not modular, as firms are always modular to some degree

REFERENCES

Arntzenius, F., 1993. "The Classical Failure to Account for Electromagnetic Arrows of Time", in G. Massey, T. Horowitz and A. Janis (eds.), Scientific Failure, Lanham: Rowman and Littlfield, pp. 29–48.

Barker, S., 2004. "Analysing Chancy Causation without Appeal to Chance-raising", in P. Dowe and P. Noordhof (eds.) 2004, pp. 120–137.

Beebee, H., 2004. "Chance-changing Causal Processes", in P. Dowe and P. Noordhof (eds.) 2004, pp. 39–57.

Beebee, H., Hitchcock, C. and Menzies, P., 2009. The Oxford Handbook of Causation, Oxford: Oxford University Press.

Bennett, J., 1987. "Event Causation: the Counterfactual Analysis", Philosophical Perspectives, 1: 367–86.

Blaauw, M., 2013. Contrastivism in Philosophy , London: Routledge.

Collins, J., 2000. "Preemptive Preemption", Journal of Philosophy, 97: 223–34.

Collins, J., Hall, E., and Paul, L., 2004. Causation and Counterfactuals, Cambridge, Mass: MIT Press.

Dowe, P., 2000. Physical Causation, Cambridge: Cambridge University Press.

Dowe, P and P. Noordhof, 2004. Cause and Chance: Causation in an Indeterministic World, London: Routledge.

Elga, A., 2000. "Statistical Mechanics and the Asymmetry of Counterfactual Dependence", Philosophy of Science, 68 (Supplement): 313–324.

Ehring, D., 1987. "Causal Relata", Synthese, 73: 319–328.

Fine, K., 1975. "Review of Lewis (1973a)", Mind, 84: 451–8.

Frisch, M., 2005. Inconsistency, Asymmetry and Non-Locality: Philosophical Issues in Classical Electrodynamics, New York: Oxford University Press.

Garfinkel, A., 1981. Forms of Explanation, New Haven: Yale University Press.

Goodman, N., 1947. "The Problem of Counterfactual Conditionals", Journal of Philosophy, 44: 113–128. Reprinted in Goodman (1983).

Hall, N., 2000. "Causation and the Price of Transitivity", Journal of Philosophy, 97: 198–222.

Halpern, J. and Pearl, J., 2001. "Causes and Explanations: A Structural-model Approach — Part I: Causes", Proceedings of the Seventeenth Conference on Uncertainty in Artifical Intelligence, San Francisco: Morgan Kaufman, pp. 194–202.

Halpern, J. and Hitchcock, C., 2015. "Graded Causation and Defaults", British Journal for the Philosophy of Science, 66: 413–57.

Hart, H. L. and Honore, A., 1965. Causation in the Law, Oxford: Clarendon Press. Second edition 1985.

Hausman, D., 1998. Causal Asymmetries, Cambridge: Cambridge University Press.

Hitchcock, C. and Knobe, J., 2009. "Cause and Norm", Journal of Philosophy, 106: 587–612.

Hitchcock, C., 1996a. "The Role of Contrast in Causal and Explanatory Claims", Synthese, 107: 395–419.

Kim, J., 1973. "Causes and Counterfactuals", Journal of Philosophy, 70: 570–72.

Kutach, D., 2013. Causation and its Basis in Fundamental Physics, Oxford: Oxford University Press.

Kvart, I., 2001. "Counterexamples to Lewis' 'Causation as Influence'", Australasian Journal of Philosophy, 79: 411–23.

Lipton, P., 1991. Inference to the Best Explanation, London: Routledge.

Loewer, B., 2007. "Counterfactuals and the Second Law" in Price and Corry 2007, pp. 293–326.

Lyon, A., 1967. "Causality", British Journal for the Philosophy of Science, 18: 1–20.

Maslen, C., 2004. "Causes, Contrasts, and the Nontransitivity of Causation", in Collins, Hall, and Paul 2004, pp. 341–358.

Maudlin, T., 2004. "Causation, Counterfactuals, and the Third Factor", in Colins, Hall, and Paul 2004, pp. 419–443.

Mill, J. S., 1843. A System of Logic.

McDermott, M., 1995. "Redundant Causation", British Journal for the Philosophy of Science, 40: 523–544.

Mackie, J. L., 1973. Truth, Probability, and Paradox, Oxford: Oxford University Press.

Menzies, P., 1989. "Probabilistic Causation and Causal Processes: A Critique of Lewis", Philosophy of Science, 56: 642–663.

Moore, M., 2009. Causation and Responsibility: An Essay In Law, Morals, and Metaphysics, Oxford: Oxford University Press.

North, J., 2003. "Understanding the Time-Asymmetry of Radiation", Philosophy of Science, 70: 1086–1097.

Northcott, R., 2008. "Causation and Contrast Classes ", Philosophical Studies, 139: 111–123.

Noordhof, P., 1999. "Probabilistic Causation, Preemption, and Counterfactuals", Mind, 108: 95–125.

Paul, L., 2004. "Aspect Causation", in Collins, Hall, and Paul 2004, pp. 205–224.

Paul, L. and Hall, N., 2013. Causation: A User's Guide, Oxford: Oxford University Press.

Pearl, J., 2000. Causality, Cambridge: Cambridge University Press.

Popper, K., 1956. "The Arrow of Time", Nature, 1777: 538.

Price, H., 1996. Time's Arrow and Archimedes' Point, Oxford: Oxford University Press.

Price, H and Corry, R., 2007. Causation, Physics, and the Constitution of Reality: Russell's Republic Revisited, Oxford: Oxford University Press.

Price, H. and Weslake, B., 2009. "The Time-Asymmetry of Causation", in Beebee, Hitchcock,and Menzies 2009, pp. 414–43.

Ramachandran, M., 1997. "A Counterfactual Analysis of Causation", Mind, 106: 263–77.

Reiss, J., 2013. "Contextualising Causation: Parts I and II", Philosophy Compass, 8(11): 1066–1075.

Schaffer, J., 2000. "Trumping Preemption", Journal of Philosophy, 9: 165–81.

Spirtes, P., Glymour, C, and Scheines, R., 1993. Causation, Prediction, and Search, New York: Springer.

Steglich-Petersen, J., 2012. "Against the Contrastive Account of Singular Causation", British Journal for the Philosophy of Science, 63: 115–43.

van Fraassen, B., 1981. The Scientific Image, Oxford: Clarendon Press.

Weslake, B., forthcoming. "A Partial Theory of Actual Causation", British Journal for the Philosophy of Science.

Woodward, J., 1984. "A Theory of Singular Causal Explanation", Erkenntnis, 21: 31–62.

Woodward, J. and Hitchcock, C., 2003. "Explanatory Generalizations. Part I: A Counterfactual Account", Noûs, 37: 1–24.

Yablo, S., 2002. "De Facto Dependence", Journal of Philosophy, 99(3): 130–48, 2004. "Advertisement for a Sketch of an Outline of a Prototheory of Causation", in Collins, Hall, and Paul (eds.) 2004, pp. 119–38.

Chapter 5

MODELS FOR SEQUENCES OF OBSERVATIONS

5.1 GENERATIVE MODELS OF RELATIONS BETWEEN DATA POINTS

5.1.1 Generative Model

Broadly, a generative model is a statistical process that outputs a synthetic set of data or observations. Usually, these synthetic data and the generative process are designed to have some properties in common with empirical data and with the process believed to have generated those data. Generative models are often parametrized, and those parameters can be chosen so as to minimize the discrepancy between observed and synthetic data. The models, themselves, can be compared against one another using standard model comparison techniques, including goodness-of-fit criteria and cross-validation approaches.

Compressibility of networks

Generative models compress our descriptions of a network, encoding the network's topology in a set of wiring rules and parameters. Naively, we could describe a network exactly given a list of its nodes and edges: that is, by consulting the list, we could correctly connect nodes that are supposed to be connected and avoid connecting nodes that are not supposed to be connected. However, connections in many networks are not independent of one another, but instead exhibit statistical regularities such that, given the wiring rule that matches those regularities, we could predict the presence/absence of connections ahead of time. In this case, it becomes unnecessary to consult the list of nodes and edges to describe the network. More importantly, we can often interpret the wiring rule itself to uncover the network's organizing principles.

As an example, consider real-world spatial networks, where the probability of observing an edge between two nodes decays as a function of distance. Often, these kinds of networks can be well approximated by a simple geometric model whose wiring rule mimics the network's distance-dependent connection formation. To perfectly describe a spatial network, we could generate a long and possibly unwieldy list of its nodes and edges. However, if the geometric model is a good approximation, e.g. synthetic networks generated by the model recapitulate many observed edges, then the model can be used to replace those edges in the list, effectively shortening our description of the network. The geometric model naturally mimics the distance dependencies of the spatial network.

5.1.2 Space of Generative Model

Is it possible to delineate classes of generative models based on their functions or characteristics? Arguably, one of the distinguishing features of any generative model is the timescale over which it operates. On one extreme are models with no timescale at all, like stochastic block models or family of exponential random graphs, which uses a regression-based framework to predict a network's link structure from node- and edge-level attributes, and which has recently been applied to brain network data.

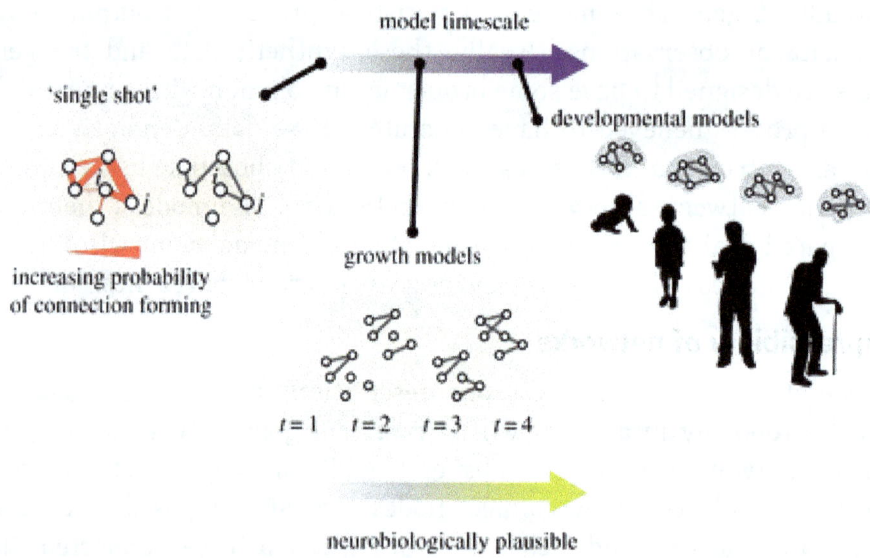

Fig: space of generative models

These kinds of models are 'single-shot' generators of networks, and can therefore be quite poor representations of real-world networks that grow and evolve over time. On the other extreme are models whose internal timescale matches that of the real system. Nodes and edges are added or rewired on a realistic timescale to match known properties of the system. The growth model is a good example where nodes and edges are added according to their empirically measured birth times; a feature that contributed to the success of that model in predicting different properties of the C. elegans connectome.

As observed, between two extremes where models operate either without any timescale or with a biologically plausible timescale where most generative models are placed. In middle ground, edges and nodes are added to or rewired in an existing network, but the timescale over which these processes occur is arbitrary. In case of BA model, new nodes are linked to an existing network over a series of steps which are ordered, so addition of one node precedes or follows that of another. Also, time is measured in arbitrary units and direct comparison to biological timescales, e.g. human development might be inappropriate. Ordering generative models based on their internal timescales is similar to ordering them according to their plausibility and mechanistic understanding. Block models and models with arbitrary timescales can do a good job compressing our description of a network and might identify general organizational principles. However, if our aim is to develop realistic mechanistic models of network growth and development, it is essential that we include the necessary components that ground the model in reality.

While a generative model's intrinsic timescale naturally results in a stratification of models according to their neurobiological plausibility, it is essential to note that increased plausibility does not necessarily imply improved fit or increased model performance. Entirely implausible models with many parameters that receive a variety of metadata as input can conceivably outperform more neurobiologically grounded mechanistic models, simply due to increased complexity

5.1.3 Generative Model Accomplishment

As observed, many current approaches for biological neural networks involve computing and comparing summary statistics between groups or continuously across individuals. While this approach is useful in identifying 'what' is different, it fails to explain 'how' those differences come to be, in the first place. On reviewing, echoing other recent reviews and call for shift in emphasis away from fact collecting studies and towards uncovering the mechanisms showing the organization of neural systems, observed that network generative modelling shows a framework that can help in moving towards addressing lofty goals.

Using correct dataset and right modelling approach, we can devise a model to reasonable approximation which can successfully take offs the growth or evolution of real-world neural system where model results in a network changes over time and whose topology evolves in a way that is consistent with known facts about real-world growth of network.

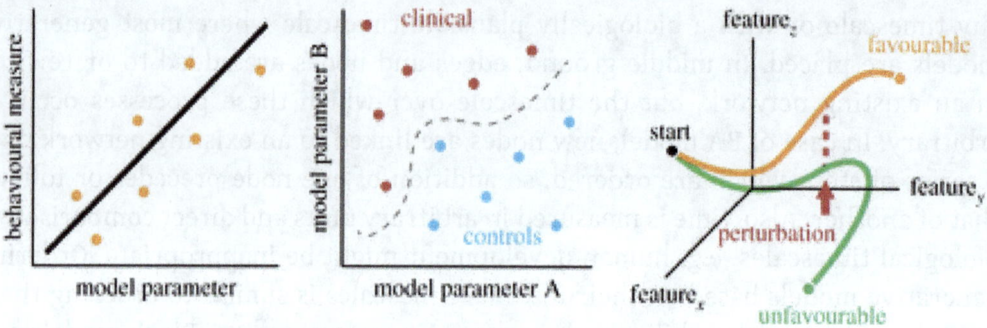

Fig: Applications using generative models

As seen, we simply maintain the status quo fit of model's parameters to individual subjects and calculate the statistical relationships among parameters and behavioural measures using machine learning techniques to partition the model's parameter space into regions associated with clinical and control populations. While useful, these approaches are quite similar to the current state of the field.

Generative models have clear utility in furthering our capacity to predict disease and identify the mechanisms that shape the development, growth and evolution of biological neural networks. A major hindrance in realizing these goals, however, is the absence of data tailored for generative models. The ideal data would

- be longitudinal, enabling one to track and incorporate individual-level changes over time in the model
- include multiple data modalities, such as functional and structural connectivity, and genetics, along with other select factors that could influence network-level organization.

In short, any metadata that could theoretically be incorporated into a model would be valuable and possibly worth collecting. Ideally, these data would be acquired at the earliest possible time point in utero and proceed through maturity.

Clearly, collecting and curetting such a dataset represents a massive undertaking. Though recent large-scale studies have made it possible to image thousands of individuals over a short period of time and a small number of individuals over a long period of time, the duration and scale of a longitudinal study of the nature proposed here seems, at present, out of reach. Furthermore, the studies that have come closest to acquiring these kinds of data have relied on MRI due to its non-invasive nature. However, this same advantage also limits the fidelity and kinds of data that can be acquired from an individual.

An attractive alternative, then, is to consider building generative models of data from non-human model organisms. Not only are the life cycles of several model organisms much shorter than that of humans, but new advances in network reconstruction techniques and the ability to make recordings of activity in unprecedented detail ensure that any generative model will be endowed with sufficiently rich data to probe for novel wiring rules. Moreover, working with model organisms also makes it possible to collect data modalities that, otherwise, would be inaccessible, including details about gene expression.

5.2 INDEPENDENT AND EXCHANGEABLE SEQUENCES

5.2.1 Independent and identically distributed random variables

In probability and statistics, a sequence or other collection of random variables is independent and identically distributed, if each random variable has similar probability distribution as the others and all are mutually independent. The annotation independent and identically distributed is particularly common in statistics , where observations in a sample are often assumed to be effectively independent and identically distributed for the purposes of statistical inference. The assumption that observations be independent and identically distributed tends to simplify the underlying mathematics of many statistical methods. However, in practical applications of statistical modeling the assumption may or may not be realistic. To test how realistic the assumption is on a given data set, the autocorrelation can be computed, lag plots drawn or turning point test performed. The generalization of exchangeable random variables is often sufficient and more easily met.

The assumption is important in the classical form of the central limit theorem, which states that the probability distribution of the sum of independent and identically distributed variables with finite variance approaches a normal distribution. Independent and identically distributed is sequences of random variables which are independent and identically distributed that shows an element in sequence is independent of random variables that came before it. Independent and identically distributed sequence is different from Markov sequence where probability distribution for the nth random variable is a function of the previous random variable in sequence. The sequence does not imply the probabilities for all elements of the sample space or event space must be the same. For example, repeated throws of loaded dice will produce a sequence that is independent and identically distributed, despite the outcomes being biased.

A more technical definition of independent and identically distributed statistics is that random variables X1, X2, . . . , Xn are independent and identically distributed if they share the same probability distribution and are independent events. Sharing the same probability distribution means that if you plotted all of the variables together, they would resemble some kind of distribution: a uniform distribution, a normal distribution or any one of the dozens of other distributions.

Each distribution has it's own characteristics, so if a sample of n random variables,

X1, X2,..., Xn, then each variable Xi has same mean (μ) and variance(σ)² which in equation form be written as:

$E(Xi) = \mu ; Var(Xi) = \sigma^2$

for all i = 1, 2,..., n.

Random variables that are identically distributed don't necessarily have to have the same probability. A flipped coin can be modeled by a binomial distribution and generally has a 50% chance of heads or tails. Further, if a coin weighted so that the probability of heads was 49.5% and tails was 50.5%, so as flipping of coin is independent and identically distributed, they do not have equal probabilities.

There are several reasons why sequences of random variables are important as often, we need to analyze a random variable X, but for some reasons is too complex to analyze directly. What we usually do in this case is to approximate X by simpler random variables X_n that are easier to study; these approximating random variables are arranged into a sequence $\{X_n\}$ and they become better and better approximations of X as n increases. This is exactly what we did when we introduced the Lebesgue integral.

Further in statistical theory, X_n is often an estimate of an unknown quantity whose value and whose properties depend on the sample size. Usually, we are able to analyze the properties of only asymptotically. Here, $\{X_n\}$ is a sequence of estimates and we analyze the properties of the limit of $\{X_n\}$, in the hope that a large sample and an infinite sample have a similar behavior. In many applications a random variable is observed repeatedly through time (for example, the price of a stock is observed every day). In this case $\{X_n\}$ is the sequence of observations on the random variable and is a time-index.

Examples:

Put m balls with numbers written on them in an urn. Draw n balls from the urn with replacement, and let X_i be the number on the ith ball. Then $X_1, X_2, ..., X_n$ will be i.i.d.

But if we draw the balls without replacement, $X_1, X_2, ..., X_n$ will not be i.i.d. - they will all have the same distribution, but will not be independent.

If we draw the balls with replacement, but let X_i be i times the number on the ith ball, then $X_1, X_2, ..., X_n$ will not be i.i.d. - they will be independent, but they will have different distributions.

5.2.2 Sums of i.i.d. random variables

Theorem: If X_1, X_2, ..., X_n are i.i.d. with the same distribution as a random variable X, then

$E(X_1 + X_2 + ... + X_n) = n\ E(X)$

$Var(X_1 + X_2 + ... + X_n) = n\ Var(X)$

$SD(X_1 + X_2 + ... + X_n) = sqrt(n)\ SD(X)$

Properties of Binomial Distributions

We can view a random variable Y that has the binomial(n,p) distribution as the sum of n i.i.d. random variables that all have the Bernoulli(p) distribution. That is, we let

$Y = X_1 + X_2 + ... + X_n$

where X_1, X_2, ..., X_n are i.i.d. with the Bernoulli(p) distribution.

Recall that the mean of a Bernoulli(p) random variable is p. We can also compute that the variance of a Bernoulli(p) random variable is

$p\ (1-p)^2 + (1-p)\ (0-p)^2 = p\ (1-p)$

From this and the theorem above about sums of i.i.d. random variables, we can conclude that if Y has then binomial(n,p) distribution, the E(Y) = np and Var(Y) =np(1-p).

5.2.3 Means of i.i.d. random variables

Define BAR-X_n = $(X_1 + X_2 + ... + X_n) / n$. This is called the "sample mean" of X_1, X_2, ..., X_n (especially if these are n observations of some quantity).

If X_1, X_2, ..., X_n are i.i.d., all having the same distribution as the random variable X, then

E(BAR-X) = $(1/n)\ E(X_1 + X_2 + ... + X_n)$ = (1/n) n E(X) = E(X)

We say that BAR-X is an "unbiased" estimate of E(X), meaning that it's "right on average".

But being unbiased doesn't guarantee that BAR-X is usually close to E(X). To see how close it is likely to be, we need to look at the standard deviation of BAR-X:

SD(BAR-X) = $(1/n)\ SD(X_1 + X_2 + ... + X_n)$ = (1/n) sqrt(n) SD(X) = (1/sqrt(n)) SD(X)

So as n gets bigger, the standard deviation of BAR-X gets smaller, and approaches zero, though because of the square root, perhaps not as fast as you might have hoped.

Law of Large Numbers

The mean of a sequence of n i.i.d. random variables can be proved to approach the expected value of (any) one of the variables, as n goes to infinity. This is called the Law of Large Numbers having many forms.

Theorem:

Let X be a random variable for which the expectation, E(X), exists, and for which the variance, Var(X), is finite. If the infinite sequence of random variables X_1, X_2, ... are i.i.d., all having the same distribution as the random variable X, then for any e > 0,

LIMIT(n->oo) P(|BAR-X_n-E(X)| > e) = 0

where BAR-X_n = (X_1 + X_2 + ... + X_n) / n.

Proof: We need to show that for any e > 0 and any d > 0, there exists some integer n^* such that for all n > n^*,

P(|BAR-X_n-E(X)| > e) < d

This will hold if we set n^* to Var(X)/de^2. Chebyshev's inequality says that

P(|BAR-X_n-E(X)| >= e) = P(|BAR-X_n-E(X)| >= (e / SD(BAR-X_n)) SD(BAR-X_n)) <= (SD(BAR-X_n) / e$)^2$

Noting that SD(BAR-X_n) = SD(X)/sqrt(n), we see that for any n > n^*,

P(|BAR-X_n-E(X)| > e) <= (SD(BAR-X_n) / e$)^2$ < ((SD(X)/sqrt(n^*)) / e$)^2$ = Var(X) / (n^*e^2) = d

which is what we needed to prove.

Law of Large Numbers shows that fraction of times an event occurs in many repetitions of a situation converges to the probability of that event, since we can define a random variable X to be 1 if event A occurs and 0 otherwise, in which case P(A)=E(X). The Law of Large Numbers therefore provides a justification of sorts for the interpretation of probability as relative frequency in many repetitions. Law of Large Numbers is also a justification for using computer simulation to estimate probabilities and expectations.

5.2.4 Directed graphical models

A directed graphical model is a way of specifying a joint probability distribution for several random variables via a simplification of the multiplication rule. As noted, any joint probability mass function for X, Y, and Z be written using multiplication rule as:

P(x,y,z) = P(x) P(y|x) P(z|x,y)

If X is conditionally independent (C.I.) of Y given Z, we can simplify P(z|x,y) to

P(z|y). When we have many random variables, such simplifications can make the task of specifying a probability distribution much easier.

A directed graphical model has a node for every random variable, with arrows from some nodes to other nodes, with there being no directed cycles. Since there are no cycles, there is always at least one way to order the variables so that all the arrows point forward. If we write the joint probability as above using the multiplication rule in this order, the absence of an arrow from X to a later node Y indicates that X is C.I. of Y given the parents of Y, so we can omit x from the factor P(y|...,x,...), thereby simplifying it.

Example:

At some ski resort, X = # of skiers on hill one day, Y = # of skiers who break a leg that day and Z = total cost of medical treatment for broken legs that day. It may be reasonable to assure that the total medical cost depends only on the number of skiers who break their leg, and not on the number of skiers, except that the number of skiers affects how many skiers break their leg. In other words, we might assume that X is C.I. of Z given Y which can be expressed by directed graphical model as:

```
X ---> Y ---> Z
```

Example:

We roll a red die and a green die, and then flip a coin as many times as the sum of the numbers showing on the red and green dice. We define R = number showing on the red die, G = number showing on the green die and X = R + G where H = number of heads when the coin is flipped X times.

Now such case can be described by directed graphical model as:

```
R --
   \
   \
    -->
       X ---> H
    -->
   /
   /
G --
```

It shows that on writing joint probability mass function for R, G, X, and H as

P(r,g,x,h) = P(r) P(g) P(x|r,g) P(h|x)

Independence and Conditional Independence in Directed Graphical Models

If we assume that some directed graphical model is valid, we can deduce various independence and conditional independence relationships from it. A theorem says that X is C.I. of Y given Z if X is "d-separated" from Y given Z, which means that all paths from X to Y in the graph are "blocked" given Z. A path is any route from X to Y, travelling along arrows in either direction. A path is blocked if any node along it blocks the path. There are three possible situations for a node W along a path:

- ... ---> W ---> ...

This is blocked if W is the variable Z that is conditioned on.

- ... <--- W ---> ...

This is also blocked if W is the variable Z that is conditioned on.

- ... ---> W <--- ...

This is blocked if W is not the variable Z that is conditioned on, and Z is also not a descendent of W.

Here, if X is not d-separated from Y given Z, it could still be the case that X is C.I. of Y given Z, but that will happen only if exact probabilities in distribution lead to their being conditionally independent - the structure of the graph doesn't imply that they are C.I.

Further it is defined separation given more than one variable where a node in a path of the form ---> W ---> or <--- W ---> blocks the path if W is any of variables conditioned on and a node of the form ---> W <--- blocks the path only if neither W nor any of its children is conditioned on.

Also, unconditional independence relationship in terms of d-separation with no variables conditioned where nodes are of the form ---> W ---> and <--- W ---> which never block a path, and node of form ---> W <--- always blocks a path.

5.2.5 The Frequentist Account

The frequentist interprets probability as limiting relative frequency. It is useful to rehearse the frequentist account of learning from experience. The weak law of large numbers reads:

Let X_i, i = 1,2,.. be independent and identically distributed variables taking values in {0,1}, and let $P\{X_i = 1\} = p$. Then for all $\varepsilon > 0$

$$P\{|(1/n)\sum_{i=1}^{n} X_i - p| > \varepsilon\} \to 0 \text{ as } n \to \infty$$

The frequentist learning model works as follows. Suppose we have a variable X taking values in {0,1} and we wish to know the probability that X = 1. If we can find a sequence of independent variables X_i with the same distribution as X, then we can observe a large number n of these variables. The relative frequency of "1"'s in $X_1,...X_n$ is then unlikely to differ greatly from the probability that X = 1. Two features of this account are noteworthy:

1. Probability exists. The person reasoning as above believes that there is some objective quantity "p".
2. p is initially unknown, but can be measured to arbitrary precision, in a probabilistic sense, by observing relative frequencies in large, finite sequences of observations

Expressed in this way, we have to know that the variables X_i are independent and identically distributed, which we could never know *before* measuring their probabilities. This circularity in the naïve frequentist account is removed in more sophisticated treatments, where probability is defined as limiting relative frequency in a *random sequence,* and "random" is defined without reference to probability.

5.2.6 Subjectivist Account

The subjectivist cannot accept this account of learning. "p" is not an objective quantity, but a subjective degree of belief. It cannot be "observed" in the sense implied by the frequentist account. It is a fact, nevertheless, that people attach importance to relative frequencies. The subjectivist must offer an explanation of this fact.

Expected Relative Frequency

Theorem: Let $p_i = p(A_i) = p(1_i{=}1)$. Then the average of the probabilities p_i equals the expected relative frequency of occurrence of $A_1,...A_n$, or

$(1/n)\Sigma p_i = \Sigma i w_i^{(n)}/n$.

Proof: Rewriting the expected relative frequency of occurrence on the right hand side, we have:

$E(1/n)\Sigma 1_i = (1/n)\Sigma E(1_i) = (1/n)\Sigma p_i$.

Here the theorem makes no independence assumptions. It also says nothing about changing our beliefs in the light of observations.

5.2.7 Exchangeability

As per De Finetti, exchangeability provides the characterization of those belief states in which we learn from relative frequencies.

In an events $A_1,..A_n$ that are exchangeable with respect to probability measure p if for all Q, Q' ∈ 2^n with #Q = #Q'; $p(1_1,..1_n = Q) = p(1_1,..1_n = Q')$. An infinite sequence of indicators is exchangeable with respect to p if every finite subsequence is exchangeable with respect to p.

After observing a sequence of outcomes Q ∈ 2^n , our probability for A_{n+1} is no longer $p(A_{n+1})$ but $p(A_{n+1}|Q)$. We wish to calculate this quantity on the assumption that $A_1,...A_{n+1}$ are exchangeable with respect to p. Suppose #Q = r.

$$P(A_{n+1} \mid Q) = P(A_{n+1} \cap Q)/p(Q) = \frac{[w_{r+1}^{(n+1)} / \binom{n+1}{r+1}]}{[w_r^{(n)} / \binom{n}{r}]}$$

$$= [w_{r+1}^{(n+1)} / w_r^{(n)}] \times [(r+1)/(n+1)]$$

To reduce this note that

$$w_r^{(n)} / \binom{n}{r} = [w_{r+1}^{(n+1)} / \binom{n+1}{r+1}] + [w_r^{(n+1)} / \binom{n+1}{r}]$$

Putting s = n - r and simplifying:

$$w_r^{(n)} = \frac{w_{r+1}^{(n+1)}(r+1) + w_r^{(n+1)}(s+1)}{n+1}$$

Since r+1 = n+2 - (s+1) which gives:

$$p(A_{n+1}|Q) = \frac{w_{r+1}^{(n+1)}(r+1)}{w_r^{(n+1)}(s+1) + w_{r+1}^{(n+1)}(r+1)}$$

$$= \frac{r+1}{(r+1) + (s+1)\,[w_r^{(n+1)} / w_{r+1}^{(n+1)}]}$$

$$= \frac{r+1}{(n+2) + (s+1)\,[w_r^{(n+1)} / w_{r+1}^{(n+1)} - 1]}$$

If the probability of 'r' occurrences in $A_1,...A_{n+1}$ is close to the probability of r+1 such occurrences, then the term in brackets is close to one and

$p(A_{n+1}|Q) \sim (r+1)/(n+2)$.

Theorem: Let A_1, A_2,...be exchangeable, and suppose there is a constant K such that for all n:

$\text{Max}\,\{r = 0...n\}\ |[w_{r+1}^{(n+1)} / w_r^{(n)}] - 1| < K/n$

then $\max Q{\in}2\omega\ \ |p(A_{n+1}|Qn) - \#Q/n| \rightarrow 0$ as $n \rightarrow \infty$.

Notice that this theorem does NOT say that the relative frequency of 1's converges to some limit as 'n' goes to infinity.

DeFinetti's representation theorem

Instead of speaking of exchangeable sequences $A_1,\ldots A_n$, we may just as well speak of exchangeable measures on the field of events generated by $A_1,\ldots A_n$.

DeFinetti's theorem states that an exchangeable measure can be uniquely represented as probabilistic mixtures of certain "extreme" measures. Any measure can be represented as a mixture of other measures via conditionalization. For example, if $\{B_i\}i=1,\ldots n$ is a partition, then

$p(A) = \Sigma p(A|B_i)p(B_i)$

represents the measure p(.) as a mixture of the measures $p_i = p(P|B_i)$, with mixing weights $p(B_i)$. Exchangeability is preserved under mixing, so if events are exchangeable under each p_i, then they are exchangeable under p as well. The question of representing exchangeable sequences can be translated into the question of representing exchangeable probability measures.

DeFinetti's representation theorem for Finite Exchangeable Sequences of Events:

(1) Any exchangeable measure on $P(2^n)$ is uniquely determined by the probabilities $w_j^{(n)}$, $j = 0,\ldots n$, and (2) any $q \in S^{n+1}$ determines an exchangeable measure by setting $w_j^{(n)} = q_{j+1}$; $j=0\ldots n$.

Proof:

(1) Partition $P(2^n)$ into sets $B_i = \{Q \in 2^n \mid \#Q = i\}$, $i = 0,\ldots n$. For any exchangeable probability measure p on $P(2^n)$,

$p = \Sigma p(\bullet|B_i)p(B_i)$.

$p(\bullet|B_i)$ is uniform on $P(2^n)$ and $p(B_i) = w_i^{(n)}$. Hence if p' is another exchangeable measure and $p'(B_i) = p(B_i)$, then p'=p.

(2) For fixed i, the probability μ_i on $P(2^n)$ which assigns B_i probability one and for which $P(\bullet|B_i)$ is uniform, is exchangeable; and for any $q \in S^{n+1}$, the measure $p = \Sigma \mu_i q_i$ is also exchangeable.

Consider drawings from an urn containing r black and n-r white balls. The probability of drawing j black and m-j white balls, with m < n, j < r is given by the hypergeometric distribution:

$$w_j^{(m)} = \frac{\binom{m}{j}\binom{n-m}{r-j}}{\binom{n}{r}}$$

If m = n, then $w_j^{(m)} = 1$ if j = r and = 0 otherwise. The probability on $P(2^n)$ induced by drawing from such an urn is exchangeable and corresponds to the measure μ_r in the above proof. Hence any exchangeable measure can be represented uniquely as a mixture of urn drawing measures. The probability $p(B_i)$ corresponds to the probability of "drawing" an urn with i black balls, i

= 0,...n; and the probabilities $p(P|B_i)$ correspond to drawings from the urn with i black balls.

DeFinetti's representation for Infinite Sequences of Exchangeable Events

For large n, drawing a few balls without replacement from an urn with r black and n-r white balls is "almost" like flipping a coin with probability r/n of "black" and (n-r)/n of "white". One can prove, letting $n \to \infty$ keeping the ratio r/n constant, that the hypergeometric distribution converges to the binomial distribution, that is

$$w_j^{(m)} \to \binom{m}{j}(r/n)^j\,((n-r)/n)^{m-j}$$

For infinite sequences of exchangeable events, DeFinetti's theorem states that any exchangeable probability measure may be uniquely represented as a mixture of binomial measures. For $Q \in 2^n$, $\#Q = r$, the probability of Q under the binomial measure with parameter $q \in (0,1)$ is

$$P(Q) = q^r\,(1-q)^{n-r}$$

Taking mixtures of such measures corresponds to integrating the above over $q \in (0,1)$, with respect to some measure dp(q) on the interval (0,1). Every exchangeable probability corresponds to a unique measure dp(q), and we may write:

$$P(Q) = \int_{[0,1]} q^{\#Q}\,(1-q)^{n-\#Q}\;dp(q)$$

where Q is a sequence of r 1's and n-r 0's.

This notation is a bit ambiguous, as the P on the left hand side is a probability on 2ω ; the p under the integral is a probability measure on (0,1). The quantity dp(q) may be thought of as the probability of "drawing" a binomial probability with parameter q.

The key to applying DeFinetti's theorem for infinite exchangeable sequences lies in finding a class of measures dp(q) for which the above integral can be evaluated easily.

5.2.8 The Subjectivist Resolution of Ellsberg Paradox

As proposed, degrees of belief cannot be represented as probability measures, so considering the following cases:

Case 1:

A subject is offered the opportunity to bet on the outcomes of tosses with a coin which the subject believes to be fair (P(heads) = 0.5, tosses independent).

Case 2:

A subject is offered the opportunity to bet on the outcomes of tosses of a coin about which he believes that the probability of heads could with equal probability be any number $r \in (0,1)$.

On the subjectivist account the subject's beliefs are modeled by, $Q \in 2^n$:

$p(Q) = \int q^{\#Q} (1-q)^{n-\#Q}\ dp(q)$.

In case 1, subject is certain that $q = 0.5$, hence the beliefs are modeled by setting $dp(q) = \delta(q-0.5)$; where $\delta(x)$ is "Dirac delta measure" assigning unit mass to point $x=0$; so for any function $F(q)$;

$\int F(q)\ \delta(q-\theta) = F(\theta)$.

In case 2, $dp(q) = dq$, so

$p(\text{heads on one toss}) = \int qd(q) = 0.5$.

The paradox is that subjects in case 1 that accept even money bets on heads, whereas in case 2 they supposedly will not, even though the subjective probabilities are the same in both cases. Hence there must be a difference in the beliefs in these two cases, even though P(heads on one toss) is the same.

In case of subjectivist account, difference in these two cases only appears when consider subject's willingness to revise betting rates on based on observations of outcomes of previous tosses.

If H_i denote event "heads on toss i" so the subject believes the tosses are independent with $P(H_i) = r$; $i = 1,2,\ldots$ .which shows that $P(H_2|H_1) = r$. Further, $dp(q)$ is not concentrated at one point, so applying Jensen's inequality to show $P(H_2|H_1) > p(H_1)$. Now if $dp(q) = dq$, using Beta integral:

$\int q^r (1-q)^{n-r} dq = r!(n-r)!/(n+1)!$

to derive Laplace's rule:

$P(H_{n+1}|r \text{ heads on n tosses}) = (r+1)/(n+2)$.

In above case, subject's beliefs are modeled as mixture of independent coin tosses, with mixing measure $dp(q)$, so the mixture of independent measures is not independent, hence the subject in above case shows willingness to learn from previous experience whereas subject in case 1 does not learn from experience.

5.3 MARKOV MODELS

5.3.1 Introduction

As per Shannon, the statistical structure of a piece of text with simple mathematical model is determined as Markov model. The Markov model of order 0 shows that each letter in the alphabet occurs with a fixed probability. We can fit a Markov model of order 0 to a specific piece of text by counting the number of occurrences of each letter in that text, and using these counts as probabilities. In case of input text "agggcagcgggcg", the Markov model of order 0 shows that every letter is 'a' with probability 2/13, 'c' with probability 3/13, and 'g' with probability 8/13, so the following sequence of letters are generated from this model as shown.

a g g c g a g g g a g c g g c a g g g g...

An order 0 model assumes that each letter is chosen independently. This does not coincide with the statistical properties of English text since there is a high correlation among successive letters in an English word or sentence. For example, the letters 'h' and 'r' are much more likely to follow 't' than either 'c' or 'x'.

It is seen a more refined model shows probability of choosing every successive letter which depends on preceding letter or letters. As per Markov model of order k, it is known that each letter occurs with fixed probability which depends on previous k consecutive letters (k-gram). In an example, if text has 100 occurrences of "th", with 60 occurrences of "the", 25 occurrences of "thi", 10 occurrences of "tha", and 5 occurrences of "tho", then as per Markov model of order 2 describes that the next letter will follow 2-gram "th" as 'e' with probability 3/5, 'i' with probability 1/4, 'a' with probability 1/10, and 'o' with probability 1/20.

5.3.2 Markov chain

Markov chain is a simple concept which can explain most complicated real time processes. Speech recognition, Text identifiers, Path recognition and many other Artificial Intelligence tools use this simple principle called Markov chain in some form.

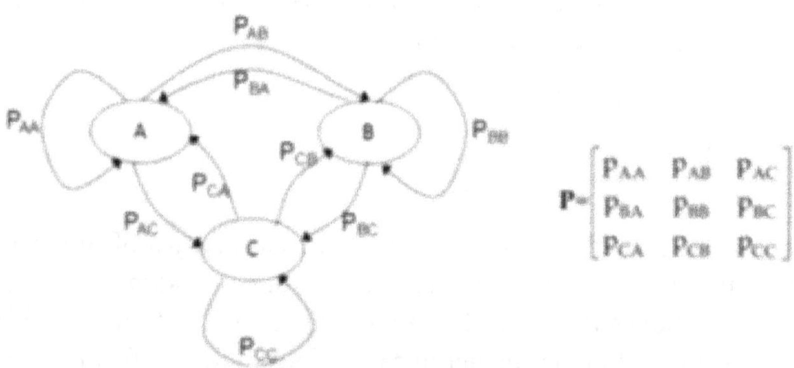

Fig: Markov chain

Markov chain is based on a principle of memorylessness where next state of the process only depends on earlier state and not the sequence of states. Such assumption makes the calculation of conditional probability easy and enables such algorithm to apply in number of scenarios.

Example

Coke and Pepsi are the only companies in country X. A soda company wants to tie up with one of these competitors. They hire a market research company to find which of the brand will have a higher market share after 1 month. Currently,

Pepsi owns 55% and Coke owns 45% of market share. Following are the conclusions drawn out by the market research company:

- P(P->P) : Probability of a customer staying with the brand Pepsi over a month = 0.7
- P(P->C) : Probability of a customer switching from Pepsi to Coke over a month = 0.3
- P(C->C) : Probability of a customer staying with the brand Coke over a month = 0.9
- P(C->P) : Probability of a customer switching from Coke to Pepsi over a month = 0.1

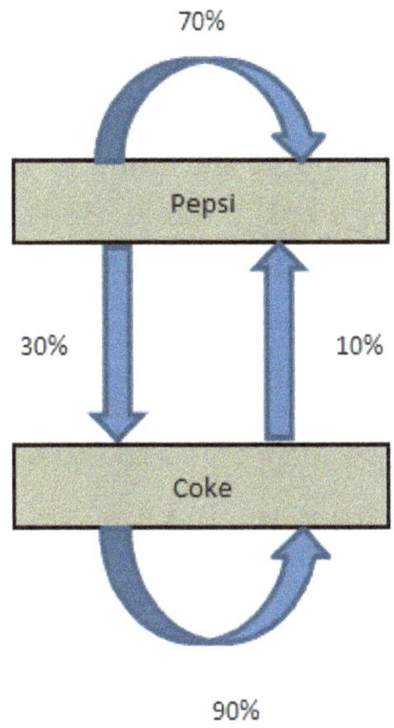

From the above statements, it is clearly observed that the customer tend to stick with Coke but Coke currently has a lower wallet share. Hence, we cannot be sure on the recommendation without making some transition calculations.

The diagram simply shows the transitions and the current market share. Now, if we want to calculate the market share after a month, we need to do following calculations :

- Market share (t+1) of Pepsi = Current market Share of Pepsi * P(P->P) + Current market Share of Coke * P(C->P)
- Market share (t+1) of Coke = Current market Share of Coke * P(C->C) + Current market Share of Pepsi * P(P->C)
- These calculations can be simply done by looking at the following matrix multiplication :
- Current State X Transition Matrix = Final State

Final state

$$\begin{matrix} \text{Pepsi} & \text{Coke} \\ 55\% & 45\% \end{matrix} \quad X \quad \begin{matrix} & \text{Pepsi} & \text{Coke} \\ \text{Pepsi} & 70\% & 30\% \\ \text{Coke} & 10\% & 90\% \end{matrix} \quad = \quad \begin{matrix} \text{Pepsi} & \text{Coke} \\ 43\% & 57\% \end{matrix}$$

Initial state

As we can clearly see that Pepsi, although has a higher market share now, will have a lower market share after one month. This simple calculation is called Markov chain. If the transition matrix does not change with time, we can predict the market share at any future time point.

Furthermore to the business case in hand, the soda company wants to size the gap in market share of the company Coke and Pepsi in a long run. This will help them frame the right costing strategy while pitching to Coke. The share of Pepsi will keep on going down till a point the number of customer leaving Pepsi and number of customers adapting Pepsi is same. Hence, we need to satisfy following conditions to find the steady state proportions:

Pepsi MS * 30% = Coke MS * 10% 1

Pepsi MS + Coke MS = 100% 2

4 * Pepsi MS = 100% => Pepsi MS = 25% and Coke MS = 75%

Let's formulate an algorithm to find the steady state. After steady state, multiplication of Initial state with transition matrix will give initial state itself. Hence, the matrix which can satisfy following condition will be the final proportions:

Initial state X Transition Matrix = Initial state

By solving for above equation, we can find the steady state matrix. The solution will be same as [25%,75%].

5.4 PROBABILISTIC CONTEXT-FREE GRAMMARS

5.4.1 Introduction

Probabilistic context free grammar have been applied in probabilistic modeling of RNA structures almost 40 years after they were introduced in computational linguistics. Probabilistic context free grammar extend context-free grammar similar to how hidden Markov models extend regular grammar. Each production is assigned a probability. The probability of a derivation is the product of the probabilities of the productions used in that derivation. These probabilities can be viewed as parameters of the model, and for large problems it is convenient to learn these parameters via machine learning. A probabilistic grammar's validity is constrained by context of its training dataset.

A probabilistic context free grammar is a context free grammar that associates a probability with each of its productions. It generates the same set of parses for a text that the corresponding context free grammar does, and assigns a probability to each parse. The probability of a parse generated by a PCFG is simply the product of the probabilities of the productions used to generate it.

More formally, let T be a terminal alphabet and N a non-terminal alphabet. A probabilistic context-free grammar G consists of a distinguished start symbol S in N plus a finite set of productions of the form

p : X -> alpha,

where

X = N

alpha = power set of N u T

p = probability value

The probability values for all production rules of X sum up to 1.0. The grammar defines a stochastic process with sentential forms as states, and leftmost rewriting steps as transitions. We denote a single rewriting operation of the grammar by a single arrow ->. If as a result of one ore more rewriting operations we are able to rewrite and element beta of the power set of N u T as a sequence gamma of non-terminals and terminals, then we write beta ->* gamma. The probability of this rewriting is the product of all probability values associated to productions used in the derivation.

Example of simple grammar generating all strings over {a,b}:

```
% s is the starting non-terminal
state([],[s])
% s -> 0.3 :: a | 0.3 :: b | 0.4 :: s s
0.3::state([a|W],S) ; 0.3::state([b|W],S) ; 0.4::state(W,[s,s|S]) :-
state(W,[s|S]).
word(W) :- reverse(W,WR),state(WR,[]).
reverse(L,R) :- reverse(L,[],R).
reverse([],L,L).
reverse([H|T],A,R) :- reverse(T,[H|A],R).
query(word([_])).
query(word([_,_])).
query(word([_,_,_])).
```

Output

Query	Location	Probability
word([a, a, a])	14:7	0.00864
word([a, a, b])	14:7	0.00864
word([a, a])	13:7	0.036
word([a, b, a])	14:7	0.00864
word([a, b, b])	14:7	0.00864
word([a, b])	13:7	0.036
word([a])	12:7	0.3
word([b, a, a])	14:7	0.00864
word([b, a, b])	14:7	0.00864
word([b, a])	13:7	0.036
word([b, b, a])	14:7	0.00864
word([b, b, b])	14:7	0.00864
word([b, b])	13:7	0.036
word([b])	12:7	0.3

Example generating well-formed sequences of brackets with a for opening and b for closing:

```
% s is the starting non-terminal
state([],[s]).
% S -> 0.4 :: O M | 0.6 :: S S
0.4::state(W,[o,m|S]) ; 0.6::state(W,[s,s|S]) :- state(W,[s|S]).
% O -> a
state([a|W],S) :- state(W,[o|S]).
% M -> 0.7 :: b | 0.3 :: S C
0.7::state([b|W],S) ; 0.3::state(W,[s,c|S]) :- state(W,[m|S]).
% C -> b
state([b|W],S) :- state(W,[c|S]).
word(W) :- reverse(W,WR), state(WR,[]).
reverse(L,R) :- reverse(L,[],R).
reverse([],L,L).
```

```
reverse([H|T],A,R) :- reverse(T,[H|A],R).
query(word([_,_])).
query(word([_,_,_,_])).
query(word([_,_,_,_,_,_])).
```

Output

Query	Location	Probability
word([a, a, a, b, b, b])	20:7	0.004032
word([a, a, b, a, b, b])	20:7	0.0056448
word([a, a, b, b, a, b])	20:7	0.0056448
word([a, a, b, b])	19:7	0.0336
word([a, b, a, a, b, b])	20:7	0.0056448
word([a, b, a, b, a, b])	20:7	0.01580544
word([a, b, a, b])	19:7	0.04704
word([a, b])	18:7	0.28

Encoding with Nonterminal-Counters

```
% s -> 0.3 :: a | 0.3 :: b | 0.4 :: s s
0.3::s_to(N,a); 0.3::s_to(N,b); 0.4::s_to(N,ss).
s([a],s(N,NN)) :-
s_to(N,a), NN is N+1.
s([b],s(N,NN)) :-
s_to(N,b), NN is N+1.
s(L,s(N,NN)) :-
s_to(N,ss),
NI is N+1,
   split(L,L1,L2),
   s(L1,s(NI,NS)),
   s(L2,s(NS,NN)).
% s is the starting symbol, and we start with the counter for s being 0
word(L) :- s(L,s(0,_)).
% split(+T,-P,-S) splits the list T into two non-empty sublists P(refix) and S(uffix)
% note that T needs to have fixed length for this to terminate
```

```
split([A,B|C],[A],[B|C]).
split([A,B|C],[A|D],E) :-
    split([B|C],D,E).
% we need to fix the length of the list to ensure split/3 has a finite number of solutions
query(word([_])).
query(word([_,_])).
query(word([_,_,_])).
```

Output

Query	Location	Probability
word([a, a, a])	26:7	0.00864
word([a, a, b])	26:7	0.00864
word([a, a])	25:7	0.036
word([a, b, a])	26:7	0.00864
word([a, b, b])	26:7	0.00864
word([a, b])	25:7	0.036
word([a])	24:7	0.3
word([b, a, a])	26:7	0.00864
word([b, a, b])	26:7	0.00864
word([b, a])	25:7	0.036
word([b, b, a])	26:7	0.00864
word([b, b, b])	26:7	0.00864
word([b, b])	25:7	0.036
word([b])	24:7	0.3

As explicitly incorporating counters into the rules as above is cumbersome, here's a general purpose encoding of the approach that allows for easy exchange of the grammar. It also adds a predicate tree/2 that generates a nested term representing a parse tree.

```
%%% model-specific part
% - one ground fact for start/1 giving the starting symbol
% - ground facts for nonterminal/1 listing all nonterminal symbols
```

```
% - for each nonterminal, an AD defining its rules, with a shared variable as last
argument, where
%  rule(X,Y,Z,_) is a rule X -> Y Z with nonterminals Y and Z
%  rule(X,A,_) is a rule X -> a with terminal "a"
%
% S -> 0.4 :: O M | 0.6 :: S S
% O -> a
% M -> 0.7 :: b | 0.3 :: S C
% C -> b
start(s).
nonterminal(s).
nonterminal(m).
nonterminal(o).
nonterminal(c).
0.4::rule(s,o,m,T); 0.6::rule(s,s,s,T).
rule(o,a,_).
0.7::rule(m,b,T); 0.3::rule(m,s,c,T).
rule(c,b,_).
% we need to fix the length of the list to ensure split/3 has a finite number of
solutions
query(word([_,_,_,_])).
query(tree([a,b,a,b,a,b],_)).
%%% model-independent part
% X -> Y Z
parse(W,X,CIn,COut) :-
   get_counter(X,CIn,N),
   rule(X,Y,Z,N),
   increment_counter(X,CIn,CC),
   split(W,W1,W2),
   parse(W1,Y,CC,CCC),
   parse(W2,Z,CCC,COut).
% X -> a
```

```
parse([A],X,CIn,COut) :-
    get_counter(X,CIn,N),
    rule(X,A,N),
    increment_counter(X,CIn,COut).
word(W) :-
    findall(X,nonterminal(X),NTs),
    init_counter(NTs,Counter),
    start(S),
    parse(W,S,Counter,_).
% building parse tree
tree(W,T) :-
    findall(X,nonterminal(X),NTs),
    init_counter(NTs,Counter),
    start(S),
    parse_tree(W,S,Counter,_,T).
% X -> Y Z
parse_tree(W,X,CIn,COut,Tree) :-
    Tree =.. [X,Left,Right],
    get_counter(X,CIn,N),
    rule(X,Y,Z,N),
    increment_counter(X,CIn,CC),
    split(W,W1,W2),
    parse_tree(W1,Y,CC,CCC,Left),
    parse_tree(W2,Z,CCC,COut,Right).
% X -> a
parse_tree([A],X,CIn,COut,Tree) :-
    Tree =.. [X,A],
    get_counter(X,CIn,N),
    rule(X,A,N),
    increment_counter(X,CIn,COut).
%%% auxiliaries
```

```
% split(+T,-P,-S) splits the (fixed length) list T into two non-empty sublists P(refix) and S(uffix)
% note that T needs to have fixed length for this to terminate
split([A,B|C],[A],[B|C]).
split([A,B|C],[A|D],E) :-
 split([B|C],D,E).
get_counter(X,Cs,N) :-
   member(count(X,N),Cs).
member(A,[A|_]).
member(A,[H|T]) :-
   A \= H,
   member(A,T).
increment_counter(X,[count(X,N)|Cs],[count(X,NN)|Cs]) :-
   NN is N+1.
increment_counter(X,[count(Y,N)|Cs],[count(Y,N)|NCs]) :-
   X \== Y,
   increment_counter(X,Cs,NCs).
init_counter([],[]).
init_counter([H|T],[count(H,0)|C]) :-
   init_counter(T,C).
```

Output

Query	Location	Probability
tree([a, b, a, b, a, b], s(s(o(a),m(b)),s(s(o(a), m(b)),s(o(a),m(b)))))	24:7	0.00790272
tree([a, b, a, b, a, b], s(s(s(o(a),m(b)),s(o(a), m(b))),s(o(a),m(b))))	24:7	0.00790272
word([a, a, b, b])	23:7	0.0336
word([a, b, a, b])	23:7	0.04704

REFERENCES

Blalock, H. (Ed.) (1971). Causal Models in the Social Sciences. Aldine-Atherton, Chicago.

Blalock, H. (1961). Causal Inferences in Nonexperimental Research. University of North Carolina Press, Chapel Hill, NC.

Costner, H. (1971). Theory, deduction and rules of correspondence. Causal Models in the Social Sciences, Blalock, H. (ed.). Aldine, Chicago.

Geiger, D. and Pearl, J. (1989b). Axioms and Algorithms for Inferences Involving Conditional Independence. Report CSD 890031, R-119-I, Cognitive Systems Laboratory, University of California, Los Angeles.

Geiger, D., Verma, T., and Pearl, J. (1990) Identifying independence in Bayesian Networks. Networks 20, 507-533.

Glymour, C., Scheines, R., Spirtes, P., and Kelly, K. (1987). Discovering Causal Structure. Academic Press, San Diego, CA.

Kiiveri, H. and Speed, T. (1982). Structural analysis of multivariate data: A review. Sociological Methodology, Leinhardt, S. (ed.). Jossey-Bass, San Francisco.

Pearl, J. (1988). Probabilistic Reasoning in Intelligent Systems. Morgan and Kaufman, San Mateo.

Pearl, J. (1995). Causal diagrams for empirical research. Biometrika, 82, pp. 669-710.

Pearl, J. and Dechter, R. (1989). Learning structure from data: A survey. Proceedings COLT '89, 30-244.

Pearl, J., Geiger, D. and Verma, T. (1990). The logic of influence diagrams. Influence Diagrams, Belief Nets and Decision Analysis. R. Oliver and J. Smith, editors. John Wiley & Sons Ltd.

Pearl, J. and Verma, T. (1991). A theory of inferred causation. Principles of Knowledge Representation and Reasoning: Proceedings of the Second International Conference, Morgan Kaufmann, San Mateo, CA.

Pearl, J. and Verma, T. (1990). A Formal Theory of Inductive Causation. Technical Report R-155, Cognitive Systems Labratory, Computer Science Dept. UCLA.

Pearl, J. and Verma, T. (1987). The Logic of Representing Dependencies by Directed Graphs. Report CSD 870004, R-79-II, University of California at Los Angeles Cognitive Systems Laboratory.

Richardson, T. (1994). Properties of Cyclic Graphical Models. MS Thesis, Carnegie Mellon University.

Richardson (1995). A Polynomial-Time Algorithm for Deciding Markov Equivalence of Directed Cyclic Graphical Models, Technical Report PHIL-63, Philosophy Department, Carnegie Mellon University.

Reichenbach, H. (1956). The Direction of Time. Univ. of California Press, Berkeley, CA.

Salmon, W. (1980). Probabilistic causality. Pacific Philosophical Quarterly 61, 50-74.

Spirtes, P. (1994a). "Conditional Independence in Directed Cyclic Graphical Models for Feedback." Technical Report CMU-PHIL-54, Department of Philosophy, Carnegie Mellon University, Pittsburgh, PA.

Spirtes, P., Glymour, C., & Scheines, R. (1993). Causation, prediction, and search. Springer-Verlag Lecture Notes in Statistics 81,. Springer-Verlag, NY.

Spirtes, P., Richardson, T., Meek, C., Scheines, R., and Glymour, C. (1996). Using d-separation to calculate zero partial correlations in linear models with correlated errors. Technical Report CMU-PHIL-72, Dept. of Philosophy, Carnegie Mellon University, Pittsburgh, PA, 15213.

Suppes, P. (1970). A Probabilistic Theory of Causality. North-Holland, Amsterdam.

Brown P.F. et al. "Class-based N-gram Models of Natural Language". Computational Linguistics, Vol.18, No.4, pp.467-479, 1992.

Chinese Knowledge Information Processing Group (CKIP). " ". Technical Report. Institute of Information Science. Academia Sinica, Taiwan. 1989.

Chinese Knowledge Information Processing Group (CKIP). " ". Technical Report 93-05. Institute of Information Science. Academia Sinica, Taiwan. 1993.

Corazza A. et al. "Stochastic ContextFree Grammars for Island-Driven Probability Parsing". Proceedings of second International Workshop on Parsing Technologies (IWPT' 91), Cancun, Mexico, pp.210-217, 1991.

Fujisaki T. et al. "A Probabilistic Parsing Method for Sentence Disambiguation". Current Issues in Parsing Technology, pp.139-152, 1991.

Jelinek J.D. et al. "Basic Methods of Probabilistic Context Free Grammar". Research Report RC 16374(#72684), IBM Research Division, T.J.Watson Research Center, 1990.

Lari K. et al. "The Estimation of Stochastic Context-Free Grammars using the Inside-Outside Algorithm". Computer, Speech and Language, Vol. 4, pp.35-56, 1990.

Resnik P. "Probabilistic Tree-Adjoining Grammar as a Framework for Statistical Natural Language Processing". Proceedings of the 14th International Conference on Computational Linguistics, 1992.

Schabes Y. et al. "Stochastic Lexicalized Context-Free Grammar". Proceedings of the 3rd International Workshop on Parsing Technologies (IWPT'93), pp.257-266, Tilburg, Netherlands, 1993

Chapter 6 INFERENCE ABOUT INFERENCE

6.1 WEBPPL FUNCTION

6.1.1 WebPPL

WebPPL is a probabilistic programming language based on Javascript. WebPPL can be used most easily through webppl.org. It can also be installed locally and run from the command line.

The deterministic part of WebPPL is a subset of Javascript. Assignment is generally not allowed . This also means looping constructs are not available; we use functional programming instead to operate on arrays. The probabilistic aspects of WebPPL come from: distributions and sampling, marginal inference, and factors.

Models

Example using distributions and sample:

```
// We build a function that returns 'H' and 'T' with equal probability:
var coin = function(){
 var aDist = Bernoulli({p: .5});
 return sample(aDist) ? 'H' : 'T';
};
var flips = [coin(), coin(), coin()];
print("Some coin flips: " + flips);
```

Here is an example using factor and Infer, and illustrating stochastic recursion.

```
// Defining the geometric distribution as a stochastic recursion:
var geometric = function(p) {
 return bernoulli(p) ? 1 + geometric(p) : 1
};
```

```
// Favoring values around 10 via factor:
var skewedGeometric = function(){
  var g = geometric(0.5);
  factor(-Math.pow(10-g,2))
  return g
}
// Finding the marginal distribution via Infer:
var m = Infer({method: 'enumerate', maxExecutions: 100},
        skewedGeometric)
print('Histogram of skewed Geometric distribution');
viz.auto(m);
```

Here, the short form bernoulli(p) which is the same as sample(Bernoulli({p: p})). We can access deterministic functions from Math (and other js standard libraries) transparently. From the command line additional libraries can be required as packages. The viz package provides easy visualization methods.

Regression

Considering simple logistic regression model:

```
//some data:
var data = [{feature: -10, label: false},
        {feature: -5, label: false},
        {feature: 2, label: true},
        {feature: 6, label: true},
        {feature: 10, label: true}]
//a helper fn:
var sigmoid = function(x) {
  return 1 / (1 + Math.exp(-x))
}
var model = function() {
  //slope, intercept, and noise for the regression:
  var m = gaussian(0, 1)
  var b = gaussian(0, 1)
```

```
  var sigmaSquared = gamma(1, 1)
  //the regression model itself
  var labelDist = function(x) {
   var y = gaussian(m * x + b, sigmaSquared);
   return Bernoulli({p: sigmoid(y)});
  }
  //include observed data
  map(function(d){factor(labelDist(d.feature).score(d.label))},
     data)
  return sample(labelDist(0))
//  return labelDist(0).score(true) //alternate return to explore confidence
}
viz.auto(Infer({method: 'MCMC',
         samples: 10000,
         callbacks: [editor.MCMCProgress()]},
        model))
```

HMM

```
var transition = function(s) {
  return s ? flip(0.7) : flip(0.3)
}
var observe = function(s) {
  return s ? flip(0.9) : flip(0.1)
}
var hmm = function(n) {
  var prev = (n == 1) ? {states: [true], observations: []} : hmm(n - 1);
  var newState = transition(prev.states[prev.states.length - 1]);
  var newObs = observe(newState);
  return {
    states: prev.states.concat([newState]),
    observations: prev.observations.concat([newObs])
  };
```

```
}
var trueObservations = [false, false, false];
var stateDist = Infer({method: 'enumerate'},
  function() {
    var r = hmm(3);
    map2(function(o,d){condition(o===d)}, r.observations, trueObservations)
    return r.states;
  }
)
viz.hist(stateDist)
```

LDA

```
var nTopics = 2;
var vocabulary = ['zebra', 'wolf', 'html', 'css'];
var docs = {
  'doc1': 'zebra wolf zebra wolf zebra wolf html wolf zebra wolf'.split(' '),
  'doc2': 'html css html css html css html css html css'.split(' '),
  'doc3': 'zebra wolf zebra wolf zebra wolf zebra wolf zebra wolf'.split(' '),
  'doc4': 'html css html css html css html css html css'.split(' '),
  'doc5': 'zebra wolf zebra html zebra wolf zebra wolf zebra wolf'.split(' ')
};
var makeWordDist = function() { dirichlet(ones([vocabulary.length,1])) };
var makeTopicDist = function() { dirichlet(ones([nTopics,1])) };
var model = function() {
  var wordDistForTopic = repeat(nTopics, makeWordDist);
  mapObject(function(docname, words) {
    var topicDist = makeTopicDist();
    map(function(word) {
      var topic = discrete(topicDist);
      var wordDist = wordDistForTopic[topic];
      var wordID = vocabulary.indexOf(word);
      factor(Discrete({ps: wordDist}).score(wordID));
```

```
   }, words);
  }, docs);
  return map(function(v) { return _.toArray(v.data); }, wordDistForTopic);
};
var post = Infer({
  method: 'MCMC',
  burn: 10000,
  samples: 1,
  callbacks: [editor.MCMCProgress()]
}, model);
var samp = sample(post);
print("Topic 1:"); viz.bar(vocabulary, samp[0]);
print("Topic 2:"); viz.bar(vocabulary, samp[1]);
```

Bayesian inference by conditioning

The most important use of inference methods is for Bayesian inference. Here, our task is to infer the value of some unknown parameter by observing data that depends on the parameter. For example, if flipping three separate coins produce exactly two Heads, what is the probability that the first coin landed Heads?

To solve this in WebPPL, we can use Infer to enumerate all values for the random variables a, b and c. We use condition to constrain the sum of the variables. The result is a distribution representing the posterior distribution on the first variable a having value true (i.e. "Heads").

```
var twoHeads = Infer({
  model() {
    var a = flip(0.5);
    var b = flip(0.5);
    var c = flip(0.5);
    condition(a + b + c === 2);
    return a;
  }
});
```

```
print('Probability of first coin being Heads (given exactly two Heads) : ');
print(Math.exp(twoHeads.score(true)));
var moreThanTwoHeads = Infer({
 model() {
  var a = flip(0.5);
  var b = flip(0.5);
  var c = flip(0.5);
  condition(a + b + c >= 2);
  return a;
 }
});
print('\Probability of first coin being Heads (given at least two Heads): ');
print(Math.exp(moreThanTwoHeads.score(true)));
```

6.1.2 Inference

WebPPL is equipped with a variety of implementations of marginalization: the operation of normalizing a (sub-) computation to construct the marginal distribution on return values. These marginalization functions (inference functions) take a random computation represented as a function with no arguments and return the marginal distribution on return values.

Considering an example of simple binomial distribution where the number of times that three fair coin tosses will appears as heads:

```
var binomial = function() {
 var a = sample(Bernoulli({ p: 0.5 }))
 var b = sample(Bernoulli({ p: 0.5 }))
 var c = sample(Bernoulli({ p: 0.5 }))
 return a + b + c
}
var binomialDist = Infer({ model: binomial })
viz(binomialDist)
```

The distribution on return values from binomial() and sample(binomialDist) are the same – but binomialDist has already collapsed out the intermediate random choices to represent this distribution as a primitive.

What if we wanted to adjust the above binomial computation to favor executions in which a or b was true? The factor keyword re-weights an execution by adding the given number to the log-probability of that execution. For instance:

```
var funnyBinomial = function(){
  var a = sample(Bernoulli({ p: 0.5 }))
  var b = sample(Bernoulli({ p: 0.5 }))
  var c = sample(Bernoulli({ p: 0.5 }))
  factor( (a || b) ? 0 : -2)
  return a + b + c}
var funnyBinomialDist = Infer({ model: funnyBinomial })
viz(funnyBinomialDist)
```

It is easier to build useful models (condition on data) with factor. But factor by itself doesn't do anything – it interacts with marginalization functions that normalize the computation they are applied to. For this reason running a computation with factor in it at the top level and not inside a marginalization operator that result in error.

WebPPL has several inference methods, including enumerate and MCMC. These are all implemented by providing a co-routine that receives the current continuation at sample and factor statements.

6.2 PRELUDE: ASSEMBLY LINES

The query operator is an ordinary Church function, in the sense that it can occur anywhere that any other function can occur. In particular, we can construct a query with another query inside of it: this represents hypothetical inference about a hypothetical inference. Nested queries are particularly useful in modeling social cognition: reasoning about another agent, who is herself reasoning.

(There are some implementation-specific restrictions on nesting queries: the rejection-query operator can always be nested, while nesting mh-query requires special syntax.)

Prelude: Thinking About Assembly Lines

Imagine a factory where the widget-maker makes a stream of widgets, and the widget-tester removes the faulty ones. You don't know what tolerance the widget tester is set to, and wish to infer it. We can represent this as:

```
(define (sample)
 (rejection-query
```

```
;;this machine makes a widget -- which we'll just represent with a real number:
(define (widget-maker) (multinomial '(.2 .3 .4 .5 .6 .7 .8) '(.05 .1 .2 .3 .2 .1 .05)))
;;this machine tests widgets as they come out of the widget-maker, letting
;; through only those that pass threshold:
(define (next-good-widget)
 (define widget (widget-maker))
 (if (> widget threshold)
   widget
   (next-good-widget)))
;;but we don't know what threshold the widget tester is set to:
(define threshold (multinomial '(.3 .4 .5 .6 .7) '(.1 .2 .4 .2 .1)))
;;what is the threshold?
threshold
;;if we see this sequence of good widgets:
(equal? (repeat 3 next-good-widget)
     '(0.6 0.7 0.8))))
(hist (repeat 20 sample))
```

But notice that the definition of next-good-widget is exactly like the definition of rejection sampling! We can re-write this as a nested-query model:

```
(define (sample)
 (rejection-query
 ;;this machine makes a widget -- which we'll just represent with a real number:
 (define (widget-maker) (multinomial '(.2 .3 .4 .5 .6 .7 .8) '(.05 .1 .2 .3 .2 .1 .05)))
 ;;this machine tests widgets as they come out of the widget-maker, letting
 ;; through only those that pass threshold:
 (define (next-good-widget)
   (rejection-query
    (define widget (widget-maker))
    widget
    (> widget threshold)))
 ;;but we don't know what threshold the widget tester is set to:
```

```
(define threshold (multinomial '(.3 .4 .5 .6 .7) '(.1 .2 .4 .2 .1)))
;;what is the threshold?
threshold
;;if we see this sequence of good widgets:
(equal? (repeat 3 next-good-widget)
    '(0.6 0.7 0.8))))
(hist (repeat 20 sample))
```

Rather than thinking about the details inside the widget tester, we are now abstracting to represent that the machine correctly chooses a good widget (by some means).

6.3 SOCIAL COGNITION

In order to capture the intuitive theory of other people, considering principle of rationality which is an agent that tends to select actions which is expected to lead outcomes which satisfy the goals. For this, consider in Church by a query where an agent infers an action that leads to the goal being satisfied:

```
(define (choose-action goal? transition state)
 (query
 (define action (action-prior))
 action
 (goal? (transition state action))))
```

The function transition describes the outcome of taking a particular action in a particular state, the predicate goal? determines whether or not a state accomplishes the goal, the input state represents the current state of the world. The function action-prior used within choose-action represents an a-priori tendency towards certain actions.

For instance, imagine that Kanika walks up to a vending machine wishing to have a cookie. Imagine also that we know the mapping between buttons (potential actions) and foods (outcomes). We can then predict Kanika's action:

```
(define (choose-action goal? transition state)
 (rejection-query
 (define action (action-prior))
 action
 (goal? (transition state action))))
(define (action-prior) (uniform-draw '(a b)))
```

```
(define (vending-machine state action)
 (case action
  (('a) 'bagel)
  (('b) 'cookie)
  (else 'nothing)))
(define (have-cookie? object) (equal? object 'cookie))
(define (sample)
 (choose-action have-cookie? vending-machine 'state))
(hist (repeat 100 sample))
```

We see, unsurprisingly, that if Kanika wants a cookie, she will always press button b. (In defining the vending machine we have used a case statement instead of a long set of ifs.) In a world that is not quite so deterministic Kanika's actions will be more stochastic:

```
;;;fold: choose-action
(define (choose-action goal? transition state)
 (rejection-query
  (define action (action-prior))
  action
  (goal? (transition state action))))
;;;
(define (action-prior) (uniform-draw '(a b)))
(define (vending-machine state action)
 (case action
  (('a) (multinomial '(bagel cookie) '(0.9 0.1)))
  (('b) (multinomial '(bagel cookie) '(0.1 0.9)))
  (else 'nothing)))
(define (have-cookie? object) (equal? object 'cookie))
(define (sample)
 (choose-action have-cookie? vending-machine 'state))
(hist (repeat 100 sample))
```

Technically, this method of making a choices is not optimal, rather it is softmax optimal.

Goal Inference

Now imagine that we don't know Kanika's goal, so observing Kanika pressing button b query to infer her goal is applied ("inverse planning" as outer query "inverts" query in choose action).

```
;;;fold: choose-action
(define (choose-action goal? transition state)
 (rejection-query
  (define action (action-prior))
  action
  (goal? (transition state action))))
;;;
(define (action-prior) (uniform-draw '(a b)))
(define (vending-machine state action)
 (case action
     (('a) (multinomial '(bagel cookie) '(0.9 0.1)))
     (('b) (multinomial '(bagel cookie) '(0.1 0.9)))
     (else 'nothing)))
(define (sample)
 (rejection-query
  (define goal-food (uniform-draw '(bagel cookie)))
  (define goal? (lambda (outcome) (equal? outcome goal-food)))
  goal-food
  (equal? (choose-action goal? vending-machine 'state) 'b)))
(hist (repeat 100 sample))
```

Now let's imagine a more ambiguous case: button b is "broken" and will (uniformly) randomly result in a food from the machine. If we see Kanika press button b, what goal is she most likely to have?

```
;;;fold: choose-action
(define (choose-action goal? transition state)
 (rejection-query
  (define action (action-prior))
  action
```

```
(goal? (transition state action))))
;;;
(define (action-prior) (uniform-draw '(a b)))
(define (vending-machine state action)
 (case action
     (('a) (multinomial '(bagel cookie) '(0.9 0.1)))
     (('b) (multinomial '(bagel cookie) '(0.5 0.5)))
     (else 'nothing)))
(define (sample)
 (rejection-query
  (define goal-food (uniform-draw '(bagel cookie)))
  (define goal? (lambda (outcome) (equal? outcome goal-food)))
  goal-food
(equal? (choose-action goal? vending-machine 'state) 'b)))
hist (repeat 100 sample))
```

Despite the fact that button b is equally likely to result in either bagel or cookie, we have inferred that sally probably wants a cookie. This is a result of the inference implicitly taking into account the counterfactual alternatives: if Kanika had wanted a bagel, she would have likely pressed button a. The inner query takes these alternatives into account, adjusting the probability of the observed action based on alternative goals.

Preferences

If we have some prior knowledge about Kanika's preferences (goals she likely to have) we can incorporate this immediately into the prior over goals (which above was uniform).

A more interesting situation is when we believe that Kanika has some preferences, but we don't know what they are. We capture this by adding a higher level prior (a uniform) over preferences. Using this we can learn about Kanika's preferences from her actions: after seeing Kanika press button b several times, what will we expect her to want the next time?

```
;;;fold: choose-action
(define (choose-action goal? transition state)
 (rejection-query
```

```
    (define action (action-prior))
    action
    (goal? (transition state action))))
  ;;;
  (define (action-prior) (uniform-draw '(a b)))
  (define (vending-machine state action)
   (case action
      (('a) (multinomial '(bagel cookie) '(0.9 0.1)))
      (('b) (multinomial '(bagel cookie) '(0.1 0.9)))
      (else 'nothing)))
  (define (sample)
   (rejection-query
    (define food-preferences (uniform 0 1))
    (define (goal-food-prior) (if (flip food-preferences) 'bagel 'cookie))
    (define (make-goal food)
     (lambda (outcome) (equal? outcome food)))
    (goal-food-prior)
     (and (equal? (choose-action (make-goal (goal-food-prior)) vending-machine
'state) 'b)
          (equal? (choose-action (make-goal (goal-food-prior)) vending-machine
'state) 'b)
          (equal? (choose-action (make-goal (goal-food-prior)) vending-machine
'state) 'b))))
  (hist (repeat 100 sample))
```

Here, try varying with amount and kind of evidence. If Kanika says "I want a cookie" (so you have directly observed her goal) how much evidence does that give you about her preferences, relative to observing her actions?

In the above preference inference, it is extremely important that sally could have taken a different action if she had a different preference (i.e. she could have pressed button a if she preferred to have a bagel). In the program below we have set up a situation in which both actions lead to cookie most of the time:

```
;;;fold: choose-action
(define (choose-action goal? transition state)
```

```
(rejection-query
 (define action (action-prior))
 action
 (goal? (transition state action))))
;;;
(define (action-prior) (uniform-draw '(a b)))
(define (vending-machine state action)
 (case action
    (('a) (multinomial '(bagel cookie) '(0.1 0.9)))
    (('b) (multinomial '(bagel cookie) '(0.1 0.9)))
    (else 'nothing)))
(define (sample)
 (rejection-query
 (define food-preferences (uniform 0 1))
 (define (goal-food-prior) (if (flip food-preferences) 'bagel 'cookie))
 (define (make-goal food)
  (lambda (outcome) (equal? outcome food)))
 (goal-food-prior)
  (and (equal? (choose-action (make-goal (goal-food-prior)) vending-machine
'state) 'b)
         (equal? (choose-action (make-goal (goal-food-prior)) vending-machine
'state) 'b)
         (equal? (choose-action (make-goal (goal-food-prior)) vending-machine
'state) 'b))))
(hist (repeat 100 sample))
```

6.4 EPISTEMIC STATES OF MODEL

6.4.1 Epistemic States

In the above models of goal and preference inference, we have assumed that the structure of the world were common knowledge as they were non-random constructs used by both the agent selecting actions and the observer interpreting these actions. What if the observer doesn't know how exactly the vending machine works, but think that however it works Kanika knows? We can capture this by placing uncertainty on the vending machine, inside the overall query but "outside" of agent inference:

```
;;;fold: choose-action
(define (choose-action goal? transition state)
  (rejection-query
   (define action (action-prior))
   action
   (goal? (transition state action))))
;;;
(define (action-prior) (uniform-draw '(a b)))
(define (make-vending-machine a-effects b-effects)
  (lambda (state action)
    (case action
        (('a) (multinomial '(bagel cookie) a-effects))
        (('b) (multinomial '(bagel cookie) b-effects))
        (else 'nothing))))
(define (sample)
  (rejection-query
   (define a-effects (dirichlet '(1 1)))
   (define b-effects (dirichlet '(1 1)))
   (define vending-machine (make-vending-machine a-effects b-effects))
   (define goal-food (uniform-draw '(bagel cookie)))
   (define goal? (lambda (outcome) (equal? outcome goal-food)))
   (second b-effects)
   (and (equal? goal-food 'cookie)
       (equal? (choose-action goal? vending-machine 'state) 'b) )))
(define samples (repeat 500 sample))
(display (list "mean:" (mean samples)))
(hist samples "Probability that b gives cookie")
```

It is seen that, we have conditioned on Kanika wanting the cookie and selecting to press button b. Thus, we have no direct evidence of the effects of pressing the buttons on the machine. What happens if you condition instead on the action and outcome, but not the intentional choice of this outcome (that is, change the condition to (equal? (vending-machine 'state 'b) 'cookie))?

Now imagine a vending machine that has only one button, but it can be pressed many times. We don't know what the machine will do in response to a given button sequence. We do know that pressing more buttons is less a priori likely.

```
;;;fold: choose-action
(define (choose-action goal? transition state)
 (rejection-query
  (define action (action-prior))
  action
  (goal? (transition state action))))
;;;
(define (action-prior) (if (flip 0.7) '(a) (pair 'a (action-prior))))
(define (sample)
 (rejection-query
  (define buttons->outcome-probs (mem (lambda (buttons) (dirichlet '(1 1)))))
  (define (vending-machine state action)
   (multinomial '(bagel cookie) (buttons->outcome-probs action)))
  (define goal-food (uniform-draw '(bagel cookie)))
  (define goal? (lambda (outcome) (equal? outcome goal-food)))
  (list (second (buttons->outcome-probs '(a a)))
      (second (buttons->outcome-probs '(a))))
  (and (equal? goal-food 'cookie)
     (equal? (choose-action goal? vending-machine 'state) '(a a)) )
  ))
(define samples (repeat 500 sample))
(hist (map first samples) "Probability that (a a) gives cookie")
(hist (map second samples) "Probability that (a) gives cookie")
```

On comparing the inferences, it shows that when Kanika presses the button twice to those if she only presses the button once. Why can we draw much stronger inferences about the machine when Kanika chooses to press the button twice? When Kanika press the button twice, she could have done "easy" action of pressing the button just once. Since she doesn't, a single press must have been unlikely to result in a cookie. This is an example of the principle of efficiency as all other things being equal, an agent will take the actions that require least effort.

Here, Kanika has an infinite space of possible actions but, because these actions are constructed by a recursive generative process, simpler actions are a priori more likely.

In these examples we have seen two important assumptions combining to allow us to infer something about the world from the indirect evidence of an agents actions. The first assumption is the principle of rational action, the second is an assumption of knowledgeability as we assumed that Kanika knows how the machine works, though we don't. Thus inference about inference, can be a powerful way to learn what others already know, by observing their actions.

Joint Inference about Beliefs and Desires

In case of social cognition, a joint inferences is consided of two kinds of mental states: agents' beliefs about world and their desires, goals or preferences. Also from an example of joint inference in vending machine scenario, when a condition on two observations such that Kanika presses the button twice which results a cookie, in such case, assuming that she knows how the machine works, we jointly infer that she wanted a cookie, that pressing the button twice is likely to give a cookie, and that pressing the button once is unlikely to give a cookie.

```
;;;fold: choose-action
(define (choose-action goal? transition state)
 (rejection-query
  (define action (action-prior))
  action
  (goal? (transition state action))))
;;;
(define (action-prior) (if (flip 0.7) '(a) (pair 'a (action-prior))))
(define (sample)
 (rejection-query
  (define buttons->outcome-probs (mem (lambda (buttons) (dirichlet '(1 1)))))
  (define (vending-machine state action)
   (multinomial '(bagel cookie) (buttons->outcome-probs action)))
  (define goal-food (uniform-draw '(bagel cookie)))
  (define goal? (lambda (outcome) (equal? outcome goal-food)))
```

```
(list (second (buttons->outcome-probs '(a a)))
    (second (buttons->outcome-probs '(a)))
    goal-food)
(and (equal? (vending-machine 'state '(a a)) 'cookie)
    (equal? (choose-action goal? vending-machine 'state) '(a a)) )
))
(define samples (repeat 500 sample))
(hist (map first samples) "Probability that (a a) gives cookie")
(hist (map second samples) "Probability that (a) gives cookie")
(hist (map third samples) "Goal probabilities")
```

Notice the U-shaped distribution for the effect of pressing the button just once. Without any direct evidence about what happens when the button is pressed just once, we can infer that it probably won't give a cookie as her aim is to have been a cookie but she didn't press the button just once---but there is a small chance that her goal was actually not to get a cookie, in which case pressing the button once could result in a cookie. This very complex inference comes naturally from joint inference of goals and knowledge.

6.5 COMMUNICATION AND LANGUAGE

Imagine playing the following two-player game. On each round the "teacher" pulls a die from a bag of weighted dice, and has to communicate to the "learner" which die it is. However, the teacher may only communicate by giving the learner examples: showing them faces of the die.

We can formalize the inference of the teacher in choosing the examples to give by assuming that the goal of the teacher is to successfully teach the hypothesis to select examples such that the learner will infer the intended hypothesis:

```
(define (teacher die)
 (query
 (define side (side-prior))
 side
 (equal? die (learner side))))
```

The goal of the learner is to infer the correct hypothesis, given that the teacher chose to give these examples:

```
(define (learner side)
 (query
```

```
(define die (die-prior))
die
(equal? side (teacher die))))
```

Such pair of mutually recursive functions shows that a teacher selecting examples or learner inferring a hypothesis, while thinking about each other. To avoid such infinite recursion say that eventually the learner will just assume that the teacher rolled the die and showed the side that came up:

```
(define (teacher die depth)
 (query
  (define side (side-prior))
  side
  (equal? die (learner side depth))))
(define (learner side depth)
 (query
  (define die (die-prior))
  die
  (if (= depth 0)
     (equal? side (roll die))
     (equal? side (teacher die (- depth 1))))))
```

To make this concrete, assume that there are two dice, A and B, which each have three sides (red, green, blue) that have weights like so:

Which hypothesis will the learner infer if the teacher shows the green side?

```
(define (teacher die depth)
 (rejection-query
  (define side (side-prior))
  side
  (equal? die (learner side depth))))
(define (learner side depth)
 (rejection-query
  (define die (die-prior))
  die
  (if (= depth 0)
```

```
    (equal? side (roll die))
    (equal? side (teacher die (- depth 1))))))
(define (die->probs die)
 (case die
  (('A) '(0.0 0.2 0.8))
  (('B) '(0.1 0.3 0.6))
  (else 'uhoh)))
(define (side-prior) (uniform-draw '(red green blue)))
(define (die-prior) (if (flip) 'A 'B))
(define (roll die) (multinomial '(red green blue) (die->probs die)))
(define depth 0)
(learner 'green depth)
```

If we run this with recursion depth 0---that is a learner that does probabilistic inference without thinking about the teacher thinking---we find the learner infers hypothesis B most of the time (about 60% of the time). This is the same as using the "strong sampling" assumption: the learner infers B because B is more likely to have landed on side 2. However, if we increase the recursion depth we find this reverses: the learner infers B only about 40% of the time. Now die A becomes the better inference, because "if the teacher had meant to communicate B, they would have shown the red side because that can never come from A."

6.5.1 Communicating with Words

Unlike the situation above, in which concrete examples were given from teacher to student, words in natural language denote more abstract concepts. However, we can use almost the same setup to reason about speakers and listeners communicating with words, if we assume that sentences have literal meanings, which anchor sentences to possible worlds. We assume for simplicity that the meaning of sentences are truth-functional: that each sentence corresponds to a function from states of the world to true/false.

From this, the speaker select what to say in order to lead listener to infer correct state:

```
(define (speaker state)
 (query
  (define words (sentence-prior))
  words
```

```
    (equal? state (listener words))))
```

The listener does an inference of the state of the world given that the speaker chose to say what they did:

```
(define (listener words)
 (query
  (define state (state-prior))
  state
  (equal? words (speaker state))))
```

However this suffers from two flaws: the recursion never halts, and the literal meaning has not been used. We slightly modify the listener function such that the listener either assumes that the literal meaning of the sentence is true, or figures out what the speaker must have meant given that they chose to say what they said:

```
(define (listener words)
 (query
  (define state (state-prior))
  state
  (if (flip literal-prob)
     (words state)
     (equal? words (speaker state)))))
```

Here the probability literal-prob controls the expected depth of recursion. Another ways to bound the depth of recursion is with an explicit depth argument. Using a standard, truth-functional, formulation for meaning of sentence where each sentence shows a predicate on world states. Hence the literal meaning of sentence shows the worlds where sentence is satisfied. Further the literal meaning of a sentence involves sorting of thing by transforming a prior over worlds into a posterior.

Also, to motivate this view, meanings are belief update operations and as right way to update beliefs coded as distributions is conditioning shows conditioning statements. Of course, the deterministic predicates can be immediately relaxed to probabilistic truth functions, that assign a probability to each world. This might be useful if we want to allow exceptions.

6.5.2 Example: Scalar Implicature

Let us imagine a situation in which there are three plants which may or may not have sprouted. We imagine that there are three sentences that the speaker could say, “All of the plants have sprouted”, “Some of the plants have sprouted”, or "None of the plants have sprouted". For simplicity we represent the worlds by the number of sprouted plants (0, 1, 2, or 3) and take a uniform prior over worlds. Using the above representation for communicating with words (with an explicit depth argument):

```
(define (state-prior) (uniform-draw '(0 1 2 3)))
(define (sentence-prior) (uniform-draw (list all-sprouted some-sprouted none-
sprouted)))
(define (all-sprouted state) (= 3 state))
(define (some-sprouted state) (< 0 state))
(define (none-sprouted state) (= 0 state))
(define (speaker state depth)
 (rejection-query
  (define words (sentence-prior))
  words
  (equal? state (listener words depth))))
(define (listener words depth)
 (rejection-query
  (define state (state-prior))
  state
  (if (= depth 0)
     (words state)
     (equal? words (speaker state (- depth 1))))))
(define depth 1)
(hist (repeat 300 (lambda () (listener some-sprouted depth))))
```

We see that if the listener hears "some" the probability of three out of three is low, even though the basic meaning of "some" is equally consistent with 3/3, 1/3, and 2/3. This is called the "some but not all" implicature.

Planning

Single step, goal-based decision problem.

```
(define (choose-action goal? transition state)
 (rejection-query
  (define action (action-prior))
  action
```

```
(goal? (transition state action))))
(define (action-prior) (uniform-draw '(a b)))
(define (vending-machine state action)
 (case action
  (('a) 'bagel)
  (('b) 'cookie)
  (else 'nothing)))
(define (have-cookie? object) (equal? object 'cookie))
(choose-action have-cookie? vending-machine 'state)
```

Single step, utility-based decision problem.

```
;;;fold:
(define (iota count start step)
 (if (equal? count 0)
   '()
   (pair start (iota (- count 1) (+ start step) step))))
(define (sample-discrete weights) (multinomial (iota (length weights) 0 1) weights))
;;;
(define (match utility)
 (sample-discrete (normalize utility)))
(define (softmax utility b)
 (sample-discrete (normalize (map (lambda (x) (exp (* b x))) utility))))
(define (normalize lst)
 (let ((lst-sum (sum lst)))
  (map (lambda (x) (/ x lst-sum)) lst)))
(define utility-function '(1 2 3 4 5))
(define b 1)
(hist (repeat 1000 (lambda () (match utility-function))) "matching")
(hist (repeat 1000 (lambda () (softmax utility-function 1))) "softmax")
```

Multi-step, suboptimal planning as inference

```
;;;fold:
```

```
(define (last l)
  (cond ((null? (rest l)) (first l))
      (else (last (rest l)))))
;;;
; states have format (pair world-state agent-position)
(define (sample-action trans start-state goal? ending)
 (rejection-query
  (define first-action (action-prior))
  (define state-action-seq (rollout trans (pair start-state first-action) ending))
  state-action-seq
  (goal? state-action-seq)))
;; input and output are state-action pairs so we can run rollout
(define (transition state-action)
 (pair (forward-model state-action) (action-prior)))
;; modified version of unfold from paper, renamed rollout
(define (rollout next init end)
 (if (end init)
   (list init)
   (append (list init) (rollout next (next init) end))))
;; red-light green-light example
(define cheat-det .9)
(define (forward-model state-action)
 (pair
  (if (flip 0.5) 'red-light 'green-light)
  (let ((light (first (first state-action)))
      (position (rest (first state-action)))
      (action (rest state-action)))
   (if (eq? action 'go)
    (if (and (eq? light 'red-light)
         (flip cheat-det))
     0
```

```
        (+ position 1))
       position))))
(define discount .95)
(define (ending? symbol) (flip (- 1 discount)))
(define goal-pos 5)
(define (goal-function state-action-seq)
  (> (rest (first (last state-action-seq))) goal-pos))
(define (action-prior) (if (flip 0.5) 'go 'stop))
;; testing
(sample-action transition (pair 'green-light 1) goal-function ending?)
```

6.6 ALGORITHMS FOR INFERENCE

6.6.1 Variable Elimination

class pgmpy.inference.ExactInference.VariableElimination(model)

induced_graph(elimination_order)

Returns the induced graph formed by running Variable Elimination on the network.

Parameters:

elimination_order: list, array like

List of variables in the order in which they are to be eliminated.

Examples

```
import numpy as np
import pandas as pd
from pgmpy.models import BayesianModel
from pgmpy.inference import VariableElimination
values = pd.DataFrame(np.random.randint(low=0, high=2, size=(1000, 5)),
...                   columns=['A', 'B', 'C', 'D', 'E'])
model = BayesianModel([('A', 'B'), ('C', 'B'), ('C', 'D'), ('B', 'E')])
model.fit(values)
inference = VariableElimination(model)
inference.induced_graph(['C', 'D', 'A', 'B', 'E'])
<networkx.classes.graph.Graph at 0x7f34ac8c5160>
```

induced_width(elimination_order)

Returns the width (integer) of the induced graph formed by running Variable Elimination on the network. The width is the defined as the number of nodes in the largest clique in the graph minus 1.

Parameters:

elimination_order: list, array like

List of variables in the order in which they are to be eliminated.

Examples

```
import numpy as np
import pandas as pd
from pgmpy.models import BayesianModel
from pgmpy.inference import VariableElimination
values = pd.DataFrame(np.random.randint(low=0, high=2, size=(1000, 5)),
...                   columns=['A', 'B', 'C', 'D', 'E'])
model = BayesianModel([('A', 'B'), ('C', 'B'), ('C', 'D'), ('B', 'E')])
model.fit(values)
inference = VariableElimination(model)
inference.induced_width(['C', 'D', 'A', 'B', 'E'])
3
```

map_query(variables=None, evidence=None, elimination_order=None)[source]

Computes the MAP Query over the variables given the evidence.

Parameters:

variables: list

list of variables over which we want to compute the max-marginal.

evidence: dict

a dict key, value pair as {var: state_of_var_observed} None if no evidence

elimination_order: list

order of variable eliminations (if nothing is provided) order is computed automatically

Examples

```
from pgmpy.inference import VariableElimination
from pgmpy.models import BayesianModel
import numpy as np
```

import pandas as pd

values = pd.DataFrame(np.random.randint(low=0, high=2, size=(1000, 5)),

... columns=['A', 'B', 'C', 'D', 'E'])

model = BayesianModel([('A', 'B'), ('C', 'B'), ('C', 'D'), ('B', 'E')])

model.fit(values)

inference = VariableElimination(model)

phi_query = inference.map_query(['A', 'B'])

max_marginal(variables=None, evidence=None, elimination_order=None)

Computes the max-marginal over the variables given the evidence.

Parameters:

variables: list

list of variables over which we want to compute the max-marginal.

evidence: dict

a dict key, value pair as {var: state_of_var_observed} None if no evidence

elimination_order: list

order of variable eliminations (if nothing is provided) order is computed automatically

Examples

import numpy as np

import pandas as pd

from pgmpy.models import BayesianModel

from pgmpy.inference import VariableElimination

values = pd.DataFrame(np.random.randint(low=0, high=2, size=(1000, 5)),

... columns=['A', 'B', 'C', 'D', 'E'])

model = BayesianModel([('A', 'B'), ('C', 'B'), ('C', 'D'), ('B', 'E')])

model.fit(values)

inference = VariableElimination(model)

phi_query = inference.max_marginal(['A', 'B'])

query(variables, evidence=None, elimination_order=None)

Parameters:

variables: list

list of variables for which you want to compute the probability

evidence: dict

a dict key, value pair as {var: state_of_var_observed} None if no evidence

elimination_order: list

order of variable eliminations (if nothing is provided) order is computed automatically

Examples

```
from pgmpy.inference import VariableElimination
from pgmpy.models import BayesianModel
import numpy as np
import pandas as pd
values = pd.DataFrame(np.random.randint(low=0, high=2, size=(1000, 5)),
...                   columns=['A', 'B', 'C', 'D', 'E'])
model = BayesianModel([('A', 'B'), ('C', 'B'), ('C', 'D'), ('B', 'E')])
model.fit(values)
inference = VariableElimination(model)
phi_query = inference.query(['A', 'B'])
```

6.6.2 Belief Propagation

class pgmpy.inference.ExactInference.BeliefPropagation(model)

Class for performing inference using Belief Propagation method.

Creates a Junction Tree or Clique Tree (JunctionTree class) for the input probabilistic graphical model and performs calibration of the junction tree so formed using belief propagation.

Parameters:

model: BayesianModel, MarkovModel, FactorGraph, JunctionTree

model for which inference is to performed

calibrate()

Calibration using belief propagation in junction tree or clique tree.

Examples

```
from pgmpy.models import BayesianModel
from pgmpy.factors.discrete import TabularCPD
from pgmpy.inference import BeliefPropagation
```

```
G = BayesianModel([('diff', 'grade'), ('intel', 'grade'),
...               ('intel', 'SAT'), ('grade', 'letter')])
diff_cpd = TabularCPD('diff', 2, [[0.2], [0.8]])
intel_cpd = TabularCPD('intel', 3, [[0.5], [0.3], [0.2]])
grade_cpd = TabularCPD('grade', 3,
...                [[0.1, 0.1, 0.1, 0.1, 0.1, 0.1],
...                 [0.1, 0.1, 0.1, 0.1, 0.1, 0.1],
...                 [0.8, 0.8, 0.8, 0.8, 0.8, 0.8]],
...                evidence=['diff', 'intel'],
...                evidence_card=[2, 3])
sat_cpd = TabularCPD('SAT', 2,
...               [[0.1, 0.2, 0.7],
...                [0.9, 0.8, 0.3]],
...               evidence=['intel'], evidence_card=[3])
letter_cpd = TabularCPD('letter', 2,
...                [[0.1, 0.4, 0.8],
...                 [0.9, 0.6, 0.2]],
...                evidence=['grade'], evidence_card=[3])
G.add_cpds(diff_cpd, intel_cpd, grade_cpd, sat_cpd, letter_cpd)
bp = BeliefPropagation(G)
bp.calibrate()
```

get_clique_beliefs()

Returns clique beliefs. Should be called after the clique tree (or junction tree) is calibrated.

get_cliques()

Returns cliques used for belief propagation.

get_sepset_beliefs()[source]

Returns sepset beliefs. Should be called after clique tree (or junction tree) is calibrated.

map_query(variables=None, evidence=None)

MAP Query method using belief propagation.

Parameters:

variables: list

list of variables for which you want to compute the probability

evidence: dict

a dict key, value pair as {var: state_of_var_observed} None if no evidence

Examples

```
from pgmpy.factors.discrete import TabularCPD
from pgmpy.models import BayesianModel
from pgmpy.inference import BeliefPropagation
bayesian_model = BayesianModel([('A', 'J'), ('R', 'J'), ('J', 'Q'),
...                    ('J', 'L'), ('G', 'L')])
cpd_a = TabularCPD('A', 2, [[0.2], [0.8]])
cpd_r = TabularCPD('R', 2, [[0.4], [0.6]])
cpd_j = TabularCPD('J', 2,
...            [[0.9, 0.6, 0.7, 0.1],
...             [0.1, 0.4, 0.3, 0.9]],
...            ['R', 'A'], [2, 2])
cpd_q = TabularCPD('Q', 2,
...            [[0.9, 0.2],
...             [0.1, 0.8]],
...            ['J'], [2])
cpd_l = TabularCPD('L', 2,
...            [[0.9, 0.45, 0.8, 0.1],
...             [0.1, 0.55, 0.2, 0.9]],
...            ['G', 'J'], [2, 2])
cpd_g = TabularCPD('G', 2, [[0.6], [0.4]])
bayesian_model.add_cpds(cpd_a, cpd_r, cpd_j, cpd_q, cpd_l, cpd_g)
belief_propagation = BeliefPropagation(bayesian_model)
belief_propagation.map_query(variables=['J', 'Q'],
...                    evidence={'A': 0, 'R': 0, 'G': 0, 'L': 1})
```

max_calibrate()

Max-calibration of the junction tree using belief propagation.

Examples

```
from pgmpy.models import BayesianModel
from pgmpy.factors.discrete import TabularCPD
from pgmpy.inference import BeliefPropagation
G = BayesianModel([('diff', 'grade'), ('intel', 'grade'),
...             ('intel', 'SAT'), ('grade', 'letter')])
diff_cpd = TabularCPD('diff', 2, [[0.2], [0.8]])
intel_cpd = TabularCPD('intel', 3, [[0.5], [0.3], [0.2]])
grade_cpd = TabularCPD('grade', 3,
...                 [[0.1, 0.1, 0.1, 0.1, 0.1, 0.1],
...                  [0.1, 0.1, 0.1, 0.1, 0.1, 0.1],
...                  [0.8, 0.8, 0.8, 0.8, 0.8, 0.8]],
...                 evidence=['diff', 'intel'],
...                 evidence_card=[2, 3])
sat_cpd = TabularCPD('SAT', 2,
...                 [[0.1, 0.2, 0.7],
...                  [0.9, 0.8, 0.3]],
...                 evidence=['intel'], evidence_card=[3])
letter_cpd = TabularCPD('letter', 2,
...                 [[0.1, 0.4, 0.8],
...                  [0.9, 0.6, 0.2]],
...                 evidence=['grade'], evidence_card=[3])
G.add_cpds(diff_cpd, intel_cpd, grade_cpd, sat_cpd, letter_cpd)
bp = BeliefPropagation(G)
bp.max_calibrate()
```

query(variables, evidence=None)

Query method using belief propagation.

Parameters:

variables: list

list of variables for which you want to compute the probability

evidence: dict

a dict key, value pair as {var: state_of_var_observed} None if no evidence

Examples

```
from pgmpy.factors.discrete import TabularCPD
from pgmpy.models import BayesianModel
from pgmpy.inference import BeliefPropagation
bayesian_model = BayesianModel([('A', 'J'), ('R', 'J'), ('J', 'Q'),
...                             ('J', 'L'), ('G', 'L')])
cpd_a = TabularCPD('A', 2, [[0.2], [0.8]])
cpd_r = TabularCPD('R', 2, [[0.4], [0.6]])
cpd_j = TabularCPD('J', 2,
...                [[0.9, 0.6, 0.7, 0.1],
...                 [0.1, 0.4, 0.3, 0.9]],
...                ['R', 'A'], [2, 2])
cpd_q = TabularCPD('Q', 2,
...                [[0.9, 0.2],
...                 [0.1, 0.8]],
...                ['J'], [2])
cpd_l = TabularCPD('L', 2,
...                [[0.9, 0.45, 0.8, 0.1],
...                 [0.1, 0.55, 0.2, 0.9]],
...                ['G', 'J'], [2, 2])
cpd_g = TabularCPD('G', 2, [[0.6], [0.4]])
bayesian_model.add_cpds(cpd_a, cpd_r, cpd_j, cpd_q, cpd_l, cpd_g)
belief_propagation = BeliefPropagation(bayesian_model)
belief_propagation.query(variables=['J', 'Q'],
...                      evidence={'A': 0, 'R': 0, 'G': 0, 'L': 1})
```

MPLP

class pgmpy.inference.mplp.Mplp(model)

Class for performing approximate inference using Max-Product Linear Programming method.

We derive message passing updates that result in monotone decrease of the dual of the MAP LP Relaxation.

Parameters:

model: MarkovModel for which inference is to be performed.

Examples

```
import numpy as np
from pgmpy.models import MarkovModel
from pgmpy.inference import Mplp
from pgmpy.factors.discrete import DiscreteFactor
student = MarkovModel()
student.add_edges_from([('A', 'B'), ('B', 'C'), ('C', 'D'), ('E', 'F')])
factor_a = DiscreteFactor(['A'], cardinality=[2], values=np.array([0.54577,
1.8323]))
factor_b = DiscreteFactor(['B'], cardinality=[2], values=np.array([0.93894,
1.065]))
factor_c = DiscreteFactor(['C'], cardinality=[2], values=np.array([0.89205,
1.121]))
factor_d = DiscreteFactor(['D'], cardinality=[2], values=np.array([0.56292,
1.7765]))
factor_e = DiscreteFactor(['E'], cardinality=[2], values=np.array([0.47117,
2.1224]))
factor_f = DiscreteFactor(['F'], cardinality=[2], values=np.array([1.5093,
0.66257]))
factor_a_b = DiscreteFactor(['A', 'B'], cardinality=[2, 2],
... values=np.array([1.3207, 0.75717, 0.75717, 1.3207]))
factor_b_c = DiscreteFactor(['B', 'C'], cardinality=[2, 2],
... values=np.array([0.00024189, 4134.2, 4134.2, 0.00024189]))
factor_c_d = DiscreteFactor(['C', 'D'], cardinality=[2, 2],
... values=np.array([0.0043227, 231.34, 231.34, 0.0043227]))
factor_d_e = DiscreteFactor(['E', 'F'], cardinality=[2, 2],
... values=np.array([31.228, 0.032023, 0.032023, 31.228]))
student.add_factors(factor_a, factor_b, factor_c, factor_d, factor_e, factor_f,
factor_a_b,
... factor_b_c, factor_c_d, factor_d_e)
```

mplp = Mplp(student)

class Cluster(intersection_set_variables, cluster_potential)

Inner class for representing a cluster. A cluster is a subset of variables.

Parameters:

set_of_variables: tuple

This is the set of variables that form the cluster.

intersection_set_variables: set containing frozensets.

collection of intersection of all pairs of cluster variables.

For eg: {{C_1 cap C_2}, {C_2 cap C_3}, {C_3 cap C_1} } for clusters C_1, C_2 & C_3.

cluster_potential: DiscreteFactor

Each cluster has a initial probability distribution provided beforehand.

Mplp.find_triangles()

Finds all the triangles present in the given model

Examples

```
from pgmpy.models import MarkovModel
from pgmpy.factors.discrete import DiscreteFactor
from pgmpy.inference import Mplp
mm = MarkovModel()
mm.add_nodes_from(['x1', 'x2', 'x3', 'x4', 'x5', 'x6', 'x7'])
mm.add_edges_from([('x1', 'x3'), ('x1', 'x4'), ('x2', 'x4'),
...               ('x2', 'x5'), ('x3', 'x6'), ('x4', 'x6'),
...               ('x4', 'x7'), ('x5', 'x7')])
phi = [DiscreteFactor(edge, [2, 2], np.random.rand(4)) for edge in mm.edges()]
mm.add_factors(*phi)
mplp = Mplp(mm)
mplp.find_triangles()
```

Mplp.get_integrality_gap()

Returns the integrality gap of the current state of the Mplp algorithm. The lesser it is, the closer we are towards the exact solution.

Mplp.map_query(init_iter=1000, later_iter=20, dual_threshold=0.0002, integrality_gap_threshold=0.0002, tighten_triplet=True, max_triplets=5, max_iterations=100, prolong=False)

MAP query method using Max Product LP method. This returns the best assignment of the nodes in the form of a dictionary.

Parameters:

init_iter: integer

Number of maximum iterations that we want MPLP to run for the first time.

later_iter: integer

Number of maximum iterations that we want MPLP to run for later iterations

dual_threshold: double

This sets the minimum width between the dual objective decrements. If the decrement is lesser than the threshold, then that means we have stuck on a local minima.

integrality_gap_threshold: double

This sets the threshold for the integrality gap below which we say that the solution is satisfactory.

tighten_triplet: bool

set whether to use triplets as clusters or not.

max_triplets: integer

Set the maximum number of triplets that can be added at once.

max_iterations: integer

Maximum number of times we tighten the relaxation. Used only when tighten_triplet is set True.

prolong: bool

If set False: The moment we exhaust of all the triplets the tightening stops. If set True: The tightening will be performed max_iterations number of times irrespective of the

triplets.

Examples

```
>>> from pgmpy.models import MarkovModel
>>> from pgmpy.factors.discrete import DiscreteFactor
>>> from pgmpy.inference import Mplp
>>> import numpy as np
>>> student = MarkovModel()
>>> student.add_edges_from([('A', 'B'), ('B', 'C'), ('C', 'D'), ('E', 'F')])
```

```
>>> factor_a = DiscreteFactor(['A'], cardinality=[2], values=np.array([0.54577,
1.8323]))
>>> factor_b = DiscreteFactor(['B'], cardinality=[2], values=np.array([0.93894,
1.065]))
>>> factor_c = DiscreteFactor(['C'], cardinality=[2], values=np.array([0.89205,
1.121]))
>>> factor_d = DiscreteFactor(['D'], cardinality=[2], values=np.array([0.56292,
1.7765]))
>>> factor_e = DiscreteFactor(['E'], cardinality=[2], values=np.array([0.47117,
2.1224]))
>>> factor_f = DiscreteFactor(['F'], cardinality=[2], values=np.array([1.5093,
0.66257]))
>>> factor_a_b = DiscreteFactor(['A', 'B'], cardinality=[2, 2],
...                     values=np.array([1.3207, 0.75717, 0.75717, 1.3207]))
>>> factor_b_c = DiscreteFactor(['B', 'C'], cardinality=[2, 2],
...                     values=np.array([0.00024189, 4134.2, 4134.2, 0.0002418]))
>>> factor_c_d = DiscreteFactor(['C', 'D'], cardinality=[2, 2],
...                     values=np.array([0.0043227, 231.34, 231.34, 0.0043227]))
>>> factor_d_e = DiscreteFactor(['E', 'F'], cardinality=[2, 2],
...                     values=np.array([31.228, 0.032023, 0.032023, 31.228]))
>>> student.add_factors(factor_a, factor_b, factor_c, factor_d, factor_e,
factor_f,
...                 factor_a_b, factor_b_c, factor_c_d, factor_d_e)
>>> mplp = Mplp(student)
>>> result = mplp.map_query()
>>> result
{'B': 0.93894, 'C': 1.121, 'A': 1.8323, 'F': 1.5093, 'D': 1.7765, 'E': 2.12239}
```

6.6.3 Dynamic Bayesian Network Inference

Elimination Ordering

class pgmpy.inference.EliminationOrder.BaseEliminationOrder(model)

Base class for finding elimination orders.

cost(node)

The cost function to compute the cost of elimination of each node. This method is just a dummy and returns 0 for all the nodes. Actual cost functions are implemented in the classes inheriting BaseEliminationOrder.

Parameters:

node: string, any hashable python object.

The node whose cost is to be computed.

fill_in_edges(node)

Return edges needed to be added to the graph if a node is removed.

Parameters:

node: string (any hashable python object)

Node to be removed from the graph.

get_elimination_order(nodes=None)

Returns the optimal elimination order based on the cost function. The node having the least cost is removed first.

Parameters:

nodes: list, tuple, set (array-like)

The variables which are to be eliminated.

Examples

```
import numpy as np
from pgmpy.models import BayesianModel
from pgmpy.factors.discrete import TabularCPD
from pgmpy.inference.EliminationOrder import WeightedMinFill
model = BayesianModel([('c', 'd'), ('d', 'g'), ('i', 'g'),
...                    ('i', 's'), ('s', 'j'), ('g', 'l'),
...                    ('l', 'j'), ('j', 'h'), ('g', 'h')])
cpd_c = TabularCPD('c', 2, np.random.rand(2, 1))
cpd_d = TabularCPD('d', 2, np.random.rand(2, 2),
...                ['c'], [2])
cpd_g = TabularCPD('g', 3, np.random.rand(3, 4),
...                ['d', 'i'], [2, 2])
cpd_i = TabularCPD('i', 2, np.random.rand(2, 1))
cpd_s = TabularCPD('s', 2, np.random.rand(2, 2),
```

```
...         ['i'], [2])
cpd_j = TabularCPD('j', 2, np.random.rand(2, 4),
...         ['l', 's'], [2, 2])
cpd_l = TabularCPD('l', 2, np.random.rand(2, 3),
...         ['g'], [3])
cpd_h = TabularCPD('h', 2, np.random.rand(2, 6),
...         ['g', 'j'], [3, 2])
model.add_cpds(cpd_c, cpd_d, cpd_g, cpd_i, cpd_s, cpd_j,
...       cpd_l, cpd_h)
WeightedMinFill(model).get_elimination_order(['c', 'd', 'g', 'l', 's'])
['c', 's', 'l', 'd', 'g']
WeightedMinFill(model).get_elimination_order(['c', 'd', 'g', 'l', 's'])
['c', 's', 'l', 'd', 'g']
WeightedMinFill(model).get_elimination_order(['c', 'd', 'g', 'l', 's'])
['c', 's', 'l', 'd', 'g']
```

6.7 COGNITIVE MODELING

Cognition is the process of acquiring and understanding knowledge through our thoughts, experiences, and senses. Learning involves acquiring knowledge through experience, study, or being taught. If you think that these two concepts are awfully similar, you're right. Both are inexorably linked - learning requires cognition and cognition involves learning. Whenever you see or hear something new, you go through a series of cognitive processes, which are the processes that result in learning.

A cognitive model is an approximation to animal cognitive processes (predominantly human) for the purposes of comprehension and prediction. Cognitive models can be developed within or without a cognitive architecture, though the two are not always easily distinguishable.

In contrast to cognitive architectures, cognitive models tend to be focused on a single cognitive phenomenon or process (e.g., list learning), how two or more processes interact (e.g., visual search and decision making), or to make behavioral predictions for a specific task or tool (e.g., how instituting a new software package will affect productivity). Cognitive architectures tend to be focused on the structural properties of the modeled system, and help constrain the development of cognitive models within the architecture. Likewise, model development helps to inform limitations and shortcomings of the architecture. Some of the most popular architectures for cognitive modeling include ACT-R and Soar.

REFERENCES

D. Ritchie, P. Horsfall, and N. D. Goodman. Deep Amortized Inference for Probabilistic Programs. arXiv:1610.05735.

L. Ouyang, M. H. Tessler, D. Ly, and N. D. Goodman. Practical optimal experiment design with probabilistic programs. arXiv:1608.05046.

M. H. Tessler and N. D. Goodman. A Pragmatic Theory of Generic Language. arXiv:1608.02926.

D. Ritchie, A. Thomas, P. Hanrahan, and N. D. Goodman. Neurally-Guided Procedural Models: Amortized Inference for Procedural Graphics Programs using Neural Networks. NIPS 2016.

D. Ritchie, A. Stuhlmüller, and N. D. Goodman. C3: Lightweight Incrementalized MCMC for Probabilistic Programs using Continuations and Callsite Caching. AISTATS 2016.

M. H. Tessler and N. D. Goodman. Communicating generalizations about events. Proceedings of the Thirty-Eighth Annual Conference of the Cognitive Science Society, 2016.

E. J. Yoon, M. H. Tessler, N. D. Goodman, and M. C. Frank. Talking with tact: Polite language as a balance between kindness and informativity. Proceedings of the Thirty-Eighth Annual Conference of the Cognitive Science Society, 2016.

C. Graf, J. Degen, R. X. D. Hawkins, and N. D. Goodman. Animal, dog, or dalmatian? Level of abstraction in nominal referring expressions. Proceedings of the Thirty-Eighth Annual Conference of the Cognitive Science Society, 2016.

O. Evans, A. Stuhlmüller, and N. D. Goodman. Learning the Preferences of Ignorant, Inconsistent Agents. AAAI 2016.

A. Stuhlmüller, R. X. D. Hawkins, N. Siddharth, and N. D. Goodman. Coarse-to-Fine Sequential Monte Carlo for Probabilistic Programs. arXiv:1509.02962.

O. Evans, A. Stuhlmüller, and N. D. Goodman. Learning the Preferences of Bounded Agents. Workshop on Bounded Optimality, NIPS 2015.

R. X. D. Hawkins, A. Stuhlmüller, J. Degen, and N. D. Goodman. Why do you ask? Good questions provoke informative answers. Proceedings of the Thirty-Seventh Annual Conference of the Cognitive Science Society, 2015.

G. Scontras and M. H. Tessler (electronic). Composition in Probabilistic Language Understanding.

O. Evans, A. Stuhlmüller, J. Salvatier, and D. Filan (electronic). Modeling Agents with Probabilistic Programs.

N. D. Goodman and J. B. Tenenbaum (electronic). Probabilistic Models of Cognition.

N. D. Goodman and A. Stuhlmüller (electronic). The Design and Implementation of Probabilistic Programming Languages.

7 Chapter
HIERARCHICAL MODELS

7.1 HIERARCHICAL GENERATIVE MODELS

7.1.1 Introduction

With the of self-similarity and quest to model needs a radical departure from earlier practices. Before this discovery, workload items were considered to be independent of each other. Modeling could then be done by sampling workload items from the relevant distributions, subject to desired correlations between workload attributes. But self-similar workloads have an internal structure. Workload items are no longer distributed uniformly along time as they come in bursts, in many different time scales.

Further, it is considered whether it is only the arrivals that are bursty or self-similarity shows workload items in bursts which says nothing about nature of items. Does the attributes of the burst items results in special characteristics, as doing job sizes as bursts, or are they just randomly selected from a distribution? And what about runtimes, memory usage, and so on?

The answer to these questions is that all workload attributes tend to come in bursts. It is common to see a burst of jobs with similar attributes, and then a burst of jobs with other attributes, and so on. Every burst is characterized by rather modal distributions, often concentrated around a single value. The wider distributions describing the entire workload are actually a combination of the modal distributions of the different bursts of activity. Thus the collective distribution does not capture the workload dynamics unless we postulate locality of sampling: instead of sampling from the whole distribution, sample first from one part, then from another, and so on.

It is observed that will all good ways to generate locality of sampling is use of hierarchical model where initially the distribution part is considered which shows on which to focus and sample from selected region. It means that it should mimic and model the processes that create the real workload. Such models are therefore called hierarchical generative models (HGM).

7.1.2 Description

Creating and training a deep neural network involves:

- Choosing a network architecture
- Choosing a learning principle
- Choosing some method for optimizing the network according to that principle

Further, all machine learning models fall into two categories:

- Discriminative
- Generative

Both models are capable of learning data distributions, as they approach the problem in different ways. Discriminative models focus on trying to simply separate different data examples, typically by some specified class. Generative models focus on trying to actually model the underlying data distribution, which can in turn be used to separate examples by class. However, by modeling the underlying data distribution, generative models can also use this distribution to generate data examples. Discriminative models can only discriminate between classes of data examples. Both types of models have pros and cons, which are often dependent on the task at hand, but both have enjoyed many successes.

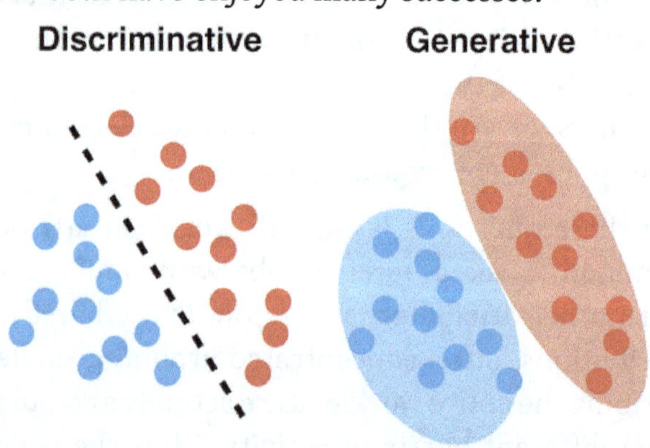

Neural networks in era of deep learning have taken on discriminative form where convolutional neural networks which trains and use object detection and classification results as discriminative. Similar types of models exist for speech recognition, reinforcement learning, and other areas. These models have had many successes in the last few years as benchmarks continue to improve and new tasks are taken on. This has mainly been fueled by better datasets, more computing power, and larger models. With this, deep learning was an unsettling feeling that these models are not truly learning in the same way in which humans do. Take object classification for example. When training a deep network to classify objects, one typically needs hundreds or thousands of example images to successfully generalize to unseen examples. Of course, one can somewhat get around this through creative forms of data augmentation and transfer learning, but the point remains that these systems need far more examples than humans do to learn new concepts. And mind you, each of those examples needs a corresponding label.

Here, there are two problems:

- The ability of model to associate some high level representation of input with some specified class, assimilating lead the information in model's body of knowledge which is normally studied in context of low-shot learning where model is expected to learn to classify a new class with minimal examples.
- The development of high level representation where a model can easily generalize among different instances of same concept has further problems.

Discriminative models have a difficult time in summarizing understanding of examples themselves as they do not model the data generation process. Unless explicitly trained to separate out different concepts, these networks tend to overfit to the data with which they are trained. They simply look for patterns in the data that are helpful for the task they are trained to perform. We can argue whether this amounts to 'understanding,' but bear with me for the time being. A discriminative model succeeds when it has access to copious amounts of data and the capacity to store this information. However, when presented with new data examples or familiar examples in new contexts, these models are often unable to generalize well.

Generative models cannot as easily get away with simply finding useful patterns in the data. They are required to build a model of how the data is generated. Depending on the expressive power of the model, this implies developing some level of understanding of the underlying data generation mechanism. When trained in an appropriate way, such a model could, in theory, disentangle the underlying factors that influence the world around us.

7.2 DIRICHLET DISTRIBUTION

7.2.1 Introduction

The Dirichlet Distribution is generalisation of Beta Distribution for many outcomes. It is parameterized with k parameters ai which must be positive. Dirichlet Distribution equals to the Beta Distribution when the number of variables k = 2.

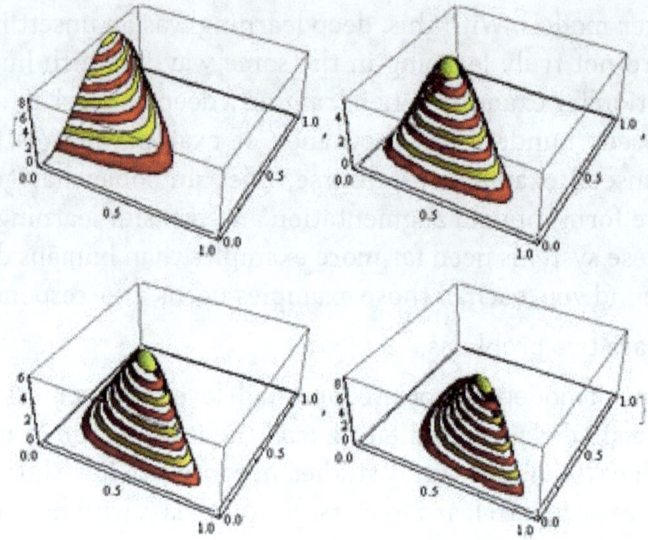

Fig: Dirichlet Distribution for various ai parameters

The Dirichlet distribution is commonly used to model a distribution over probabilities and has the following probability density:

$$P(p_1, p_2, \ldots, p_k | a_1, a_2, \ldots, a_k) = \frac{\Gamma(\sum a_i)}{\prod_{i=1}^{k} \Gamma(a_i)} p_1^{a_1 - 1} p_2^{a_2 - 1} \ldots p_k^{a_k - 1}$$

In this, Γ(x) is gamma function, where p_i take the values in [0,1] and $\Sigma p_i=1$. The Dirichlet distribution models the joint distribution of p_i gives the likelihood of $P_1=p_1, P_2=p_2, \ldots, P_{k-1}=p_{k-1}$ with $P_k=1 - \Sigma P_i$. In Beta, the a_i parameters can be considered as pseudocounts of the appearances of each i event. The Dirichlet distribution is used to model the probability of k rival events occurring and is often denoted as Dirichlet(a).

Beta Distribution

The Beta distribution is a family of continuous distributions which is defined in the interval of [0,1]. It is parameterized by two positive parameters a and b and its form heavily depends upon the selection of those two parameters.

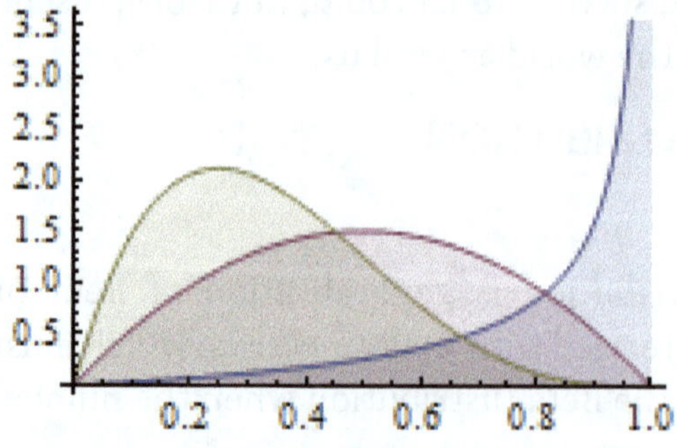

Fig: Beta Distribution for different a, b parameters

The Beta distribution is commonly used to model a distribution over probabilities and has the following probability density:

$$P(p, a, b) = \frac{\Gamma(a+b)}{\Gamma(a)\Gamma(b)} p^{a-1}(1-p)^{b-1}$$

Here, Γ(x) is the gamma function and a, b the parameters of the distribution. Beta is commonly used as a distribution of probability values and gives us the likelihood that the modelled probability equals to a particular value P = p0. By its definition Beta distribution is able to model the probability of binary outcomes which take values true or false. The parameters a and b can be considered as the pseudocounts of success and failure respectively. Thus the Beta Distribution models the probability of success given a successes and b failures.

7.2.2 Dirichlet Prior with Multinomial Likelihood

As mentioned earlier the Dirichlet distribution can be seen as a distribution over probability distributions. In cases where we want to model the probability of k events occurring, a Bayesian approach would be to use Multinomial Likelihood and Dirichlet Priors. In a graphical model as shown:

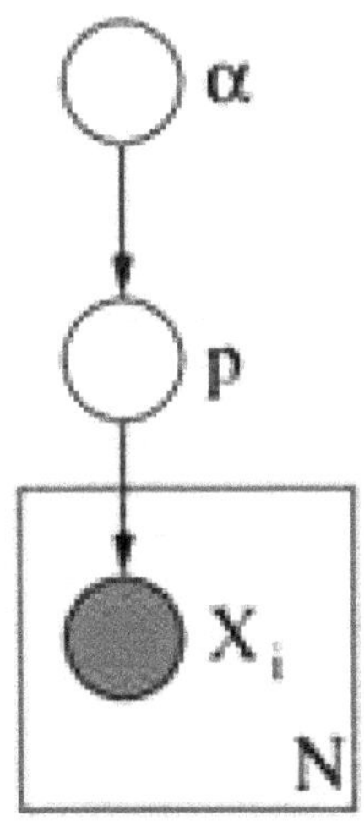

Fig: Graphical Model of Dirichlet Priors with Multinomial Likelihood

α is a k dimensional vector with the hyperparameters of Dirichlet priors, p is a k dimensional vector with the probability values and xi is a scalar value from 1 to k which tells us which event has occurred. It is observed that, P follows the Dirichlet distribution parameterized with vector α and thus P ~ Dirichlet(α), while the xi variables follow the Discrete distribution (Multinomial) parameterized with the p vector of probabilities. Similar hierarchical models can be used in document classification to represent the distributions of keyword frequencies for in different topics.

7.2.3 Finite Mixture Model with Dirichlet Distribution

By using Dirichlet Distribution we can construct a Finite Mixture Model which can be used to perform clustering. Let's assume that we have the following model:

$$\varphi_c \sim G_0$$

$$p \sim Dirichlet\left(\frac{a}{k}, \ldots, \frac{a}{k}\right)$$

$$c_i \mid p \sim Discrete(p)$$

$$x_i \mid c, \varphi \sim F(\varphi_{c_i})$$

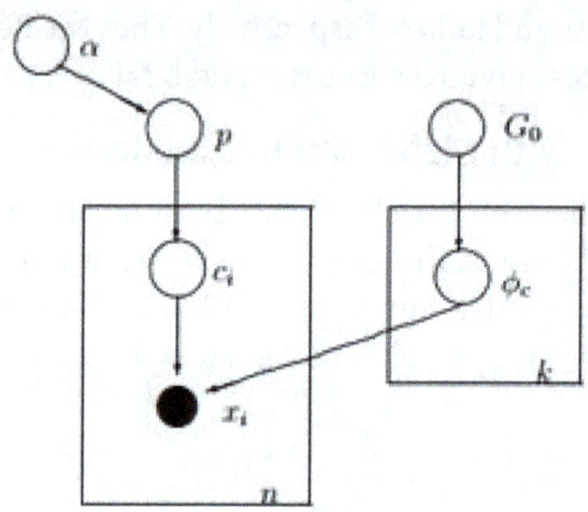

Fig: Graphical Model of Finite Mixture Model with Dirichlet Distribution

In the model, a dataset X with n observations are to perform cluster analysis where k is a constant finite number showing the number of clusters/components. The c_i variables stores the cluster assignment of observation X_i, they take values from 1 to k and follow the Discrete Distribution with parameter p which are the mixture probabilities of the components. The F is the generative distribution of our X and it is parameterized with a parameter φ_{c_i} which depends on the cluster assignment of each observation. In total we have k unique φ_{c_i} parameters equal to the number of our clusters. The φ variable stores the parameters that parameterize the generative F Distribution and we assume that it follows a base G_0 distribution. The p variable stores the mixture percentages for every one of the k clusters and follows the Dirichlet with parameters α/k. Finally the α is a k dimensional vector with the hyperparameters of Dirichlet distribution.

The previous mixture model allows us to perform unsupervised learning, follows a Bayesian approach and can be extended to have a hierarchical structure. Nevertheless it is a finite model because it uses a constant predefined k number of clusters. As a result it requires us to define the number of components before performing Cluster Analysis and as we discussed earlier in most applications this is unknown and can't be easily estimated.

One way to resolve this is to imagine that k has a very large value which tends to infinity. In other words we can imagine the limit of this model when k tends to infinity. If this is the case, then we can see that despite that the number of clusters k is infinite, the actual number of clusters that are active (the ones that have at least one observation), can't be larger than n (which is the total number of the observations in our dataset). In fact, the number of active clusters will be significantly less than n and they will be proportional to $a * \log(n)$.

Of course taking the limit of k to infinity is non-trivial. Several questions rise such as whether it is possible to take such a limit, how would this model look like and how can we construct and use such a model.

7.3 LEARNING OVERHYPOTHESES

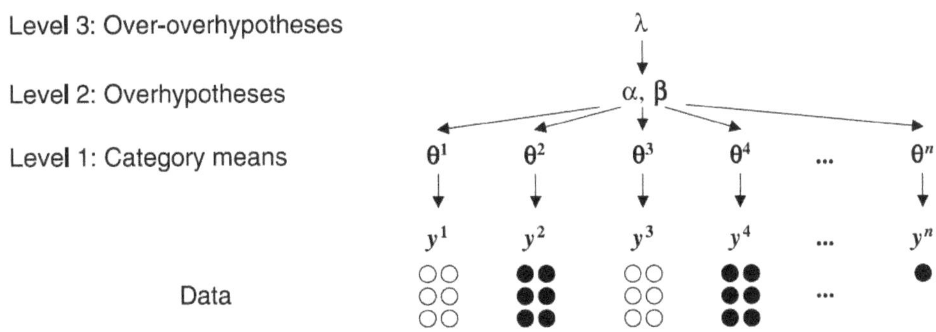

Fig: Hierarchical Bayesian model.

On applying Gibbs sampling to get overhypotheses is about featuring variability for the bags of marbles model as shown. If S is a stack containing many bags of marbles, then on emptying several bags and discovering marbles in similar bag will have certain features where some bags may have black marbles while others have white marbles, but that marbles in each bag are uniform in color.

Given a new bag – bag n - and a single marble (e.g. a black marble) drawn from this bag we are interested in the probability of the colors of all other marbles within this bag. On its own, a single draw would provide little information about the contents of the new bag, but experience with previous bags may lead us to endorse certain hypothesis (e.g. all marbles in a bag have uniform colors).

Learning over-hypothesis is used to refer to any form of abstract knowledge that sets up a hypothesis space at a less abstract level. By this criterion, an over-hypothesis sets up a space of hypotheses about the marbles in bag n as they could be uniformly black, uniformly white, and so on. Hierarchical Bayesian models capture the notion of overhypothesis by allowing hypothesis spaces at several levels of abstraction. In this example we wish to explain how a certain kind of inference can be drawn from a given body of data. In this case, the data are observations of several bags and we are working with a set of 2 colors.

Bags of marbles model: Let y^i shows a set of observations of the marbles in bag i. If we have drawn five marbles from bag 7 and all but one are black, then $y^7 = [4,1]$. We are interested in the ability to predict the color of the next marble to be drawn from bag n. The first step is to identify a kind of knowledge (level 1 knowledge) that explains the data and that supports the ability of interest. In this case, level 1 knowledge is knowledge about the color distribution of each bag. Let θ^i indicate the true color distribution for the ith bag in the stack, so on assuming $y^{i \text{ and}}$ drawing from a binomial distribution with parameter θ^i, the marbles responsible for the observations in y^i are drawn independently at random from the ith bag, and the color of each depends on the color distribution θ^i for that bag. If 60% of the marbles in bag 7 are black, then $\theta^7 = [0.6,0.4]$.

For the marbles scenario, level 2 knowledge is knowledge about the distribution of the θ variables. This knowledge is represented using two parameters, α and β. The vectors θ^i are drawn from a Beta distribution parameterized by a scalar α and a vector β = (β1, β2) with β1 + β2 = 1. The parameter α determines the extent to which the colors in each bag tend to be uniform, and β represents the distribution of colors across the entire collection of bags. We need to formalize our a priori expectations about the values of these variables.

Level 2 knowledge is acquired by relying on a body of knowledge at an even higher level, level 3. We use a uniform distribution on β1 and an exponential distribution on α, which captures a weak prior expectation that the marbles in any bag will tend to be uniform in color. The mean of the exponential distribution is λ=1, i.e. P(α) = exp(-α). The parameter λ and the pair (α, β) are both overhypotheses, since each sets up a hypothesis space at the next level down. Since the level 3 knowledge is specified in advance (λ), you should analyze how an overhypothesis can be learned at level 2.

The joint probability distribution for this model is therefore given by

$$P(\mathbf{y}^1, ..., \mathbf{y}^n, \theta^1, ..., \theta^n, \alpha, \beta | \lambda) = \prod_{i=1}^{n} P(\mathbf{y}^i | \theta^i) P(\theta^i | \alpha, \beta) P(\alpha | \lambda) P(\beta)$$

with

$$\begin{aligned} \alpha &\sim Exponential(\lambda) \\ \beta_1 &\sim Beta(1,1) \\ \theta^i &\sim Beta(\alpha\beta_1, \alpha\beta_2) \\ \mathbf{y}^i | n^i &\sim Binomial(\theta^i) \end{aligned}$$

where n^i is the number of observations for bag i. On performing Gibbs sampling for this joint distribution to estimate the marginal distributions for each single θ^i, α and β (the overhypotheses) where the observation y^i are kept fixed for the following situations:

- After observing 10 all-white bags, 10 all-black bag and a single black marble in the last bag.
- After observing 20 mixed bags, where half of the marbles are white and half of the marbles are black, and a single black marble in the last bag.
- Same as in 1 but with fixed α = 1and $\beta1=\beta2=0.5$
- Same as in 2 but with fixed α = 1and $\beta1=\beta2=0.5$

Calculating average distributions across 50 Markov chains, each of which was run for 100000 iterations. Hand in plots for all estimated distributions and interpret your results.

7.4 X-BAR THEORY

7.4.1 Introduction

The X-bar theory was first proposed by Noam Chomsky which postulates that all human languages share certain structural similarities, including the same underlying syntactic structure, which is known as X-bar. It is a theory about the internal structure of syntactic constituents which was originally intended to place constraints on the power of phrase structure rules. X-bar theory captures the insight that all phrases share some essential structural properties. Its main tenet is that all phrase structure can be reduced to recursive specifier-head configurations.

Constituency grammars are a method of sentence analysis that divides a sentence into major parts, which are in turn further divided into smaller parts in a process that continues until irreducible constituents are reached, i.e., until each constituent consists of only a word or a meaningful part of a word. The end result is presented in a visual diagrammatic form that reveals the hierarchical immediate constituent structure of the sentence at hand. For example:

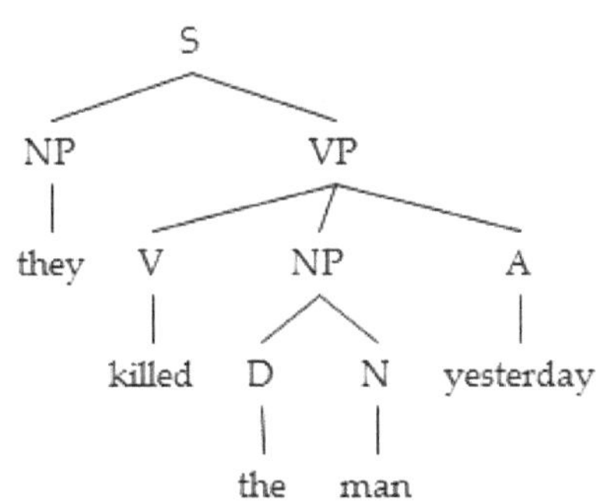

Fig: Tree

This tree illustrates the manner in which the entire sentence is divided first into two constituents (NP and VP, i.e., subject and predicate), which are further divided into immediate constituents (V, NP, A), and so on, until the smallest constituents (N, V, D, A) are reached.

Example

The structure shown below have in common that the head has an element to its right, which can be construed as its complement.

- a lookV [for you]
- b the searchN [for you]
- c angryA [with you]
- d onP [with you]

These structural properties are conventionally represented as:

```
          X”
         /\
         / \
specifier   X’
            /\
            / \
         X  complement
```

In the arrangement:

- X = head of phrase
- X’ and X” = projections of X

Typographically, these projections are marked by one or more primes (X’ and X”), called bars. Thus, X’ is pronounced X-bar; X”, X-double-bar etc.. The head is called the zero projection (also written as X0). The topnode X” (or XP) is called the maximal projection of X. All other projections between the head and the maximal projection are called intermediate projections. The sister(s) of X are called the complements of the head), and the sister(s) of X’ is/are the specifier(s) (of the phrase).

The structure above shown has following assumptions about internal structure of constituents:

- Each phrase XP has one unique, structurally obligatory element: head X0 of the phrase.

- There is one maximal projection, or X-max, corresponding to the phrasal node (XP). There is no strong consensus about whether the X-max node always has two bars.
- All other elements within the XP besides the head are structurally optional, their presence being determined by principles of licensing (theta-theory, case theory). They can appear both on the left and on the right hand side of the head.
- The intermediate projection X' between the head and the maximal projection can be iterated.
- In case of adjunction, the maximal projection XP can also be iterated.
- Except for the possibilities of iteration, projections must obey condition: Xn -> Xn-1
- Such condition excludes possibility of endless projection loops, i.e. phrases like as shown:

```
X''
/\
  \
 X'
  |
X''
  |
X0
  |
 X''
```

The value of X ranges over at least the categories N, A, V, P, the so-called lexical categories. Such categories can be characterized in terms of features [Â±N] (substantive) and [Â±V] (predicative) as:

a [+N,+V] = A

b [+N,-V] = N

c [-N,+V] = V

d [-N,-V] = P

This notation allows crosscategorical reference to sets of categories.

7.4.2 Features

The X-bar is a specific implementation of constituency grammars: it is a method of sentence analysis that divides the sentence into constituents, but it states some very specific rules for doing that:

- The topmost node (S, in the diagram above) is called XP (X-phrase) and is considered to be the maximal projection of a head X. This means that the whole process must be understood bottom-up (from a head to its projections) instead of top-down.
- Tthe "X" is actually a variable that must be replaced by any of the possible heads: noun (N), verb (V), adjective (J), adverb (A), etc. In that sense, there is no real XP, but NP's, VP's, JP's, etc. A VP (verbal phrase) is the maximal projection of a verb (V); a NP (noun phrase) is the maximal projection of a noun (N); and so on. The sentence above, for instance, can be considered to be the maximal projection of a V (killed) and, therefore, constitutes a VP (verbal phrase), instead of "S". The use of the "X" (and therefore "XP") comes from the fact that one of the claims of the theory is that all these phrases (NP, VP, JP, etc.) share the same underlying structure, i.e., a NP is a specific implementation of a general XP.
- Projections are always binary, i.e., the tree cannot bring more than two branches at a time. In the example above, for instance, there is a VP (killed the man yesterday) with three branches. This is not possible in X-bar. In order to avoid this, the head may have intermediate projections before the maximal projection. These intermediate projections are called XB (from X-bar), and again must be replaced by the specific categories of the head (NB is the intermediate projection of N, VB is the intermediate projection of V, etc.).
- The maximal projection is "maximal", i.e., there can be one single maximal projection of the same head. If we simply replace "S" by "VP" in the example above, the VP would project a VP, which is not possible according to the X-bar. We have then to proliferate the intermediate projections (VB's in our case). One head can have as many intermediate projections as necessary, but it can have one single maximal projection.
- There can be four different types of arguments inside the X-bar structure: the head, which projects the whole structure ("killed", in the example above); the complement (or comp), that complements the head ("the man"); the adjunct (or adjt), that modifies the head ("yesterday"); and the specifier (or spec), that determines the head ("they"). The head can have as many complements and adjuncts as necessary, but it can have one single specifier.

- The intermediate projections (NB's, VB's, JB's, etc.) are actually combinations of the head with its complements and adjuncts, if any, where as the maximal projection (NP, VP, JP, etc.) is the combination of the head with its specifier, if any.
- The complements, adjuncts and specifiers are themselves maximal projections (of different categories other than the head). For instance, the complement of "killed" is not simply a noun but a NP ("the man"), which is the maximal projection of the noun head ("man"). Likewise, the adjunct of "killed" is not the word "yesterday" but the AP ("yesterday"), which is the maximal projection of the adverbial head "yesterday".

On having all required changes shown in above tree, an X-bar representation of sentence will be shown as:

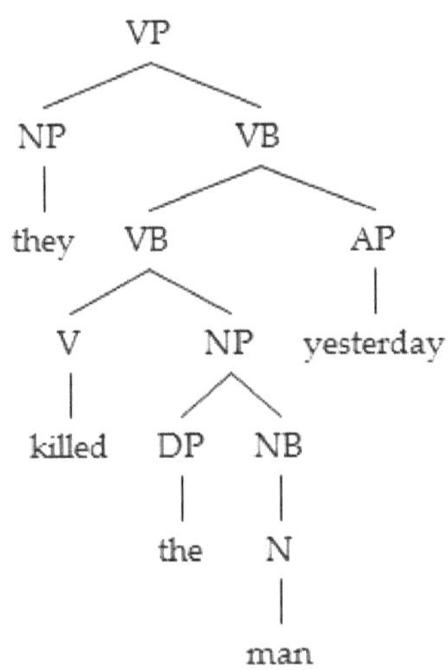

- "they" is a NP, i.e., a maximal projection of nominal head (the personal pronoun "they"). It plays the role of the specifier of the VP.
- "killed" is the head of the VP, which is actually a projection of it.
- "the man" is a NP, i.e., a maximal projection of a nominal head (the noun "man"). It plays the role of the complement of the VP (and, therefore, constitutes a VB).
- "the" is a DP, i.e., a maximal projection of a determiner head (the article "the"). It plays the role of the specifier of the NP, which is inside the VB.
- "yesterday" is an AP, i.e., a maximal projection of an adverbial head (the adverb "yesterday"). It plays the role of the adjunct of the VP (and, therefore, constitutes a VB).
- VP, NP, DP, AP are maximal projections
- VB and NB are intermediate projections

7.4.3 Structure

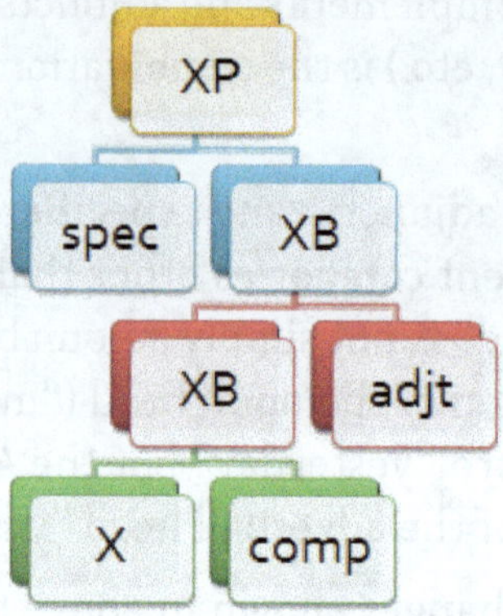

Fig: Structure of X bar

The X-bar abstract configuration is described below:

- X is the head, the nucleus or the source of the whole syntactic structure, which is actually derived (or projected) out of it. The letter X is used to signify an arbitrary lexical category (part of speech). When analyzing a specific utterance, specific categories are assigned. Thus, the X may become an N for noun, a V for verb, an J for adjective, a P for preposition, etc.
- comp (i.e., complement) is an internal argument, i.e., a word, phrase or clause which is necessary to the head to complete its meaning (e.g., objects of transitive verbs)
- adjt (i.e., adjunct) is a word, phrase or clause which modifies the head but which is not syntactically required by it (adjuncts are expected to be extra-nuclear, i.e., removing an adjunct would leave a grammatically well-formed sentence)
- spec (i.e., specifier) is an external argument, i.e., a word, phrase or clause which qualifies (determines) the head
- XB (X-bar) is the general name for any of the intermediate projections derived from X
- XP (X-bar-bar, X-double-bar, X-phrase) is the maximal projection of X.

Heads

In X-bar diagram shown, X is used to signify an arbitrary category, N for noun, V for verb, and so on. In Default Grammar, there are eight different types of heads such as:

- N = nouns and nominals: personal pronouns, demonstrative pronouns, nominalizations, etc
- V = verbs

- J = adjectives
- A = adverbs[2]
- P = prepositions
- D = determiners: articles, demonstrative determiners, possessive determiners, quantifiers
- I = auxiliary verbs
- C = conjunctions

Specifiers

Specifiers are used to narrow the meaning intended by the head. They include:

- articles: the (book), a (book), etc.
- possessive determiners: my (book), your (book), etc.
- demonstrative determiners: this (book), that (book), etc.
- quantifiers: no (answer), every (hour), etc.
- intensifiers (emphasizers, amplifiers, downtoners): very (expensive), quite (well), nearly (under), etc.

Complements

Complements are used to complete the meaning intended by the head which are:

- Direct objects: (do) something, (give) something
- Indirect objects: (laugh at) something, (give to) someone
- Complement of deverbals (i.e., nouns deriving from verbs): (construction of) the city, (arrival of) Peter
- Complement of adjectives: (loyal) to the queen, (interested) in Chemistry
- Complement of adverbs: (contrarily) to popular belief, (independently) from her
- Complement of prepositions: (under) the table, (after) today
- Complement of conjunctions: (and) Peter, (I don't know if) he'll come

Adjuncts

Adjuncts are used to modify the meaning intended by the head:

- Adjectives: beautiful (table)
- Adverbs: (speak) slowly
- Prepositional phrases: (table) of wood

Projections

In the X-bar theory, the heads (X) project two different types of structures:

- XB (x-bar) is the intermediate projection, and is derived from the combination of the head or any of its intermediate projections with complements and adjuncts
- XP (x-bar-bar, or x-phrase) is the maximal projection, and is derived from the combination of the topmost intermediate projection and the specifier

There can be as many intermediate projections as adjuncts and complements, but any head projects one single maximal projection, because it may have one single specifier. The heads define the nature of the intermediate and maximal projections, thus:

- A head N projects NB's and a Noun Phrase (NP)
- A head V projects VB's and a Verbal Phrase (VP)
- A head J projects JB's and an Adjective Phrase (JP)
- A head A projects AB's and an Adverbial Phrase (AP)
- A head P projects PB's and a Prepositional Phrase (PP)
- A head D projects DB's and a Determiner Phrase (DP)
- A head I projects IB's and an Inflectional Phrase (IP)
- A head C projects CB's and Complementizer Phrase (CP)

7.5 LAMBDA ABSTRACTION

λ-expressions are formed out of ordinary first order formulas using the λ -operator. We can prefix the λ-operator, followed by a variable, to any first order formula or λ-expression. We call expressions with such prefixes λ-abstraction. We say that the variable following a λ-operator is abstracted over . And we say that the variable abstracted over is *(λ-)*bound by its respective λ-operator within an abstraction, just as we say that a quantified variable is bound by its quantifier inside a quantification.

The following two are examples of λ-abstractions:

$$\lambda x.\textsc{woman}(x)$$

$$\lambda u.\lambda v.\textsc{love}(u, v)$$

In the first example, we have abstracted over x. Thus the x in the argument slot of WOMAN is bound by the λ in the prefix. In the second example, we have abstracted twice: Once over v and once over u. So the u in the first argument slot of LOVE is bound by the first λ, and the v is bound by the second one.

Considering an occurrences of variables bound by λ as placeholders for missing information, it is observed that, each will serve to mark *explicitly* on substituting many bits and pieces obtained in semantic construction. Consider an example of λ-expression where the prefix λx. states that there is information missing in the formula following it, and it gives this ``information gap" the name x. The same way in our second example, the two prefixes λu. and λv. give us separate handles on *each of the two* information gaps in the following two-place predication.

It is noticed that lambda abstraction starts with lower case lambda (represented as "\" in this document), followed by a variable name ("bound variable"), a full stop and a lambda expression (the body). The body is taken to extend as far to the right as possible so, for example an expression,

\x.\y.x+y

is read as

\x.(\y.x+y).

A nested abstraction such as this is often abbreviated to:

\xy.x+y

The lambda expression (\v.E) denotes a function which takes an argument and returns the term E with all free occurrences of v replaced by the actual argument. Application is represented by juxtaposition so

(\x.x) 42

represents the identity function applied to the constant 42. A lambda abstraction in Lisp is written as the symbol lambda, a list of zero or more variable names and a list of zero or more terms, e.g.

(lambda (x y) (plus x y))

Lambda expressions in Haskell are written as a backslash, "\", one or more patterns (e.g. variable names), "->" and an expression, e.g. \x -> x.

8 Chapter | OCCAM'S RAZOR

8.1 FITTING CURVES

8.1.1 Introduction

Occam's razor is a logical principle attributed to the mediaeval philosopher William of Occam (or Ockham). The principle states that one should not make more assumptions than the minimum needed. This principle is often called the principle of parsimony. It underlies all scientific modelling and theory building. It admonishes us to choose from a set of otherwise equivalent models of a given phenomenon the simplest one. In any given model, Occam's razor helps us to "shave off" those concepts, variables or constructs that are not really needed to explain the phenomenon. By doing that, developing the model will become much easier, and there is less chance of introducing inconsistencies, ambiguities and redundancies.

Though the principle may seem rather trivial, it is essential for model building because of what is known as the "under determination of theories by data". For a given set of observations or data, there is always an infinite number of possible models explaining those same data. This is because a model normally represents an infinite number of possible cases, of which the observed cases are only a finite subset. The non-observed cases are inferred by postulating general rules covering both actual and potential observations.

For example, through two data points in a diagram you can always draw a straight line, and induce that all further observations will lie on that line. However, you could also draw an infinite variety of the most complicated curves passing through those same two points, and these curves would fit the empirical data just as well. Only Occam's razor would in this case guide you in choosing the "straight" (i.e. linear) relation as best candidate model. A similar reasoning can be made for n data points lying in any kind of distribution.

Occam's razor is especially important for universal models such as the ones developed in General Systems Theory, mathematics or philosophy, because there the subject domain is of an unlimited complexity. If one starts with too complicated foundations for a theory that potentially encompasses the universe, the chances of getting any manageable model are very slim indeed. Moreover, the principle is sometimes the only remaining guideline when entering domains of such a high level of abstraction that no concrete tests or observations can decide between rival models. In mathematical modelling of systems, the principle can be made more concrete in the form of the principle of uncertainty maximization: from your data, induce that model which minimizes the number of additional assumptions.

This principle is part of epistemology, and can be motivated by the requirement of maximal simplicity of cognitive models. However, its significance might be extended to metaphysics if it is interpreted as saying that simpler models are more likely to be correct than complex ones, in other words, that "nature" prefers simplicity.

8.1.2 Fitting Curves

Under traditional approaches to model fitting where we adjust each model's parameters until it fits best, then choose the best-fitting model — a model with strictly more free parameters will tend to be preferred regardless of whether it actually comes closer to describing the true processes that generated the data. But this is not the way the mind works. We assess models with a natural eye for complexity, balancing fit to the data with model complexity in subtle ways that will not inevitably prefer the most complex model. Instead we often seem to judge models using Occam's razor: we choose the least complex hypothesis that fits the data well. In doing so we avoid "over-fitting" our data in order to support successful generalizations and predictions.

Fitting curves (or smooth functions) to sparsely sampled, noisy data provides a familiar example of the problem.

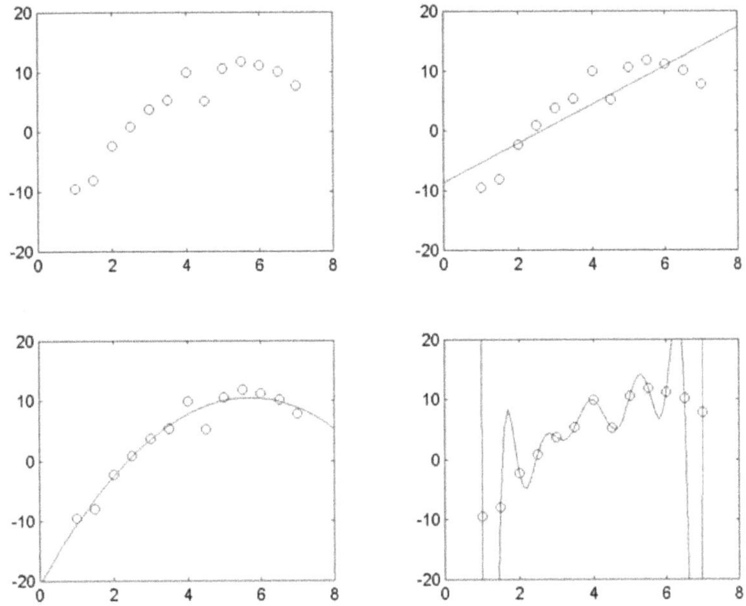

Fig: Fitting Curves

The figure above shows three polynomial fits: a 1st-order (linear), a 2nd-order (quadratic), and a 12th-order polynomial. How do our minds decide which of these functions provides the best account of the data? The 1st-order model captures the rough trend of the data but seems too coarse; it attributes some of the variation that we see as "signal" to "noise". The 2nd-order model seems best; it seems to be just complex enough to fit the main shape of the data without over-fitting the noise. The 12th-order model seems ridiculously over-fit; with 13 data points, the parameters can be adjusted so as to make the curve pass exactly through every data point, thus taking as "signal" all of what we see as "noise". Again we can think of this as a causal inference problem: each function represents a hypothesis about the causal process that gave rise to the observed data, including the shape of the function from inputs to outputs, as well as the level of noise added to the output.

8.2 LAW OF CONSERVATION OF BELIEF

It is convenient to emphasize an aspect of probabilistic modeling that seems deceptively trivial, but comes up repeatedly when thinking about inference. In Bayesian statistics we think of probabilities as being degrees of belief. Our generative model reflects world knowledge and the probabilities that we assign to the possible sampled values reflect how strongly we believe in each possibility. The laws of probability theory ensure that our beliefs remain consistent as we reason.

A consequence of belief maintenance is known as the Law of Conservation of Belief (LCB). Here are two equivalent formulations of this principle:

- Sampling from a distribution selects exactly one possibility (in doing so it implicitly rejects all other possible values).
- The total probability mass of a distribution must sum to 1. That is, we only have a single unit of belief to spread around.

The latter formulation leads to a common metaphor in discussing generative models: We can usefully think of belief as a "currency" that is "spent" by the probabilistic choices required to construct a sample. Since each choice requires "spending" some currency, an outcome that requires more choices to construct it will generally be more costly, i.e. less probable.

It is this conservation of belief that gives rise to the Bayesian Occam's razor. A hypothesis that spends its probability on many alternatives that don't explain the current data will have less probability for the alternatives that do, and will hence do less well overall than a hypothesis which only entertains options that fit the current data. We next examine a special case where this tradeoff plays out clearly, the size principle, then come back to the more general cases.

8.3 THE SIZE PRINCIPLE

A simple case of Bayes Occam's razor comes from the size principle [1]: Of hypotheses which generate data uniformly, the one consistent with the data and with smallest extension is the most probable.

The following Church program demonstrates the size principle with a very simple model. Here we have two hypothesized sets: Big has 6 elements and Small has 3 elements. The generative model chooses one of the hypotheses at random and samples some number of symbols from it uniformly. We then wish to infer the hypothesis given observed elements.

```
(define samples
 (mh-query
  100 100
  (define (hypothesis->set  hyp)
   (if (equal? hyp  'Big) '(a b c d e f) '(a b c)))
  (define hypothesis (if (flip) 'Big 'Small))
  (define (observe N)
   (repeat N (lambda () (uniform-draw (hypothesis->set hypothesis)))))
  hypothesis
```

```
(equal? (observe 1) '(a))
)
)
(hist samples "Size Principle")
```

With a single observed a, we already favor hypothesis small. What happens when we increase the amount of observed data? Consider the learning trajectory:

```
(define (samples data)
  (mh-query
  100 10
  (define (hypothesis->set  hyp)
    (if (equal? hyp  'Big) '(a b c d e f) '(a b c)))
(define hypothesis (if (flip) 'Big 'Small))
  (define (observe N)
    (repeat N (lambda () (uniform-draw (hypothesis->set hypothesis)))))
hypothesis
(equal? (observe (length data)) data)
  )
  )
(define (big-freq data) (mean (map (lambda (hyp) (if (equal? hyp 'Big) 1.0 0.0))
(samples data))))
(lineplot-value (pair 1 (big-freq '(a))) "Prob. of hypothesis Big")
(lineplot-value (pair 3 (big-freq '(a b a))) "Prob. of hypothesis Big")
(lineplot-value (pair 5 (big-freq '(a b a b b))) "Prob. of hypothesis Big")
(lineplot-value (pair 7 (big-freq '(a b a b b a b))) "Prob. of hypothesis Big")
```

As the number of data points increases, the hypothesis Small rapidly comes to dominate the posterior distribution. Why is this happening? We sample observations uniformly from hypotheses, the law of conservation of belief and the symmetry between observations imply that the probability of a draw from Big is $\frac{1}{6}$, while the probability of a draw from Small is $\frac{1}{3}$. Thus, by the product rule of probabilities, the probability of drawing a set of N observations from Big is $(\frac{1}{6})^N$, while the probability of drawing a set of observations from Small is $(\frac{1}{3})^N$. The later probability decreases much more slowly than the former as the number of observations increases. Using Bayes' rule, the posterior distribution over hypotheses is given by:

$P(hypothesis | observations) \propto P(observations|hypothesis) P(hypothesis)$

Because our hypotheses are equally probable a priori, this simplifies to

$P(hypothesis | observations) \propto P(observations|hypothesis)$

So we see that the the posterior distribution over hypotheses in this case is just the normalized likelihood $P(observations|hypothesis)$. The likelihood ratio $P(observations|Big)/P(observations|Small) = (\frac{1}{2})^N$ determines how quickly the simpler hypothesis Small comes to dominate the posterior.

The size principle is related to an influential proposal in linguistics known as the subset principle. Intuitively the subset principle suggests that when two grammars both account for the same data, the grammar that generates a smaller language should be preferred.

8.4 BAYESIAN OCCAM'S RAZOR

Occam's razor describes that when two models fit equally well, the simpler model is likely to be a better description of reality. A simple model makes sharper predictions than a more complex model. For example, consider fitting a linear model and a cubic model. The cubic model is more general and fits more data. The linear model is more restrictive and hence easier to falsify. But when the linear and cubic models both fit, Bayes' theorem "rewards" the linear model for making a bolder prediction.

Bayes' Occam razor says that all else being equal the hypothesis that assigns the highest likelihood to the data will dominate the posterior. Because of the law of conservation of belief, assigning higher likelihood to the observed data requires assigning lower likelihood to other possible data. Consider the following example

```
(define observed-letters '(a b a b c d b b))
(define samples
 (mh-query
 100 100
 (define (hypothesis->parameters hyp)
  (if (equal? hyp 'A)
    (list '(a b c d) '(0.375 0.375 0.125 0.125))
```

```
        (list '(a b c d) '(0.25 0.25 0.25 0.25))))
  (define hypothesis  (if (flip) 'A 'B))
    (define (observe) (apply multinomial (hypothesis->parameters hypothesis)))
  hypothesis
  (equal? observed-letters (repeat (length observed-letters) observe))
    )
   )
  (hist samples "Bayes-Occam-Razor")
```

In this example, unlike the size principle cases above, both hypotheses lead to the same possible observed values. However, hypothesis A is skewed toward examples a and b—while it can produce c or d, it is less likely to do so. In this sense hypothesis A is less flexible than hypothesis B. The data set we conditioned on also has exemplars of all the elements in the support of the two hypotheses. However, because there are more exemplars of elements favored by hypothesis A, this hypothesis is favored in the posterior. The Bayesian Occam's razor emerges naturally here, and is often described as favoring the less flexible hypothesis.

Similar effects emerge if hypothesis B is not uniform, but favors different examples that hypothesis A:

```
(define observed-letters '(a b a c d))
(define samples
  (mh-query
   100 100
(define (hypothesis->parameters  hyp)
    (if (equal? hyp  'A)
       (list '(a b c d) '(0.375 0.375 0.125 0.125))
       (list '(a b c d) '(0.125 0.125 0.375 0.375))))


   (define hypothesis  (if (flip) 'A 'B))
   (define (observe) (apply multinomial (hypothesis->parameters hypothesis)))
hypothesis
(equal? observed-letters (repeat (length observed-letters) observe))
   )
  )
(hist samples "Bayes-Occam-Razor")
```

Note that it takes less evidence here to favor hypothesis A that when B is uniform, but still more that in a size principle case (where A wouldn't be able to generate c or d at all)—but the size principle case would be unable to handle the "exceptional" observations of c and d. This examples suggest another way to understand Bayes Occam's razor: the posterior distribution will favor hypotheses for which the data set is simpler in the sense that it is more "easily generated." Here more "easily" generated, means generated with higher probability.

REFERENCES

Ariew, Roger (1976). Ockham's Razor: A Historical and Philosophical Analysis of Ockham's Principle of Parsimony. Champaign-Urbana, University of Illinois.

Charlesworth, M. J. (1956). "Aristotle's Razor". Philosophical Studies (Ireland) [clarification needed]. 6: 105–112. doi:10.5840/philstudies1956606.

Churchland, Paul M. (1984). Matter and Consciousness. Cambridge, Massachusetts: MIT Press. ISBN 0-262-53050-3.

Crick, Francis H. C. (1988). What Mad Pursuit: A Personal View of Scientific Discovery. New York, New York: Basic Books. ISBN 0-465-09137-7.

Dowe, David L.; Steve Gardner; Graham Oppy (December 2007). "Bayes not Bust! Why Simplicity is no Problem for Bayesians". British J. for the Philosophy of Science. 58 (4): 709–754. doi:10.1093/bjps/axm033. Archived from the original on 16 December 2008. Retrieved 24 September 2007.

Duda, Richard O.; Peter E. Hart; David G. Stork (2000). Pattern Classification (2nd ed.). Wiley-Interscience. pp. 487–489. ISBN 0-471-05669-3.

Epstein, Robert (1984). "The Principle of Parsimony and Some Applications in Psychology". Journal of Mind Behavior. 5: 119–130.

Hoffmann, Roald; Vladimir I. Minkin; Barry K. Carpenter (1997). "Ockham's Razor and Chemistry". HYLE – International Journal for the Philosophy of Chemistry. 3: 3–28. Retrieved 2006-04-14.

Jacquette, Dale (1994). Philosophy of Mind. Engleswoods Cliffs, New Jersey: Prentice Hall. pp. 34–36. ISBN 0-13-030933-8.

Jaynes, Edwin Thompson (1994). "Model Comparison and Robustness". Probability Theory: The Logic of Science. ISBN 0-521-59271-2.

Jefferys, William H.; Berger, James O. (1991). "Ockham's Razor and Bayesian Statistics (Preprint available as "Sharpening Occam's Razor on a Bayesian Strop)"," (PDF). American Scientist. 80: 64–72.

Katz, Jerrold (1998). Realistic Rationalism. MIT Press. ISBN 0-262-11229-9.

Kneale, William; Martha Kneale (1962). The Development of Logic. London: Oxford University Press. p. 243. ISBN 0-19-824183-6.

MacKay, David J. C. (2003). Information Theory, Inference and Learning Algorithms. Cambridge University Press. ISBN 0-521-64298-1. Retrieved 2016-02-24.

Menger, Karl (1960). "A Counterpart of Ockham's Razor in Pure and Applied Mathematics: Ontological Uses". Synthese. 12 (4): 415–428. doi:10.1007/BF00485426.

Morgan, C. Lloyd (1903). "Other Minds than Ours". An Introduction to Comparative Psychology (2nd ed.). London: W. Scott. p. 59. ISBN 0-89093-171-2. Archived from the original on 12 April 2005. Retrieved 2006-04-15.

Newton, Isaac (2011) [1726]. Philosophiæ Naturalis Principia Mathematica (3rd ed.). London: Henry Pemberton. ISBN 978-1-60386-435-0.

Nolan, D. (1997). "Quantitative Parsimony". British Journal for the Philosophy of Science. 48 (3): 329–343. doi:10.1093/bjps/48.3.329.

Pegis, A. C., translator (1945). Basic Writings of St. Thomas Aquinas. New York: Random House. p. 129. ISBN 0-87220-380-8.

Popper, Karl (1992). "7. Simplicity". The Logic of Scientific Discovery (2nd ed.). London: Routledge. pp. 121–132. ISBN 84-309-0711-4.

Rodríguez-Fernández, J. L. (1999). "Ockham's Razor". Endeavour. 23 (3): 121–125. doi:10.1016/S0160-9327(99)01199-0.

Schmitt, Gavin C. (2005). "Ockham's Razor Suggests Atheism". Archived from the original on 2007-02-11. Retrieved 2006-04-15.

Smart, J. J. C. (1959). "Sensations and Brain Processes". Philosophical Review. The Philosophical Review. 68 (2): 141–156. doi:10.2307/2182164. JSTOR 2182164.

Sober, Elliott (1975). Simplicity. Oxford: Oxford University Press.

Sober, Elliott (1981). "The Principle of Parsimony" (PDF). British Journal for the Philosophy of Science. 32 (2): 145–156. doi:10.1093/bjps/32.2.145. Archived from the original (PDF) on 15 December 2011. Retrieved 4 August 2012.

Sober, Elliott (1990). "Let's Razor Ockham's Razor". In Dudley Knowles. Explanation and its Limits. Cambridge: Cambridge University Press. pp. 73–94.

Sober, Elliott (2002). Zellner; et al., eds. "What is the Problem of Simplicity?" (PDF). Archived from the original (PDF) on 8 November 2006. Retrieved 4 August 2012.

Swinburne, Richard (1997). Simplicity as Evidence for Truth. Milwaukee, Wisconsin: Marquette University Press. ISBN 0-87462-164-X.

9 Chapter

MIXTURE MODELS

9.1 INTRODUCTION

A Gaussian mixture model is a probabilistic model that assumes all the data points are generated from a mixture of a finite number of Gaussian distributions with unknown parameters. One can think of mixture models as generalizing k-means clustering to incorporate information about the covariance structure of the data as well as the centers of the latent Gaussians.

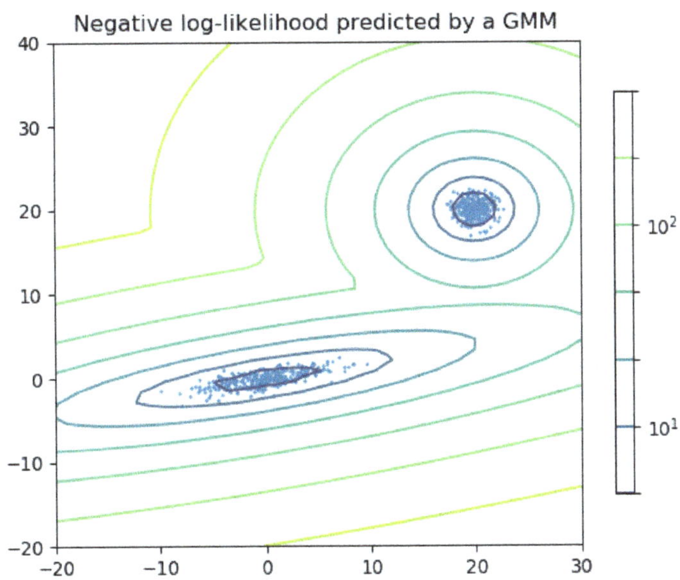

Fig: Two-component Gaussian mixture model

Gaussian Mixture represents Gaussian mixture model of probability distribution which allows to estimate the parameters of Gaussian mixture distribution. Gaussian Mixture object implements the expectation maximization algorithm for fitting mixture-of-Gaussian models which can be drawn ellipsoids for multivariate models and finding Bayesian Criterion so as to know the number of clusters in a data. The method learns about Gaussian Mixture Model from train data, with given test data by assigning every sample Gaussian. The GaussianMixture appears with different options to constrain covariance of difference classes like spherical, diagonal, tied or full covariance.

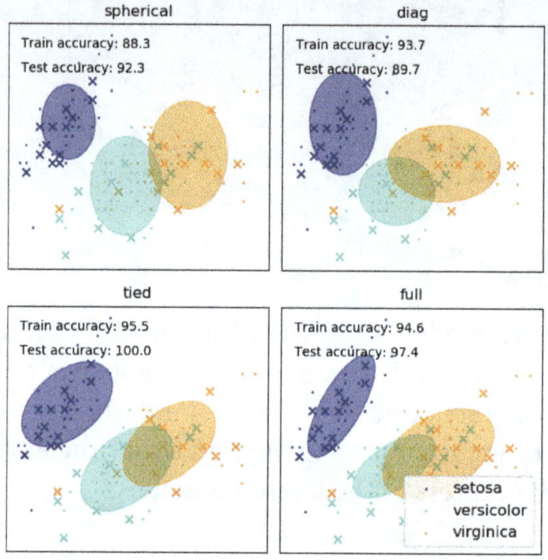

There appears difficulty in studying Gaussian mixture models from unlabeled data as it will not show clear points that appears from latent component. Expectation-maximization is a well-founded statistical algorithm to get around this problem by an iterative process. First one assumes random components and computes for each point a probability of being generated by each component of the model. Repeating this process is guaranteed to always converge to a local optimum.

Considering the clusters as Gaussian distributions centred on barycentres as shown where grey circle represents the first variance of the distribution:

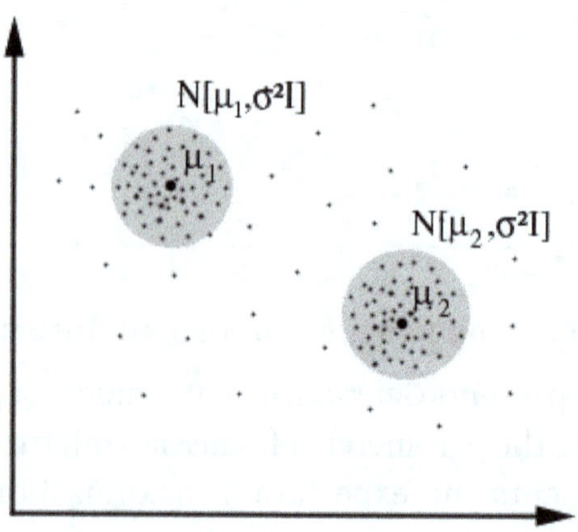

The algorithm shows:

selecting component (the Gaussian) at random with probability $P(\omega_i)$;

sampling a point $N(\mu_i, \sigma^2 I)$.

Let's suppose:

$x_1, x_2, \dots, x_N$

$P(\omega_1), \dots, P(\omega_K), \sigma$

From the likelihood of sample $P(x \mid \omega_i, \mu_1, \mu_2, \dots, \mu_K)$, maximising $P(x \mid \mu_1, \mu_2, \dots, \mu_K)$ (probability of a datum given the centres of the Gaussians) as

$$P(x \mid \mu_i) = \sum_i P(\omega_i) P(x \mid \omega_i, \mu_1, \mu_2, \dots, \mu_K)$$

is base to write likelihood function:

$$P(\text{data} \mid \mu_i) = \prod_{i=1}^{N} \sum_i P(\omega_i) P(x \mid \omega_i, \mu_1, \mu_2, \dots, \mu_K)$$

Now we should maximise the likelihood function by calculating $\partial L / \partial \mu = 0$, but it would be too difficult. That's why we use a simplified algorithm called Expectation-Maximization.

Considering an example of Expectation-Maximization, where x_k are the marks got by the students of a class, with these probabilities:

$x_1 = 30 \qquad P(x_1) = \frac{1}{2}$

$x_2 = 18 \qquad P(x_2) = \mu$

$x_3 = 0 \qquad P(x_3) = 2\mu$

$x_4 = 23 \qquad P(x_4) = \frac{1}{2} - 3\mu$

First case: we observe that the marks are so distributed among students:

x_1: a studentsx_2: b studentsx_3: c studentsx_4: d students

$$P(a, b, c, d \mid \mu) \propto \left(\frac{1}{2}\right)^a * (\mu)^b * (2\mu)^c * \left(\frac{1}{2} - 3\mu\right)^d$$

We should maximise this function by calculating $\partial P / \partial \mu = 0$. Let's instead calculate the logarithm of the function and maximise it:

$$P_L = \log\left(\frac{1}{2}\right)^a + \log(\mu)^b + \log(2\mu)^c + \log\left(\frac{1}{2} - 3\mu\right)^d$$

$$\frac{\partial P_L}{\partial \mu} = \frac{b}{\mu} + \frac{2c}{2\mu} - \frac{3d}{\frac{1}{2} - 3\mu} = 0$$

$$\Rightarrow \mu = \frac{b+c}{6(b+c+d)}$$

Supposing a = 14, b = 6, c = 9 and d = 10 we can calculate that μ = 1/10.

Second case: we observe that marks are so distributed among students:

$x_1 + x_2$: h studentsx_3: c studentsx_4: d students

We have so obtained a circularity which is divided into two steps:

expectation: $\mu \rightarrow a = \frac{\frac{1}{2}}{\frac{1}{2}+\mu} h, b = \frac{\mu}{\frac{1}{2}+\mu} h$

maximization: $, b \rightarrow \mu = \frac{b+c}{6(b+c+d}$

This circularity can be solved in an iterative way.

EM algorithm works for a mixture of Gaussians

Initialize parameters:

$$_0 = \{\mu_1^{(0)}, \mu_2^{(0)}, \ldots, \mu_K^{(0)}, p_1^{(0)}, p_2^{(0)}, \ldots, p_K^{(0)}$$

E-step:

$$P(\omega_j \mid x_k, \lambda_t) = \frac{P(x_k \mid \omega_j, \lambda_t) P(\omega_j \mid \lambda_t)}{P(x_k \mid \lambda_t)} = \frac{P(x_k \mid \omega_i, \mu_i^{(t)}, \sigma^2) p_i^{(t)}}{\sum_k P(x_k \mid \omega_j, \mu_j^{(t)}, \sigma^2) p_j^{(t)}}$$

M-step:

$$_i^{(t+1)} = \frac{\sum_k P(\omega_i \mid x_k, \lambda_t) x_k}{\sum_k P(\omega_i \mid x_k, \lambda_t)}$$

$$_i^{(t+1)} = \frac{\sum_k P(\omega_i \mid x_k, \lambda_t)}{R}$$

where R is the number of records.

9.2 MIXTURE MODEL WITH GAUSSIAN COMPONENTS

Gaussian mixture models are a probabilistic model for representing normally distributed subpopulations within an overall population. Mixture models in general don't require knowing which subpopulation a data point belongs to, allowing the model to learn the subpopulations automatically. Since subpopulation assignment is not known, this constitutes a form of unsupervised learning.

For example, in modeling human height data, height is typically modeled as a normal distribution for each gender with a mean of approximately 5'10" for males and 5'5" for females. Given only the height data and not the gender assignments for each data point, the distribution of all heights would follow the sum of two scaled (different variance) and shifted (different mean) normal distributions. A model making this assumption is an example of a Gaussian mixture model (GMM), though in general, a GMM may have more than two components. Estimating the parameters of the individual normal distribution components is a canonical problem in modeling data with GMMs.

Since many simple distributions are unimodal, an obvious way to model a multimodal distribution would be to assume that it is generated by multiple unimodal distributions. For several theoretical reasons, the most commonly used distribution in modeling real-world unimodal data is the Gaussian distribution. Thus, modeling multimodal data as a mixture of many unimodal Gaussian distributions makes intuitive sense. Furthermore, GMMs maintain many of the theoretical and computational benefits of Gaussian models, making them practical for efficiently modeling very large datasets.

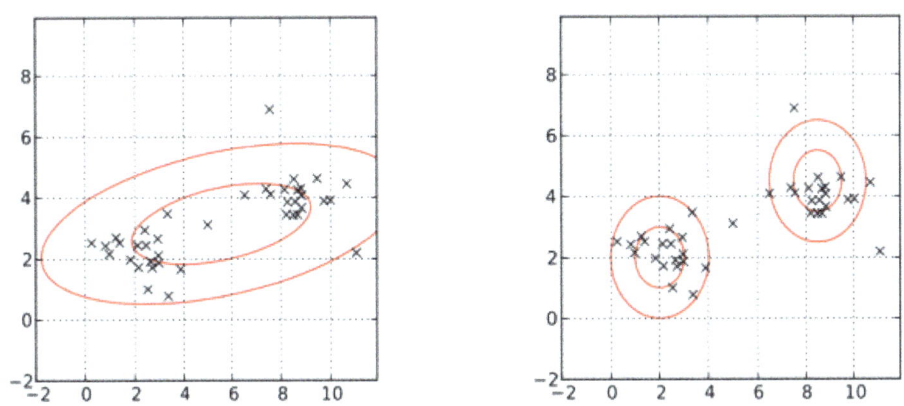

Fig: One and Two components Gaussian mixture model

9.3 LATENT DIRICHLET ALLOCATION

Latent Dirichlet Allocation is a common method of topic modeling where describes different models in a document. Such model builds a system hich looks at other sports articles or mathematics papers that directly decides whether this unseen document's topic is of what category.

For such model, a document exists as collection of topics where every topic has certain probability of generating a particular word. For potential sports article, average appears four times, so finding the probability of sports topic that generates many instances of average, can be done by looking at each training document as bag of words that are pulled from distribution selected by Dirichlet process.

Dirichlet is basically distribution specified by vector parameter α having some αi corresponding to each topic i, that can be written as Dir(α). The formula for computing the probability density function for each topic vector x is proportional to the product over all topics i of xiαixiαi. xixi is the probability that the topic is i, so the items in x must sum to 1. That keeps you from getting arbitrarily large probabilities by giving arbitrarily large values of x.

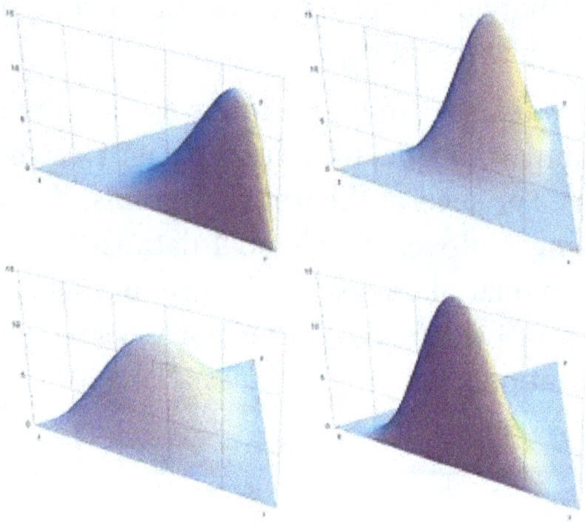

The above graphs show Dirichlet distributions for three topics which triangles at the bottom with one side for each topic and closer a point on triangle is to side i the higher the probability of topic i. Here the curve is probability density function over mixture of topics where the edges of the triangle have probability 0, so pdf is proportional to xiαi, so if xi is 0, then probability of mixture of topics will be 0. Such thing will restricts our model a bit and ensures that we never are totally certain about the topic of a document.

To have a mixture of topics for document, initially determine the value of each xi which shows that we have another Dirichlet distribution in the model for every topic i where instead of sides of triangle being topics, they're words. Now picture the topic sports article similar to distributions, so rather than sitting on triangles, they are on shapes with many sides where shape goes into many dimensions with the topics. If average appears in a sports article, the bump pushes closer to the side for average.

The Latent part of LDA comes into play because in statistics, a variable we have to infer rather than directly observing is called latent variable. We're only directly observing the words and not the topics, so the topics themselves are latent variables. LDA assumes that each document k is generated by:

- From our Dirichlet distribution for k, sample a random distribution of topics. That is, pick a place on that triangle that is associated with a certain probability of generating each topic. If we choose a place very close to the "sports article" edge, we have a higher probability of picking "sports article". The probability of picking a particular place on the triangle is described by the pdf of the Dirichlet distribution (the placement of the purple mound).
- For each topic, pick a distribution of words for that topic from the Dirichlet for that topic.
- For each word in document k,
- From the distribution of topics selected for k, sample a topic, like "sports article".
- From the distribution selected for "sports article", pick the current word.

REFERENCES

Ackley D., Hinton G. E., Sejnowski T. J. (1985). A learning algorithm for Boltzmann machines.

Albert R., Barabasi A. L. (2002). Statistical mechanics of complex networks. Rev. Mod. Phys. 74, 47–97. 10.1103/RevModPhys.74.47

Bullmore E., Sporns O. (2009). Complex brain networks: graph theoretical analysis of structural and functional systems. Nat. Rev. Neurosci. 10, 186–198. 10.1038/nrn2575

Cappelletti M., Didino D., Stoianov I., Zorzi M. (2014). Number skills are maintained in healthy ageing. Cogn. Psychol. 69, 25–45. 10.1016/j.cogpsych.2013.11.004

Deco G., Jirsa V. K., McIntosh A. R. (2013). Resting brains never rest: computational insights into potential cognitive architectures. Trends Neurosci. 36, 268–274. 10.1016/j.tins.2013.03.001

Elman J. L., Bates E., Johnson M., Karmiloff-smith A., Parisi D., Plunkett K. (1996). Rethinking Innateness: A Connectionist Perspective on Development. Cambridge, MA: MIT Press.

Farah M. J. (2004). Visual Agnosia. Cambridge, MA: MIT Press.

Griffiths T. L., Kemp C., Tenenbaum J. B. (2008). "Bayesian models of cognition," in Cambridge Handbook of Computational Cognitive Modeling, ed. Sun R., editor. (Cambridge, MA: Cambridge University Press;), 59–100.

Hinton G. E., Dayan P., Frey B., Neal R. M. (1995). The "wake-sleep" algorithm for unsupervised neural networks. Science 268, 1158–1161. 10.1126/science.7761831

Hinton G. E., Salakhutdinov R. (2006). Reducing the dimensionality of data with neural networks. Science 313, 504–507. 10.1126/science.1127647

Hinton G. E., Shallice T. (1991). Lesioning an attractor network: investigations of acquired dyslexia. Psychol. Rev. 98, 74–95. 10.1037/0033-295x.98.1.74

Humphreys G. W., Forde E. M. (2001). Hierarchies, similarity and interactivity in object recognition: "category-specific" neuropsychological deficits. Behav. Brain Sci. 24, 453–476;

Itti L., Baldi P. (2009). Bayesian surprise attracts human attention. Vision Res. 49, 1295–1306. 10.1016/j.visres.2008.09.007 [PMC free article] [PubMed] [Cross Ref]

Jirsa V. K., Sporns O., Breakspear M., Deco G., McIntosh A. R. (2010). Towards the virtual brain: network modeling of the intact and the damaged brain. Arch. Ital. Biol. 148, 189–205.

Joanisse M., Seidenberg M. S. (1999). Impairments in verb morphology after brain injury: a connectionist model. Proc. Natl. Acad. Sci. U S A 96, 7592–7597. 10.1073/pnas.96.13.7592

Jordan M. I., Sejnowski T. J. (2001). Graphical Models: Foundations of Neural Computation. Cambridge, MA: MIT Press.

Kelso J. A. S. (2012). Multistability and metastability: understanding dynamic coordination in the brain. Philos. Trans. R. Soc. Lond. B Biol. Sci. 367, 906–918. 10.1098/rstb.2011.0351

Koller D., Friedman N. (2009). Probabilistic Graphical Models: Principles and Techniques. Cambridge, MA: The MIT Press.

Lake B. M., Salakhutdinov R., Tenenbaum J. B. (2015). Humal-level concept learning through probabilistic program induction. Science 350, 1332–1338. 10.1126/science.aab3050

Le Q. V., Ranzato M. A., Monga R., Devin M., Chen K., Corrado G. S., et al. (2012). "Building high-level features using large scale unsupervised learning," in Proceedings of the 29th International Conference on Machine Learning.

LeCun Y., Bengio Y., Hinton G. E. (2015). Deep learning. Nature 521, 436–444. 10.1038/nature14539 [PubMed] [Cross Ref]

Mathers C., Fat D. M., Boerma T. J. (2008). The Global Burden of Disease: 2004 Update. Geneva, Switzerland: World Health Organization.

Medaglia J. D., Lynall M.-E., Bassett D. S. (2015). Cognitive network neuroscience. J. Cogn. Neurosci. 27, 1471–1491. 10.1162/jocn_a_00810

Mnih V., Kavukcuoglu K., Silver D., Rusu A. A., Veness J., Bellemare M. G., et al. . (2015). Human-level control through deep reinforcement learning. Nature 518, 529–533. 10.1038/nature14236

Nessler B., Pfeiffer M., Buesing L., Maass W. (2013). Bayesian computation emerges in generic cortical microcircuits through spike-timing-dependent plasticity. PLoS Comput. Biol. 9:e1003037. 10.1371/journal.pcbi.1003037

Newman M. (2010). Networks: An Introduction. New York, NY: Oxford University Press.

Ngiam J., Khosla A., Kim M., Nam J., Lee H., Ng A. Y. (2011). "Multimodal deep learning," in Proceedings of the 28th International Conference on Machine Learning (ICML-11), Bellevue, WA, 689–696.

O'Reilly R. C., Munakata Y. (2000). Computational Exploration in Cognitive Neuroscience. Cambridge, MA: MIT Press.

Plaut D. C., Shallice T. (1993). Deep dyslexia: a case study of connectionist neuropsychology. Cogn. Neuropsychol. 10, 377–500. 10.1080/02643299308253469

Raichle M. E. (2015). The restless brain: how intrinsic activity organizes brain function. Philos. Trans. R. Soc. Lond. B Biol. Sci. 370:20140172. 10.1098/rstb.2014.0172

Raina R., Madhavan A., Ng A. Y. (2009). "Large-scale deep unsupervised learning using graphics processors," in International Conference on Machine Learning, (New York, NY: ACM Press), 873–880.

Reichert D. P., Series P., Storkey A. (2013). Charles bonnet syndrome: evidence for a generative model in the cortex? PLoS Comput. Biol. 9:e1003134. 10.1371/journal.pcbi.1003134

Rotzer S., Kucian K., Martin E., von Aster M., Klaver P., Loenneker T. (2008). Optimized voxel-based morphometry in children with developmental dyscalculia. Neuroimage 39, 417–422. 10.1016/j.neuroimage.2007.08.045 [PubMed] [Cross Ref]

Rumelhart D. E., McClelland J. L. (1986). Parallel Distributed Processing: Explorations in the Microstructure of Cognition, Vol. 1: Foundations. Cambridge, MA: MIT Press.

Stoianov I., Zorzi M. (2013). "Developmental trajectories of numerosity perception," in Poster Presented at the Workshop: Interactions Between Space, Time and Number: 20 Years of Research (Paris:).

Stoianov I., Zorzi M., Umiltà C. (2004). The role of semantic and symbolic representations in arithmetic processing: insights from simulated dyscalculia in a connectionist model. Cortex 40, 194–196. 10.1016/s0010-9452(08)70948-1

Sutskever I., Hinton G. E., Taylor G. (2008). The recurrent temporal restricted Boltzmann machine. Adv. Neural Inf. Process. Syst. 20, 1601–1608.

Tenenbaum J. B., Kemp C., Griffiths T. L., Goodman N. D. (2011). How to grow a mind: statistics, structure and abstraction. Science 331, 1279–1285. 10.1126/science.1192788 [PubMed] [Cross Ref]

Testolin A., Stoianov I., Zorzi M. Human-like letter perception emerges from unsupervised deep learning and recycling of natural image statistics.

10 Chapter

NON-PARAMETRIC MODELS

10.1 SAMPLING FROM DISCRETE DISTRIBUTION

Considering a sample from discrete distribution of nucleotides as shown:

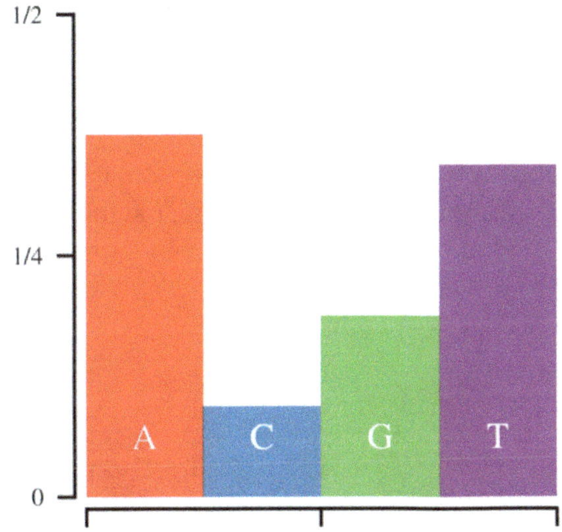

Here the heights of these bars will be h_0, h_1, h_2 and h_3. As these heights correspond to probability that a random base is A, C, G, or T, the total area of histogram will be 1. For sampling from histogram, draw a uniform random number and mark it as u between 0 and 1 and find which bar corresponds to that number. If $u < h_0$, in such case, sample A while if $u < h_0+h_1$, then sample C, etc. In such case, it is inefficient as it needs to search through the histogram from left to right every time on sampling. If you were sampling from 64 codons, in such case a more efficient method is to sample a point uniformly in a box having all the bars as shown:

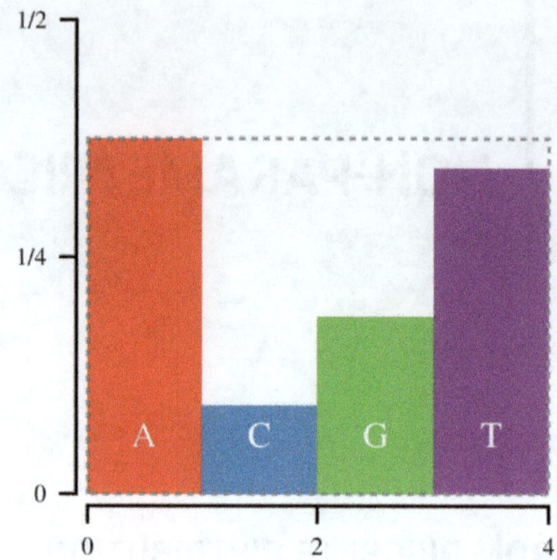

The (x, y) coordinates of the sampled point are defined by uniform random numbers between [0, 4) and 0,3/8)], so when such point is in white space, it gets rejected. This approach is more efficient as on selecting x, you only need to compare y against $h_{floor}(x)$. Also, white space makes up 1/3 of space in a box, and so on average, you will have to sample 1.5 points for every sampled nucleotide.

Using Alias Method, we can bring this down to 1 point for every sampled nucleotide, so start by constructing following box, having an area 1.

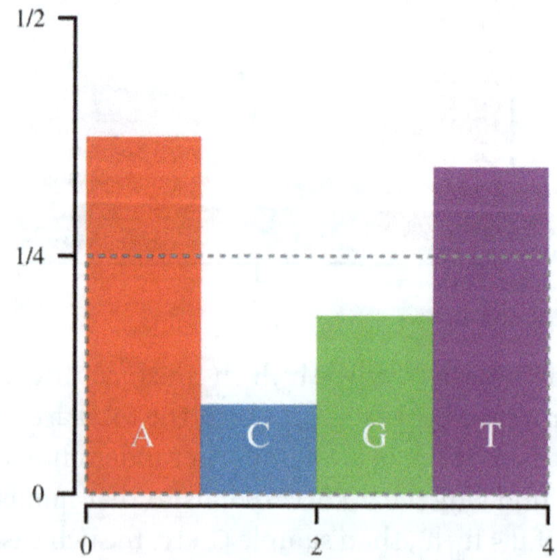

It is observed that amount of white space in the box will be equal to amount of filled space outside it, hence it is possible to cut the histogram in blocks and rearrange such that the entire box is filled.

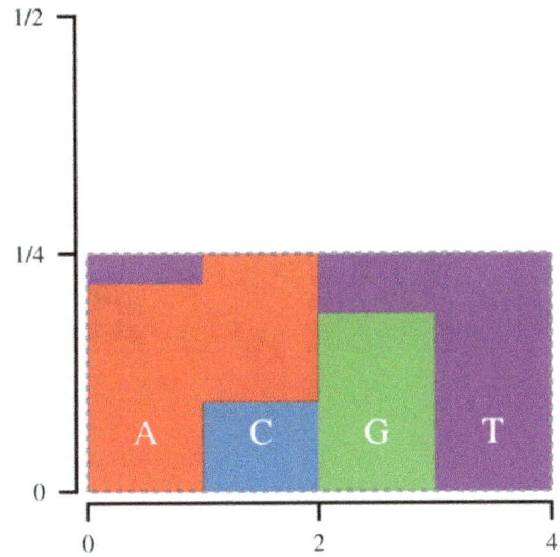

It is noticed that all bar is defined by lower, normal and upper regions. On drawing a point (x, y) uniformly in the box, x shows which bar to look at while y shows whether we return the normal or alias value. As there is no white space, so only 1 point per sampled nucleotide is drawn.

```
/*
 * C++ code for sampling from an alias table
 */
uint32_t a[64]; //aliases
uint64_t h[64]; //bar heights
uint32_t get_codon() {
    uint64_t u = rand_uint64();
    uint32_t x = u&63;
    return (u < h[x]) ? x : a[x];
}
```

It is seen that the hard part comes in slicing and moving the blocks around where Vose's method appears. In this, the list of bars are kept above or below the top line of box known as large and small with poping of element of both lists and using large element to fill in small element. If the large element is above the line, put it back in large list or put it in small list. On repeating the process, the box gets filled and will look as shown:

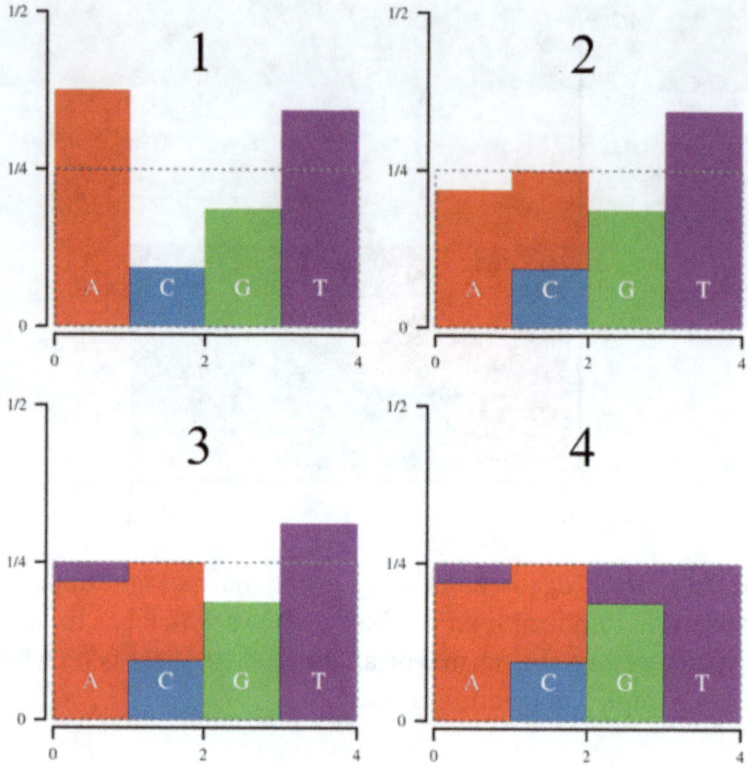

While Vose's method is typically implemented using arrays, where manipulation is expensive. However, it is possible to implement Vose's method without using temporary arrays to hold large and small elements. As shown, indices are there in the code that walk through the histogram linearly where only three indices are needed as:

g for current large bar

m for current small bar

mm for next possible small bar

Among the indices, as g and mm are keeping track of positions that have been examined and never decrease, in such case, m sometimes will jump backwards wwhen large bar becomes small.

```
/*
 * Initialize alias table from discrete distribution, pp
 */
void create_alias_table(const double *pp) {
   // normalize pp and copy into buffer
```

```
double f=0.0, p[64];
for(int i=0;i<64;++i)
   f += pp[i];
f = 64.0/f;
for(int i=0;i<64;++i)
   p[i] = pp[i]*f;

// find starting positions
std::size_t g,m,mm;
for(g=0; g<64 && p[g] <  1.0; ++g)
   /*noop*/;
for(m=0; m<64 && p[m] >= 1.0; ++m)
   /*noop*/;
mm = m+1;
// build alias table until we run out of large or small bars
while(g < 64 && m < 64) {
   // convert double to 64-bit integer, control for precision
   h[m] = (static_cast<uint64_t>(
         ceil(p[m]*9007199254740992.0)) << 11);
   a[m] = g;
   p[g] = (p[g]+p[m])-1.0;
   if(p[g] >= 1.0 || mm <= g) {
      for(m=mm;m<64 && p[m] >= 1.0; ++m)
         /*noop*/;
      mm = m+1;
   } else
      m = g;
   for(; g<64 && p[g] <  1.0; ++g)
      /*noop*/;
}
// any bars that remain have no alias
```

```
    for(; g<64; ++g) {
      if(p[g] < 1.0)
        continue;
      h[g] = std::numeric_limits<boost::uint64_t>::max();
      a[g] = g;
    }
    if(m < 64) {
      q[m] = std::numeric_limits<boost::uint64_t>::max();
      a[m] = m;
      for(m=mm; m<64; ++m) {
        if(p[m] > 1.0)
          continue;
        h[m] = std::numeric_limits<boost::uint64_t>::max();
        a[m] = m;
      }
    }
}
```

Note that if the values in pp were not immutable, then we would not need p.

10.2 THE DIRICHLET PROCESSES

The Bayesian approach allows for a coherent framework for dealing with uncertainty in machine learning. By integrating out parameters, Bayesian models do not suffer from overfitting, thus it is conceivable to consider models with infinite numbers of parameters, aka Bayesian nonparametric models. An example of such models is the Gaussian process, which is a distribution over functions used in regression and classification problems. Another example is the Dirichlet process, which is a distribution over distributions. Dirichlet processes are used in density estimation, clustering, and nonparametric relaxations of parametric models. It has been gaining popularity in both the statistics and machine learning communities, due to its computational tractability and modelling flexibility.

The Dirichlet process is a stochastic proces used in Bayesian nonparametric models of data, particularly in Dirichlet process mixture models. It is a distribution over distributions, i.e. each draw from a Dirichlet process is itself a distribution.

10.3 MARKOV MODELS

10.3.1 Introduction

Markov model consists of a list of the possible states of that system, the possible transition paths between those states, and the rate parameters of those transitions. In reliability analysis the transitions usually consist of failures and repairs. When representing a Markov model graphically, each state is usually shown as bubble, with arrows denoting the transition paths between states, as depicted in the figure below for a single component that has just two states: healthy and failed.

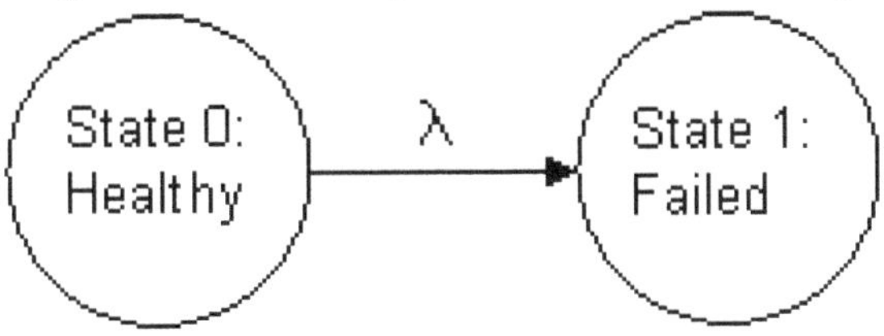

Fig: Single component with two states

In this, symbol l denotes the rate parameter of the transition from State · to State '. In addition, we denote by $P_j(t)$ the probability of the system being in State j at time t. If the device is known to be healthy at some initial time t = 0, the initial probabilities of the two states are $P_0(0) = 1$ and $P_1(0) = 0$. Thereafter the probability of State 0 decreases at the constant rate l, which means that if the system is in State 0 at any given time, the probability of making the transition to State 1 during the next increment of time dt is ldt. Therefore, the overall probability that the transition from State 0 to State 1 will occur during a specific incremental interval of time dt is given by multiplying (1) the probability of being in State 0 at the beginning of that interval, and (2) the probability of the transition during an interval dt given that it was in State 0 at the beginning of that increment. This represents the incremental change dP_0 in probability of State · at any given time, so we have the fundamental relation

$$dP_0 = -(P_0)(\lambda dt)$$

Dividing both sides by dt, we have the simple differential equation

$$\frac{dP_0}{dt} = -\lambda P_0$$

It shows that a transition path from a given state to any other state reduces the probability of the source state at a rate equal to the transition rate parameter l multiplied by the current probability of the state. Now, since the total probability of both states must equal 1, it follows that the probability of State 1 must increase at the same rate that the probability of State 0 is decreasing, so the equations for simple model will result as:

$$= -\lambda P_0 \qquad \frac{dP_1}{dt} = \lambda P_0 \qquad P_0 + P$$

The solution of these equations, with the initial conditions P0(0) = 1 and P1(0) = 0, is

$$= e^{-\lambda t} \qquad P_1(t) =$$

It shows why transitions with constant rates are called as exponential transitions, as the transition times are exponentially distributed. Further, it is clear that the total probability of all the states is conserved. Probability simply flows from one state to another. It's worth noting that the rate of occurrence of a given state equals the flow rate of probability into that state divided by the probability that the system is not already in that state. Thus in the simple example above the rate of occurrence of State 1 is given by (lP0)/(1-P1) = l.

As seen, many Markov are elaborated as compared to simple example as Markov model of real system includes full-up state and set of intermediate states showing partially failed condition, leading to fully failed state, i.e., the state in which the system is unable to perform its design function. The model may include repair transition paths as well as failure transition paths. The analyst defines the transition paths and corresponding rate between the various states, and then writes the system equations whose solution represents the time-history of the system. In general, each transition path between two states reduces the probability of the state it is departing, and increases the probability of the state it is entering, at a rate equal to the transition parameter l multiplied by the current probability of the source state.

The state equation for each state equates the rate of change of the probability of that state (dP/dt) with the "probability flow into and out of" that state. The total probability flow into a given state is the sum of all transition rates into that state, each multiplied by the probability of the state at the origin of that transition. The probability flow out of the given state is the sum of all transitions out of the state multiplied by the probability of that given state. To illustrate, the flows entering and exiting a typical state from and to the neighboring states are depicted in figure.

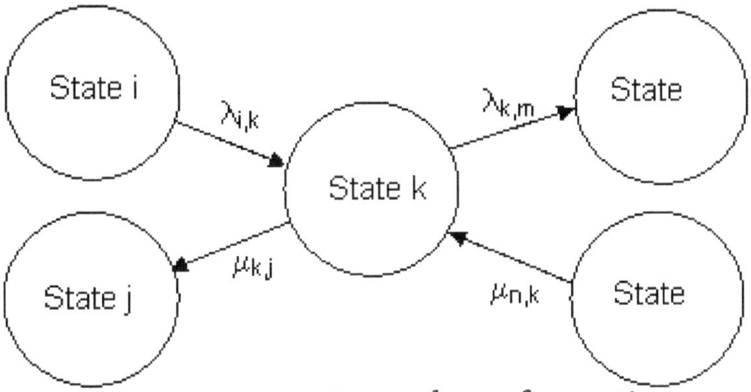

Fig: Transitions into and out-of State Pj

It is not showing complete Markov model, but shows only single state with some surrounding states and transition paths. It's conventional in field of reliability to denote failure rates by the symbol l and repair rates by the symbol m, sometimes with subscripts to designate the source and destination states. The state equation for State k sets the time derivative of Pk(t) equal to the sum of the "probability flows" corresponding to each of the transitions into and out of that state, hence:

$$\frac{dP_k}{dt} = \sum_i \lambda_{i,k} P_i + \sum_n \mu_{n,k} P_n - \left(\sum_j \mu_{k,j} + \sum_n \lambda_{k,n} \right) P_k$$

Each state in the model has an equation of this form, and these equations together determine the behavior of the overall system. In this generic description we have treated repair transitions as if they occur at constant rates, but, as noted in the Introduction, actual repairs in real-world applications are usually not characterized by constant rates. Nevertheless, with suitable care, repairs can usually be represented in Markov models as continuous constant-rate transitions from one state to another, by choosing each repair rate m such that 1/m is the mean time to repair for the affected state.

10.3.2 Markov Model for Two-Unit System

Consider a case of 2-unit system as shown where the system perform its intended function if Unit 1 or Unit 2 or both are operational.

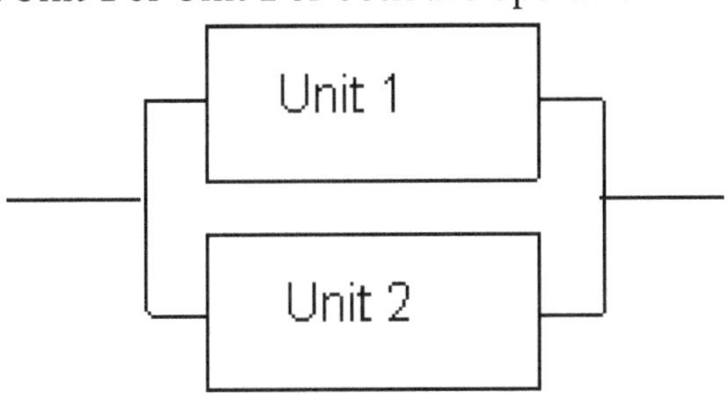

Fig: Simple 2-unit System

It is noted that an individual units will have constant failure rates of l_1 = 50E-06 and l_2 = 20E-06. Such system can be in one of four possible states:

(1) both units healthy

(2) Unit 1 failed but Unit 2 healthy

(3) Unit 2 failed but Unit 1 healthy

(4) both units failed

For maintaining such system, follow the strategy as follows:

- Status of unit 1 is monitored continuously and if it fails, operator will repair it in 100 hours of failure.
- Status of Unit 2 is not monitored regularly, but operator is required to inspects it every 1000 hours, and if it failed during one of such periodic checks, it is repaired at that time.
- If overall system fails, both units are immediately repaired, returning the system to the full-up state.

When we include these repair transitions, the two-unit model can be depicted as shown below.

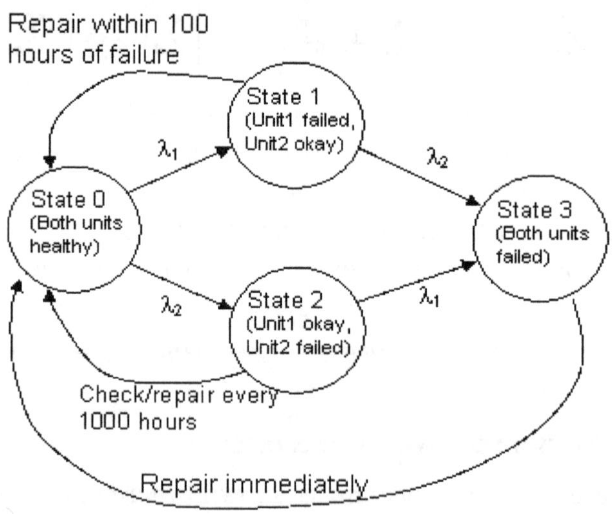

Fig: Repair of model

The immediate repair of the fully-failed state can be accurately represented by a constant-rate transition with a very large rate. However, the repair transitions for the two partially failed states are not strictly "Markovian", because the repair times of Unit 1 depend on the time of failure and repair times of Unit 2 have a discrete rather than continuous density distribution, i.e., they occur only at discrete intervals so, strictly speaking, they cannot be assigned a constant rate.

However, the repairs of Unit 1, which occur within 100 hours of failure, can be conservatively represented by a constant repair rate of 1/100 per hour. Admittedly it might be repaired more quickly, but in the absence of any data to substantiate the quicker repairs, it is usually best to just assume that the operator waits the full 100 hours before making the repair.

Likewise for the periodic inspection/repairs of Unit 2, we can always conservatively represent such repairs by a transition with a constant rate of 1/1000 per hour, because the time from failure to repair can never exceed 1000 hours. However, this may be considered excessively conservative, because it assumes every failure occurs at the very beginning of an inspection interval, so that the fault exists for nearly the full interval before being found and repaired. This would be fairly accurate if the MTBF of the unit was small in comparison with the inspection interval, but in practice this is almost never the case. To the contrary, an inspection interval for a unit is ordinarily chosen to be a small fraction of the unit's MTBF, because we don't want the system to be operating with latently failed units for any significant length of time. Therefore, in practice the distribution of failures in an interval is normally uniform, so the expected time between failure and repair is actually half of the inspection interval. In such cases we are justified in using a repair rate of 2/T, instead of 1/T, where T is the periodic inspection/repair interval.

On this basis the Markov model for the simple two-unit system, including all the failure and repair transitions, is as shown in the figure below.

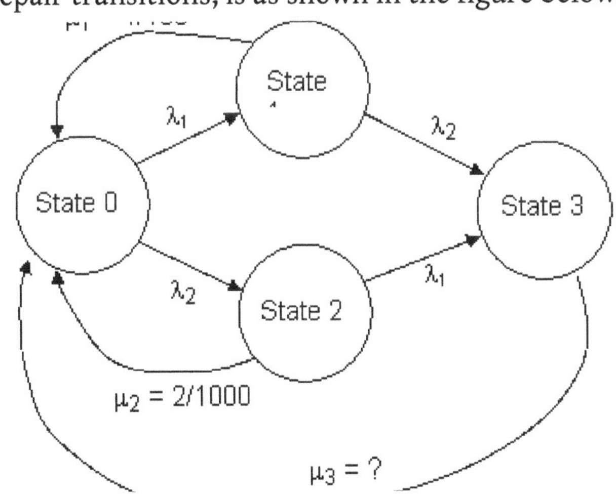

Notice that, since the repair rate of the fully-failed state (State 3) is infinite, the probability of that state will be zero, but we will leave it in the model for conceptual clarity. The total system failure rate is the total flow rate into that state, which is l2 P1 + l1 P2. To determine the long-term average system failure rate we need consider only the steady-state condition, i.e., the flow entering each state equals the flow exiting the state. Hence the system equations are simply;

$$\lambda_1 + \lambda_2) P_0 = \mu_1 P_1 + \mu_2 P_2 + \mu_3 P_3$$

$$\lambda_1 P_0 = (\lambda_2 + \mu_1) P_1$$

$$\lambda_2 P_0 = (\lambda_1 + \mu_2) P_2$$

$$\lambda_2 P_1 + \lambda_1 P_2 = \mu_3 P_3$$

The quantity m3 P3 represented by the fourth equation might seem to be indeterminate, because it equals zero multiplied by infinity. However, the left side of that equation defines the value of this quantity, which (as noted above) is the overall system failure rate. Substituting from the fourth equation into the first, we eliminate the empty state P3, and the system equations can be written as

$$\lambda_1 + \lambda_2) P_0 = (\lambda_2 + \mu_1) P_1 + (\lambda_1 + \mu_2) I$$

$$_1 P_0 = (\lambda_2 + \mu_1) P_1$$

$$_2 P_0 = (\lambda_1 + \mu_2) P_2$$

The second two equations immediately give

$$= \frac{\lambda_1}{\lambda_2 + \mu_1} P_0 \qquad\qquad P_2 = \frac{\lambda_2}{\lambda_1 + \mu_2}$$

We also know that the sum of all the probabilities must always equal 1, and since P3 = 0, the conservation equation is simply

$$+ P_1 + P_2$$

Substituting for the values of P1 and P2 from the preceding equations and solving for P0, we get the steady-state value of P0

$$_0 = \frac{1}{1 + \frac{\lambda_1}{\lambda_2 + \mu_1} + \frac{\lambda_2}{\lambda_1 + \mu_2}}$$

The steady-state values of P1 and P2 are given in terms of P0 by the preceding equations, so this enables us to write the overall average system failure as

$$_{ys} = \lambda_2 P_1 + \lambda_1 P_2 = \frac{\lambda_2 \frac{\lambda_1}{\lambda_2 + \mu_1} + \lambda_1 \frac{\lambda_2}{\lambda_1 + \mu}}{1 + \frac{\lambda_1}{\lambda_2 + \mu_1} + \frac{\lambda_2}{\lambda_1 + \mu_2}}$$

Inserting the values l1 = 50E-06, l2 = 20E-06, m1 = 1/100, and m2 = 2/1000, this gives the average total system failure rate of lsys = 5.79E-07 per hour.

REFERENCES

Aldous, D. (1985). Exchangeability and related topics. In École d'Été de Probabilités de Saint-Flour XIII–1983, pages 1–198. Springer, Berlin. Antoniak, C. E. (1974).

Mixtures of Dirichlet processes with applications to Bayesian nonparametric problems. Annals of Statistics, 2(6):1152–1174.

Beal, M. J., Ghahramani, Z., and Rasmussen, C. E. (2002). The infinite hidden Markov model. In Advances in Neural Information Processing Systems, volume 14.

Blackwell, D. and MacQueen, J. B. (1973). Ferguson distributions via Pólya urn schemes. Annals of Statistics, 1:353–355.

Blei, D., Griffiths, T., Jordan, M., and Tenenbaum, J. (2004). Hierarchical topic models and the nested Chinese restaurant process. In Advances in Neural Information Processing Systems, volume 16.

Blei, D. M. and Jordan, M. I. (2006). Variational inference for Dirichlet process mixtures. Bayesian Analysis, 1(1):121–144.

Caron, F., Davy, M., and Doucet, A. (2007). Generalized Polya urn for time-varying Dirichlet process mixtures. In Proceedings of the Conference on Uncertainty in Artificial Intelligence, volume 23.

Cowans, P. (2004). Information retrieval using hierarchical Dirichlet processes. In Proceedings of the Annual International Conference on Research and Development in Information Retrieval, volume 27, pages 564–565.

Cowans, P. (2006). Probabilistic Document Modelling. PhD thesis, University of Cambridge.

Daume III, H. (2007). Fast search for Dirichlet process mixture models. In Proceedings of the International Workshop on Artificial Intelligence and Statistics, volume 11.

Ewens, W. J. (1972). The sampling theory of selectively neutral alleles. Theoretical Population Biology, 3:87–112.

Fearnhead, P. (2004). Particle filters for mixture models with an unknown number of components. Statistics and Computing, 14:11–21.

Ferguson, T. S. (1973). A Bayesian analysis of some nonparametric problems. Annals of Statistics, 1(2):209–230.

Finkel, J. R., Grenager, T., and Manning, C. D. (2007). The infinite tree. In Proceedings of the Annual Meeting of the Association for Computational Linguistics.

Fox, E. B., Choi, D. S., and Willsky, A. S. (2006). Nonparametric Bayesian methods for large scale multi-target tracking. In Proceedings of the Asilomar Conference on Signals, Systems, and Computers, volume 40.

Fox, E. B., Sudderth, E. B., Choi, D. S., and Willsky, A. S. (2007a). Tracking a non-cooperative maneuvering target using hierarchical Dirichlet processes. In Proceedings of the Adaptive Sensor Array Processing Conference.

Fox, E. B., Sudderth, E. B., and Willsky, A. S. (2007b). Hierarchical Dirichlet processes for tracking maneuvering targets. In Proceedings of the International Conference on Information Fusion.

Goldwater, S. (2006). Nonparametric Bayesian Models of Lexical Acquisition. PhD thesis, Brown University.

Goldwater, S., Griffiths, T., and Johnson, M. (2006a). Interpolating between types and tokens by estimating power-law generators. In Advances in Neural Information Processing Systems, volume 18.

Goldwater, S., Griffiths, T. L., and Johnson, M. (2006b).

Contextual dependencies in unsupervised word segmentation. In Proceedings of the 21st International Conference on Computational Linguistics and 44th Annual Meeting of the Association for Computational Linguistics.

Görür, D. (2007). Nonparametric Bayesian Discrete Latent Variable Models for Unsupervised Learning. PhD thesis, Technischen Universität Berlin.

Görür, D., Jäkel, F., and Rasmussen, C. E. (2006). A choice model with infinitely many latent features. In Proceedings of the International Conference on Machine Learning, volume 23.

Griffin, J. E. (2007). The Ornstein-Uhlenbeck Dirichlet process and other time-varying processes for Bayesian nonparametric inference.

Griffiths, T. L., Canini, K. R., Sanborn, A. N., and Navarro, D. J. (2007a). Unifying rational models of categorization via the hierarchical Dirichlet process. In Proceedings of the Annual Conference of the Cognitive Science Society, volume 29.

Griffiths, T. L. and Ghahramani, Z. (2006). Infinite latent feature models and the Indian buffet process. In Advances in Neural Information Processing Systems, volume 18.

Griffiths, T. L., Ghahramani, Z., and Sollich, P. (2007b). Bayesian nonparametric latent feature models (with discussion and rejoinder). In Bayesian Statistics, volume 8.

Haghighi, A. and Klein, D. (2007). Unsupervised coreference resolution in a nonparametric Bayesian model. In Proceedings of the Annual Meeting of the Association for Computational Linguistics.

Heller, K. A. and Ghahramani, Z. (2005). Bayesian hierarchical clustering. In Proceedings of the International Conference on Machine Learning, volume 22.

Heller, K. A. and Ghahramani, Z. (2007). A nonparametric Bayesian approach to modeling overlapping clusters. In Proceedings of the International Workshop on Artificial Intelligence and Statistics, volume 11.

Hjort, N. L. (1990). Nonparametric Bayes estimators based on beta processes in models for life history data. Annals of Statistics, 18(3):1259–1294.

Ishwaran, H. and James, L. F. (2001). Gibbs sampling methods for stick-breaking priors. Journal of the American Statistical Association, 96(453):161–173.

Jain, S. and Neal, R. M. (2004). A split-merge Markov chain Monte Carlo procedure for the Dirichlet process mixture model. Technical report, Department of Statistics, University of Toronto.

Johnson, M., Griffiths, T. L., and Goldwater, S. (2007). Adaptor grammars: A framework for specifying compositional nonparametric Bayesian models. In Advances in Neural Information Processing Systems, volume 19.

Kemp, C., Tenenbaum, J. B., Griffiths, T. L., Yamada, T., and Ueda, N. (2006).

Learning systems of concepts with an infinite relational model. In Proceedings of the AAAI Conference on Artificial Intelligence, volume 21.

Kim, S. (2007). Learning Hierarchical Probabilistic Models with Random Effects with Applications to Time-series and Image Data. PhD thesis, Information and Computer Science, University of California at Irvine.

Kim, S. and Smyth, P. (2007). Hierarchical dirichlet processes with random effects. In Advances in Neural Information Processing Systems, volume 19.

Kingman, J. F. C. (1982a). The coalescent. Stochastic Processes and their Applications, 13:235–248.

Kingman, J. F. C. (1982b). On the genealogy of large populations. Journal of Applied Probability, 19:27–43. Essays in Statistical Science.

Kivinen, J., Sudderth, E., and Jordan, M. I. (2007). Image denoising with nonparametric hidden Markov trees. In International Conference on Image Processing.

Kurihara, K., Welling, M., and Vlassis, N. (2007). Accelerated variational DP mixture models. In Advances in Neural Information Processing Systems, volume 19.

Li, W., Blei, D., and McCallum, A. (2007). Nonparametric Bayes pachinko allocation. In Proceedings of the Conference on Uncertainty in Artificial Intelligence.

Liang, P., Jordan, M. I., and Taskar, B. (2007a). A permutation-augmented sampler for Dirichlet process mixture models. In Proceedings of the International Conference on Machine Learning.

Liang, P., Petrov, S., Jordan, M. I., and Klein, D. (2007b). The infinite PCFG using hierarchical Dirichlet processes. In Proceedings of the Conference on Empirical Methods in Natural Language Processing.

MacEachern, S., Kottas, A., and Gelfand, A. (2001). Spatial nonparametric Bayesian models. Technical Report 01-10, Institute of Statistics and Decision Sciences, Duke University.

Mansingkha, V. K., Roy, D. M., Rifkin, R., and Tenenbaum, J. B. (2007). AClass: An online algorithm for generative classification. In Proceedings of the International Workshop on Artificial Intelligence and Statistics, volume 11.

Meeds, E., Ghahramani, Z., Neal, R. M., and Roweis, S. T. (2007).

Neal, R. M. (2000). Markov chain sampling methods for Dirichlet process mixture models. Journal of Computational and Graphical Statistics, 9:249–265.

GLOSSARY

Algorithm.

A series of steps that are repeated.

Break-Even Point (BEP).

Number of units sold that will result in total revenue equaling total costs (i.e., profit is $0).

Break-Even Point in Dollars (BEP$).

Sum of fixed and total variable cost if the number of units sold equals the break-even point.

Decision Analyst.

An individual who is responsible for developing a decision model.

Decision Modeling.

A scientific approach that uses quantitative (mathematical) techniques as a tool in managerial decision making. Also known as quantitative analysis, management science, and operations research.

Decision Problem.

A statement, which should come from a manager, that indicates a problem to be solved or an objective or goal to be reached.

Deterministic Model.

A model that assumes that all the relevant input data and parameters are known with certainty.

Formulation.

The process by which each aspect of the problem scenario is translated and expressed in terms of a mathematical model.

Garbage In, Garbage Out.

The principle that improper data will result in misleading results.

Goal Seek.

A feature in Excel that allows users to specify a goal or target for a specific cell and automatically manipulate another cell to achieve this target.

Input Data.

Data that are used in a model in arriving at the final solution.

Model.

A representation (usually mathematical) of a practical problem scenario or environment.

Parameter.

A measurable quantity that is inherent in the problem. It typically has a fixed and known value (i.e., a constant).

Probabilistic Model (also called stochastic).

A model that assumes that some input data are not known with certainty.

Sensitivity Analysis (also called post-optimality analysis).

Determining how sensitive a solution is to changes in the formulation of a problem.

Variable.

A measurable quantity that may vary or is subject to change.

INDEX

A

Abstract 2, 12-13, 215

Actions 49-50, 177, 181-182, 185

Acyclic 96

Adaptive 70-72

Agreement 87

Algebra 2, 10, 13

Algorithms 34-37

Analysis v, 13, 22-23, 34, 37, 44-45, 57, 93, 166, 214, 259, 264

Annals 44, 259

Arbitrary 143, 222

Arithmetic 37

Assignment 121, 214

Asymmetry 93-94, 138

Athletic 109

B

Bayesian 23, 36-37, 84-86, 96-97, 173, 198, 200, 215, 234, 252, 259-261

B-effects 183

Bernoulli 147, 169-170, 174-175

Binomial 15, 147, 154, 174

Bivariate 52

Bloodgene 104-105

Bloodtrial 105

Bloodtype 104-108

Brains 82

Buttons 184

C

Chemistry 234

Children 132

C-language 37

Clusters 55, 214-215, 238

Cognition 49, 81, 88, 206

Cognitive 82, 166, 206-207, 243, 245

Collins 137, 139

Components 136, 214, 241

Compound 41

Computer 47

Concrete 2-3, 13, 228

Conference 86, 207, 245, 259-262

Cortex 83, 87

Coughing 96

Covariance 79, 238

Currency 230

Customer 157

Cycles 149

D

Dataframe 195
Decoder 31-32
Density 25, 59, 62, 71-72, 75-76, 242
Dental 58
Detector 132
Die-prior 187
Disorders 44
Domain 34, 49, 60, 62-63
Dynamics 44-45

E

Electronic 208
Elements 4, 230, 233
Encoding 32, 114
Epistemic 182

F

Forecasts 33
Framework 1, 37

G

Garbage 263
Gender 53, 241
Generation 211
Geometric 142, 169-170
Geometry 2-3, 5
Goal-food 179-180, 183-185
Goal-pos 193
Goldfine 44
Goldwater 260
Growth 143

H

Histogram 50, 61, 64, 247
Hypothesis 186-187, 215, 230-233

I

Integral 154

L

Lambda 41-43, 48, 63, 130, 183-185, 191, 225, 231
Learners 27
Library 36-37
Linewidth 66, 69

M

Matrix 79, 157-158
Matters 93
Modular 89, 133, 136-137
Multimodal 241

N

Nature 83, 85-87, 93, 144, 244-245
Networks 26, 82, 84, 86, 141-142, 166, 210, 243-244
Neural 28, 31, 82-84, 86-87, 143, 210, 244, 259-261
Neuroimage 87, 245
Neuron 82-83
Notation 120
Nuclear 94
Nucleotide 248

O

Operations 6-8, 11, 34
Operators 34
Orthodox 12

P

Patients 17, 44
Phenomenon 125, 227

Philosophy 137-140, 167, 234-235

Planning 49

Polynomial 229

Propagate 101

Python 37, 205

Q

Quantity 151, 258, 264

R

Radius 67

Random 1-15, 28, 37-40, 52, 55, 58-60, 64-66, 72-74, 76-78, 120-121, 145-149, 151, 174, 195, 205-206, 247, 261

Reasonable 55

Reasoning 116, 122, 129, 166, 175

Recursion 169, 188-189

Regression 170

Reverse 159-161

Robust 34

S

Segments 72

Semantics 90

Signal 229

Squeezing 72

Statistics 22, 29, 145, 246, 259, 261-262

Students 130, 239-240

Symbol 8, 255

Symptoms 96-97, 123

Synthetic 141

Systems 2, 34-35, 136, 166, 228, 259-261

T

Timescales 143

Training 27-30, 33

Transition 157-158, 171, 177-181, 183-185, 253-254

Triplets 203

V

Vaccine 17

Variance 55, 58, 134-135

Vocabulary 172-173

W

Weather 100, 102

Widget 176-177

Workshop 167

X

Xproposal 64

www.ingramcontent.com/pod-product-compliance
Lightning Source LLC
LaVergne TN
LVHW062227200926
848484LV00006B/1495